Critical Essays on Emily Dickinson

Critical Essays on Emily Dickinson

Paul J. Ferlazzo

G. K. Hall & Co. • Boston, Massachusetts

Library of Congress Cataloging in Publication Data
Main entry under title:

Critical essays on Emily Dickinson.

   (Critical essays on American literature)
   Includes index.
   1. Dickinson, Emily, 1830–1886 — Criticism and interpretation — Addresses, essays, lectures.
I. Ferlazzo, Paul J. II. Series.
PS1541.Z5C7   1984   811'4   83-18635
ISBN 0-8161-8463-1

CRITICAL ESSAYS ON AMERICAN LITERATURE

This series seeks to anthologize the most important criticism on a wide variety of topics and writers in American literature. Our readers will find in various volumes not only a generous selection of reprinted articles and reviews but original essays, bibliographies, manuscript sections, and other materials brought to public attention for the first time. Paul J. Ferlazzo's volume on Emily Dickinson is a welcome addition to our list in that it is the most substantial collection of scholarship yet assembled on this important writer. Among the thirty-three essays are reprinted selections from Thomas Wentworth Higginson, William Dean Howells, Norman Foerster, Amy Lowell, Allen Tate, Richard Chase, Robert E. Spiller, Arlin Turner, and Hyatt Waggoner. In addition to Paul Ferlazzo's extensive introduction, which surveys the history of Dickinson criticism, are original essays by Jane Donahue Eberwein and Barbara Antonina Clarke Mossberg. We are confident that this collection will make a permanent and significant contribution to American literary study.

James Nagel, GENERAL EDITOR

Northeastern University

To
Michael and John

CONTENTS

INTRODUCTION

BIBLIOGRAPHY

The premiere bibliography for the study of Emily Dickinson is Willis J. Buckingham, *Emily Dickinson: An Annotated Bibliography*.[1] The book contains over 2,600 items emphasizing the scholarly and critical growth in her reputation. Well indexed and cross-referenced, it includes not only foreign language material, but also fiction and drama based on Dickinson's life, tributes by other artists, and miscellaneous categories. It also annotates dissertations and theses, recordings, broadcasts, films, and contains lists of unpublished papers read at scholarly meetings. About half of all the entries are in the core section of critical analysis entitled, "Parts of Books and Signed Articles."

This volume has been supplemented with two addenda published in the *Emily Dickinson Bulletin*.[2] The annual checklists in the *Emily Dickinson Bulletin*, renamed *Dickinson Studies* in 1978, together with the annual editions of *American Literary Scholarship* and the PMLA *Bibliography*, give the most current and readily accessible bibliographic information on Dickinson.

Another useful and important bibliography is Sheila Clendenning, *Emily Dickinson, A Bibliography: 1859-1966*.[3] Although it contains fewer than half the items found in Buckingham, it is well annotated, indexed, and cross-referenced. She excludes many categories that Buckingham includes, such as creative tributes and fictional portrayals, but lists 12 pages of explications. Of special significance is her insightful introductory essay on the literary reputation of Emily Dickinson.

Although superseded by Buckingham and Clendenning, several other bibliographies deserve notice. A general list of 456 items is found in Susan Freis, *Emily Dickinson: A Checklist of Criticism, 1930-1966*.[4] William White, "Emily Dickinsoniana: An Annotated Checklist of Books About the Poet," is useful for its annotations and critical reviews of other bibliographies.[5] Clear, concise commentaries on the major Dickinson studies is found in James Woodress's bibliographic essay, "Emily Dickinson" in *Fifteen American Authors*.[6]

Of historic interest only, indicating the initial efforts at gathering

1

bibliographical information, are Alfred Leete Hampson, *Emily Dickinson: A Bibliography*,[7] and compiled by the Jones Library staff, *Emily Dickinson, December 10, 1830–May 15, 1886: A Bibliography*.[8]

Despite the continuing work done with the Dickinson bibliography a comprehensive ordering of the field is yet to be done. The issues raised by Willis J. Buckingham in a 1974 article "The Bibliographical Study of Emily Dickinson," have yet to be addressed.[9] Among other things he called for "a complete descriptive bibliography" and "a full-length handbook to Dickinson studies that will winnow and appraise the mass of accumulating materials."

Two remaining items of utmost usefulness to the Dickinson scholar should be mentioned. S. P. Rosenbaum, *A Concordance to the Poems of Emily Dickinson*, indexes over one hundred thousand of Dickinson's words.[10] It gives the word in context, the first line of the poem in which the word appears, and is keyed to the Johnson edition of her poetry. Word-frequency lists are included in an appendix. Joseph Duchac, *The Poems of Emily Dickinson: An Annotated Guide to Commentary Published in English, 1890–1977*, is a massive collection of over 6000 brief excerpts from explications and criticism published in English.[11] Over 1300 poems are listed and over 750 books, chapters, and articles are cited. This important compilation reveals that there are over 400 of Dickinson's poems that have received no critical attention at all. A study of these "neglected" poems seems to be called for. Such an examination may reveal gems which have been wrongly ignored, and patterns of theme, tone, or technique in certain poems which account for critical neglect.

EDITIONS AND MANUSCRIPTS

The publication history of Emily Dickinson's poetry and letters is a complicated and absorbing tale. The place to read about it is in Millicent Todd Bingham, *Ancestors' Brocades*, R. W. Franklin, *The Editing of Emily Dickinson*, John S. van E. Kohn, "Giving Emily Dickinson to the World," and for the history of Dickinson's letters only, Robert B. Laurence, "The Mind Alone."[12] After Emily Dickinson's death, Lavinia found the poems among her sister's effects and engaged Mabel Loomis Todd, a family friend, and Col. Thomas Wentworth Higginson, a personal correspondent and early literary advisor of Dickinson's, to edit the poems and see to their publication. Together they brought out two well received volumes, *Poems by Emily Dickinson*, and *Poems by Emily Dickinson, Second Series*.[13] Todd brought out a third volume alone, *Poems by Emily Dickinson, Third Series*.[14] The poems in these three volumes were significantly edited to make the lines rhyme and the meter regular according to the popular taste of the time for poetry. The three volumes together contained some 450 poems, less than half of those transcribed by Todd from manuscripts given her by Lavinia Dickinson.

Because of the popular reception of the poetry, Todd also edited two volumes of the poet's letters.[15]

An unpleasant legal battle during 1896–97 between the Dickinsons and the Todds over a debated piece of land brought further publication of Dickinson's poems, now in the possession of the Todds, to a halt. Mabel Loomis Todd reportedly stored away into a camphorwood chest her remaining Dickinson materials. They remained untouched for 35 years.

The next phase of publishing activity was taken up by Martha Dickinson Bianchi, the daughter of Emily Dickinson's brother, Austin, and Susan Gilbert Dickinson. In 1914 she edited *The Single Hound*, which contained 147 poems chosen from the 276 which had been in the possession of her mother.[16] During the following years Bianchi continued to edit the poetry with the aid of Alfred Leete Hampson and brought out four more editions of the poetry: *The Complete Poems of Emily Dickinson, Further Poems of Emily Dickinson, The Poems of Emily Dickinson, Centenary Edition*, and *Unpublished Poems by Emily Dickinson*.[17] Bianchi also brought out two volumes which contained biographical sketches and selections from Dickinson's letters: *The Life and Letters of Emily Dickinson*, and *Emily Dickinson Face to Face*.[18] At this point a total of 908 of Dickinson's poems had been published, a little more than half the total left by the poet.

The only edition of the poetry thus far to appear edited by an "outsider" was Conrad Aiken's selection of poems from the Todd-Higginson texts entitled *Selected Poems*.[19] He criticized Bianchi's editorial work for being distorted and misrepresenting the poet. In a review article, "Emily Dickinson and Her Editors," Aiken called for a new, corrected edition of the poetry.[20] His opinions regarding the textual state of Dickinson's poetry was typical of the academic and literary communities of this time, and helps to explain why her poetry was not yet receiving serious scholarly attention.

After the death of Mabel Loomis Todd in 1932, her daughter, Millicent Todd Bingham brought the camphorwood chest out of storage and reopened it to resume the work her mother had abandoned years before because of the lawsuit with the Dickinson family. Bingham, trained as a scientist and having in mind the sense of a modern editor's responsibilities, prepared a carefully edited collection of Dickinson's poetry, *Bolts of Melody*, and two volumes of letters, *Emily Dickinson: A Revelation*, containing the correspondence with Judge Otis Lord, and *Emily Dickinson's Home*.[21] With *Bolts of Melody* 668 new poems appeared, leaving some 200 of Dickinson's poems yet to see the light of publication.

It was not until the 1950s that the Dickinson manuscripts finally became available for examination and study to a scholar outside of the small circle of family and friends who had controlled them for more than fifty years. Thomas H. Johnson edited *The Poems of Emily Dickinson*, a three-volume work containing all 1775 poems known to have been written by Dickinson.[22] This historic edition is still recognized as the definitive one. It records previous publication data for the poems and changes made by previous editors. Dickinson's idiosyncratic punctuation, unmetrical verse, off-rhymes, and other innovations that had been regularized by previous editors, are restored here to their original. Johnson arranged the poems chronologically, attempting to date them according to their original locations in the packets left by Dickinson, and by a study of handwriting changes that occurred over the years. The introductory essays and appendices contain a great deal of information on the origin and editing of the poems, the recipients of the poems, and the manuscripts themselves. The Johnson version was issued in a one-volume edition without critical apparatus as *The Complete Poems of Emily Dickinson*, and in an edition of 575 selected poems entitled *Final Harvest*.[23]

In over thirty years since the Johnson edition appeared only two significant challenges to the definitive nature of the work have surfaced. R. W. Franklin, in *The Editing of Emily Dickinson*, after having examined the manuscripts believes that the Johnson chronology can be corrected, and that Dickinson's own intended arrangement of the poems can be established accurately from a more thorough study of the packets.[24] And Edith Wylder, in *The Last Face*, claims that the variety of dashes in shape, size, and direction scattered throughout the poems in manuscript which Johnson regularized in his edition, are actually nineteenth-century elocution symbols that Dickinson intentionally used to indicate "inflection, pause, and stress."[25] In an extensive introductory essay, Wylder develops and clarifies the theory she first introduced in 1963 under the name Edith Perry Stamm in the *Saturday Review*.[26] Thirty five poems are reprinted from the manuscripts attempting to keep the dashes as originally written. However, since Dickinson also used the dashes in her prose, even in a recipe for gingerbread as noticed by Brita Lindberg,[27] acceptance of Wylder's theory awaits a closer and more thorough scrutiny of all the manuscripts, both the poetry and prose.

Thomas H. Johnson followed his edition of Dickinson's poems with *The Letters of Emily Dickinson* edited with an associate, Theodora Ward.[28] The three-volume work prints all her known letters, notes, and prose fragments chronologically. The critical apparatus includes biographical sketches of the recipients of the letters and persons mentioned.

Nearly all the known Dickinson manuscripts are available in two large collections. In 1950 the Houghton Library of Harvard University received the Dickinson papers owned by Martha Dickinson Bianchi and Alfred Leete Hampson. In 1956 The Amherst College Library received the collection in possession of Millicent Todd Bingham. The latter collection is available on microfilm. An indispensable volume to be consulted before working with either collection is R. W. Franklin, *The Editing of Emily Dickinson*.[29] Franklin has also edited a facsimile edition of Dickinson's poetry manuscripts. *The Manuscript Books of Emily Dickinson* reproduces in two volumes 1,147 poems as they were written and sewn in packets or fascicles by Dickinson herself.[30] The poems and packets are arranged in their original sequence and chronology as determined by Franklin, and show with remarkable clarity every detail, from pencilled revisions to sewing holes and inkspots. With the availability of this book, one may now expect wider scholarly response to the problems associated with the manuscripts.

BIOGRAPHY

The early biographies of Emily Dickinson were sensational mixtures of romance and legend, fact and fantasy, and helped to create a myth about the poet which remains vivid to this day in the popular consciousness. The central element of the legend has to do with a secret lover or lovers. Martha Dickinson Bianchi, the poet's niece, gave voice to the core of the myth by writing in an introductory essay to *The Single Hound*, "The list of those whom she bewitched . . . included college boys, tutors, law students, the brothers of her girl friends,—several times their affianced bridegrooms even; and then the maturer friendships,—literary, Platonic, Plutonic; passages varying in intensity, and at least one passionate attachment, whose tragedy was due to the integrity of the lovers, who scrupled to take their bliss at another's cost."[31] In her 1924 volume, *The Life and Letters of Emily Dickinson*, she enhanced speculation by offering a brief but suggestive description of an overpowering love for an unnamed married man that Dickinson met in Philadelphia in the spring of 1854.[32] Because she could not violate the moral codes of her society and destroy the happy life of the man's wife, according to Bianchi, Dickinson withdrew completely, and forever, into the protection of her father's house. The man, unable to live with such sacrifice, withdrew with his family to the other side of the continent.

Two biographies in 1930 attempted to solve the mystery surrounding Dickinson's life. With an undue emphasis on the love story as the central fact of her life, what both finally achieved was to romanticize and make even more remote the heart and soul of the poet. Each biographer introduced a candidate for the role of paramour and heaped a good deal of sentimentality on both men. To Josephine Pollitt in *Emily Dickinson: The Human Background of Her Poetry*, Major Edward B. Hunt, the first husband of Dickinson's childhood friend Helen Hunt Jackson, was the secret man in Dickinson's life.[33] Genevieve Taggard, whose biography *The Life and Mind of Emily Dickinson* was published six months after Pollitt's, proposed the name of George H. Gould, a student at Amherst College, as Dickinson's unknown lover.[34]

These earliest biographies are now considered inadequate for serious study of Emily Dickinson because their arguments were based on unfounded assumptions, hearsay, coincidence, and erroneous evidence. However, they did succeed in creating the idea of a love story too delicious for the public imagination to willingly surrender, and a heroized image of the poet which obscured the facts of the real woman and poet.

It was not until 1938 that the first reliable biography was published. George Frisbie Whicher, in *This Was a Poet*, suggests the names of two men who were important to Dickinson, Benjamin Franklin Newton, an apprentice in her father's law firm, and Rev. Charles Wadsworth, a Presbyterian minister she met in Philadelphia in 1855.[35] While Whicher discusses their influence upon Dickinson, he wisely avoids the presumptions of a sensational love affair with either. The strengths of Whicher's study lie in his placement of the poet firmly in the context of her New England background, and in his suggestive interpretations of the first person voice in her poetry.

The search for Dickinson's supposed lover has been a fairly consuming interest of many scholars and biographers. In addition to the several candidates already proposed, Samuel Bowles, editor of the *Springfield Republican* and longtime friend of the Dickinson family, has been suggested by Winfield Townley Scott, David Higgins, and Ruth Miller.[36]

Still another name for the mysterious lover was put forward by Rebecca Patterson, in the person of Kate Scott Anthon.[37] Patterson sees Dickinson engaged in a lesbian love affair that has been mostly ignored by other Dickinson scholars until recently. Lillian Faderman in "Emily Dickinson's Homoerotic Poetry," lends support to Patterson's theory by examining a group of love poems she feels are clearly addressed to a woman or women.[38] In an essay reviewing the critical reception of Dickinson as a homosexual, Frederick L. Morey in "ED's Elusive Lover," suggests there has been a significant change over the years.[39] The early reactions to Patterson's biography ranged from outrage to silence. Recent and more positive assessments, Morey suggests, reflect the broader changes in society's attitudes in general toward human sexuality.

The most recent candidate to emerge as Dickinson's early lover is found in Dorothy Waugh, *Emily Dickinson's Beloved*.[40] Working with fragments of poems and letters, a great deal of supposition and conjecture, Waugh names Richard Salter Storrs Dickinson, a distant relative of the poet.

Strange and difficult evidence for an early unrequited love affair are the three drafts of letters found among Dickinson's papers addressed to an unnamed "Master." They are puzzling documents because of their cryptic content and distorted rhetoric that appear to be the product of extreme tension. They are painfully moving letters which plead desperately for love and attention from the "Master." The sense of rejection and unfulfilled desire echo throughout the letters. David Higgins in *Portrait of Emily Dickinson: The Poet and Her Prose*, and Ruth Miller in *The Poetry of Emily Dickinson*, agree that the identity of the "Master" is Samuel

Bowles.[41] In Miller's thorough and convincing discussion of these important letters, she states her belief that the letters were never sent, but were written to seek relief from her feelings of frustration at the indifference of Samuel Bowles. Miller's close examination of the letters reveals that they served as the source material for later poems and letters that Dickinson did send to Bowles. Miller's evidence is based upon similarities in imagery, tone, subject matter, and allusions.

The emotional life of anyone is complex and usually sufficiently private to make reconstruction difficult, if not altogether impossible. In the case of Emily Dickinson, an elusive personality who clung to her privacy perhaps more than many in literary history, the hidden areas of her life may prove to be impervious to illumination. Whether the man she loved in her early years was Bowles, or Wadsworth, or some other person yet to be revealed, the fact remains that during the period from 1858 to 1864 she not only learned about the beauty and pain of love, but transformed her experience into some of the finest lyrics in the English language.

While uncertainty may always cloud the identity of an early lover, biographers are now convinced of an important love that came to Dickinson late in life. One of the most interesting and well documented relationships for Dickinson appears in Millicent Todd Bingham, *Emily Dickinson: A Revelation*.[42] Bingham published a collection of love letters written by Dickinson during the late 1870's and early 1880's to Otis P. Lord, judge of the Massachusetts Supreme Court and friend of Dickinson's father. The letters reveal Dickinson's loving though Platonic attachment that was apparently reciprocated by the elderly widower. It seems she wore a ring he gave her, and a few weeks after his death in 1884 she suffered a nervous collapse which marked the beginning of a protracted illness from which she died in 1886. While not secret and sensational as the supposed earlier romance in her life, Dickinson's relationship with Judge Lord appears to have been serious, wholesome, and rewarding for both.

After George Whicher's 1938 biography, another significant one did not appear until the 1950's. Richard Chase, *Emily Dickinson*, and Thomas H. Johnson, *Emily Dickinson: An Interpretive Biography*, are critical works and add to our understanding of Dickinson's poetry, background, and friendships, but neither add data not found in Whicher.[43]

An important and unique source of biographical material appeared in 1960. Jay Leyda's *The Years and Hours of Emily Dickinson* is a two-volume collection of chronologically arranged letters and selections from diaries of many people surrounding Dickinson, as well as items from periodicals and other printed sources from the period, which gives a multi-sided view of her life and environs.[44]

The other items of biographical significance to appear in the 1960's are Theodora Ward, *The Capsule of the Mind*, and Jack L. Capps, *Emily*

Dickinson's Reading 1836–1886.[45] Ward traces the inner life of Dickinson through the self-relevation found in the poetry and deals thoroughly with several of her important friendships. Capps provides a full-scale discussion of the influence of her reading upon her mind and art.

In 1974 appeared what is generally considered the finest and final summation to date of Dickinson's biography. Richard B. Sewall's *The Life of Emily Dickinson* is a comprehensive two-volume study of her life summarizing and concluding all the known facts, as well as all the theories, guesses, and legends about the poet, her family, and her surroundings.[46] Issues that have been unresolved because of a lack of complete information—for example, the identity of Dickinson's supposed lover, and the exact nature of her relationship to Sue Gilbert—remain unresolved in Sewall's study. But his presentation of all available material regarding such issues is meticulous and thorough. He includes new material about the love affair between Dickinson's brother, Austin, and the first editor of her poems, Mabel Todd. Sewall has covered the territory so completely that the need for another major biography seems unnecessary until, and unless, new evidence is found to significantly alter our understanding of her life as he has presented it.

A unique and important contribution to an understanding of Emily Dickinson's biography was made by John Cody, M.D., a practicing psychiatrist, who began in 1967 to issue articles recreating her psychological life through an interpretation of her writings. In 1971 his complete study appeared, *After Great Pain*, tracing her emotional and mental states from poems, letters, and the evidence of her contemporaries who knew her.[47] Two chief hypotheses about Dickinson's personality are that she experienced early in life a psychological separation from her mother, and that she suffered a severe mental breakdown during her late twenties. Out of this suffering and psychological instability, Cody claims, grew the voice of a great poet. Other sections of the book dealing with her relationships with her brother and his wife seem convincing, as does Cody's analysis of the love poems as imaginary attempts to fulfill deep personal longings.

Negative reception of Cody's book has focused more on method than content. Eleanor Lyons in "A Psychiatric Look at Emily Dickinson," criticizes the use of poems as biographical evidence rather than as works of art.[48] She feels Cody's method forces him to wrench the meaning of a poem to fit his theory. Cynthia Chaliff, who has herself written on Dickinson from a psychological point of view, also feels Dr. Cody has forced poems to fit a preconceived thesis, and has ignored the cultural factors regarding Dickinson's relationship with her mother.[49] While Cody sees the weak mother and dominating father as crucial and unique to Dickinson's development, Chaliff sees Dickinson's domestic arrangements as extremely typical of the Victorian world.

In recent years the study of Emily Dickinson from the women's studies perspective has revealed significant new understanding about her life and times and much further work in this area may yet be done. Among the most substantial items recently is Adrienne Rich's, "Vesuvius at Home: The Power of Emily Dickinson."[50] Instead of seeing Dickinson's withdrawal from society as the result of female psychic frailty, Rich suggests that Dickinson withdrew in order to conceal her poetic power from a disapproving patriarchal culture. In her day, only men were accorded the strength of mind Dickinson sensed in herself. In a similar vein, Suzanne Juhasz in " 'A Privilege So Awful': Emily Dickinson as Woman Poet," believes that Dickinson mocked the limiting roles allowed for women in the mid-nineteenth century, and withdrew to maintain the power and dignity of herself as both woman and poet.[51]

Among larger studies of the life of women in America there are frequently references to Dickinson. Among several which may be mentioned is a sociological approach to the world in which Dickinson lived, Barbara Welter, *Dimity Convictions: The American Woman in the Nineteenth Century*,[52] and a good overall view of the relation of Dickinson to other women writers of the time, Ellen Moers, *Literary Women*.[53]

A matter of continuing interest for biographers has been Dickinson's physical ailments. Of particular concern has been the eye problem she sought treatment for in Boston during 1864–65. Dr. Cody in *After Great Pain* suggested it was actually counseling she sought in Boston, perhaps for a psychosomatic problem related to her eyes. A new and plausible observation concerning her eyes is Martin Wand and Richard B. Sewall, " 'Eyes Be Blind, Heart Be Still': A New Perspective on Emily Dickinson's Eye Problem."[54] After examining daguerreotypes and paintings of the poet, her sister, and mother, the authors conclude the three women suffered from a condition in which one eye turns out, called exotropia. The illness has a set of behavior patterns associated with it which they hypothesize may account for certain of Dickinson's characteristics.

Jerry Ferris Reynolds seems to go too far when he suggests a physical reason for Dickinson's withdrawal from society. In " 'Banishment from Native Eyes': The Reason for Emily Dickinson's Seclusion Reconsidered," he believes that certain of her letters and poems make reference to a disease called lupas erythematosus which causes disfiguring skin blotches.[55] To hide the embarrassing rash from view, he concludes, Dickinson withdrew.

CRITICISM

A good overview of the first seventy years of Dickinson criticism is Klaus Lubbers, *Emily Dickinson: The Critical Revolution*.[56] It is a detailed, chronological survey of the growth of Dickinson's reputation from 1862–1962. The book succeeds in charting the changes in her fame, as it charts the changes in taste over the hundred year period.

The earliest published critical commentary about Emily Dickinson's poetry is found in several essays by Thomas Wentworth Higginson and in the short periodical reviews of the early editions of her poetry. Higginson's essay, "An Open Portfolio," is the first essay about Dickinson's poetry, and his introduction to *Poems*, 1890, is a serious attempt to introduce the reader to the irregularities of her poetry.[57] He defended her lack of rhyme and regular meter, and her use of ellipsis and compression. He affirmed that "when a thought takes one's breath away, a lesson in grammar is an impertinence."

The surprisingly large number of early reviews of her poetry (many of them unsigned) are typically mixed in their enthusiasm. Few were totally negative. William Dean Howells's "The Poems of Emily Dickinson," is perhaps the extreme statement of appreciation for her work.[58] He touches upon her New England character, her isolation, and sees a variety of influences upon her poetry. He declared her poems were "the perfect expression of her ideals." To the opposite extreme is Andrew Lang's "Some American Poets."[59] He found nothing to admire and referred to her as incomprehensible, illiterate, and uneducated. Her challenge to accepted notions of rhyme, meter, and correct grammar were the major targets of his dislike.

In 1896, in response to the publication of a third volume of her poems, three essays appeared which summed up all of her work thus far published, and looked forward to the future development of her reputation: Bliss Carmen, " A Note on Emily Dickinson," Harry Lyman Koopman, "Emily Dickinson," and Rupert Hughes, "The Ideas of Emily Dickinson."[60] All three admired her originality and expressed confidence that her place in world poetry was assured.

It was not until after the appearance of *The Single Hound* in 1914 that there was another outpouring of critical response to Emily Dickinson. Things which had bothered earlier critics, such as her irregular poetic form, were now seen as her original attempts at liberating American poetry from a stale heritage. Elizabeth Shepley Sergeant in "An Early Imagist," drew the similarities sharply into focus between Dickinson and the Imagists by emphasizing Dickinson's experimental quality, her stark, bold expression, and her freedom with form.[61] Amy Lowell, the leading Imagist poet of the time, began to include Dickinson in her lectures on the new poetry and wrote her into *A Critical Fable*.[62]

Other young poet-critics wrote admiringly about Dickinson and recognized her as a precursor to the modern spirit. Robert S. Hillyer wrote over a dozen pieces on her, and Louis Untermeyer and Conrad Aiken both, in addition to editing volumes of her poems, wrote a number of appreciative essays, reviews, and commentaries about her. Aiken's introduction to his *Selected Poems of Emily Dickinson* is perhaps the most important essay of the period.[63] He analyzed the poetry and isolated a number of important topics that have been of interest to critics ever since.

He saw the influence of Transcendentalism but discounted that of Puritanism. Her treatment of death in a large number of poems and her profoundly metaphysical tendencies he noted were part of the singular nature of her genius.

Although there was growing enthusiasm and much favorable commentary about Dickinson's work among creative writers and staff editors, the academic critics of the 1920's were relatively uninterested in her. For example, in the singularly important *Cambridge History of American Literature*, Norman Foerster assigns a very minor role for her in the future study of American letters, by declaring her place "inconspicuous but secure."[64]

In the 1930's the situation began to change. Practitioners of the New Criticism with their de-emphasis on biography, their appreciation for irony and poetic tension, and their innovative practice of poetry explication, began to uncover what was often misunderstood or unappreciated about Dickinson's poetic genius. The first significant essay of this new era is Allen Tate's "New England Culture and Emily Dickinson."[65] Tate described the tension evident in Dickinson's poetry resulting from the decline of Puritanism under the impact of emerging Emersonian Transcendentalism. Dickinson lived during this time of change, a period which created for her what Tate calls the perfect literary situation.

Two other important scholars of the time wrote evaluative and influential essays on Dickinson. Yvor Winters in "Emily Dickinson and the Limits of Judgment" and R. P. Blackmur in "Emily Dickinson: Notes on Prejudice and Fact," attempted to give balanced judgments of what was good and bad in Dickinson's art.[66] However, both have an apologetic and condescending flavor which tend to date them.

Between the publication of the first reliable biography of Dickinson, Whicher's *This Was a Poet* (1938), and the appearance of the Johnson variorum edition of her poetry in 1955, critical response to her was steady but relatively slight. During the 1940's only three books of criticism were produced. Sister Mary James Power, *In the Name of the Bee: The Significance of Emily Dickinson*, interpreted Dickinson in the spirit of Roman Catholic mysticism, and Henry W. Wells's *Introduction to Emily Dickinson* was a good overall introduction to her but suffers from excessive enthusiasm and hyperbolic evaluations.[67] A small third book privately printed in 1945 is Clement Wood, *Emily Dickinson: The Volcanic Heart*.[68] It is a heavily Freudian interpretation of the poetry which views a renounced lover as the key element in the poet's life.

In 1950 Sister Mary Humiliata in "Emily Dickinson—Mystic Poet?" corrected the excesses of Sister Power's claims for Dickinson as a mystic.[69] Two final critical studies appearing before the publication of the Johnson edition are Richard Chase, *Emily Dickinson*, and Donald E. Thackrey, *Emily Dickinson's Approach to Poetry*.[70] Chase's is a discriminating study full of illuminations into her poetry. He observed her major theme to be "the achievement of status through crucial experiences." Thackrey's is a useful analysis of Dickinson's attitudes toward language.

With the appearance of the three-volume Johnson variorum edition of Dickinson's poetry, the number of critical studies produced every year has grown enormously. Articles and explications appeared in the decade after 1955 at the rate of ten to twenty a year. In recent years the output has been significantly greater. Theses and dissertations on Dickinson have been steadily increasing as well. Within the limitations of this essay, it seems prudent to touch lightly on a selection of the most significant works, and to indicate, where possible, trends or directions in the criticism.

The first book based upon a close examination of the poems and letters arranged chronologically was Johnson's own *Emily Dickinson: An Interpretive Biography*.[71] Largely biographical in nature, it does contain valuable information about her prosody. The first comprehensive reading of the poems based upon the Johnson edition is Charles R. Anderson, *Emily Dickinson's Poetry: Stairway of Surprise*.[72] His analyses of 103 of her best poems remain substantial and perceptive contributions to our understanding of her craft.

Many poets have written about Dickinson, both critically and creatively, but few have been as interesting as Archibald MacLeish, Louise Bogan, and Richard Wilbur. They appeared together at a Dickinson celebration at Amherst College and their papers were published as *Emily Dickinson: Three Views*.[73] MacLeish in "The Private World" gives attention to the tone of Dickinson's poetic voice; Bogan focused on her mystical nature; and Wilbur wrote of her as the poet with a "sense of privation." Marguerite Harris's *Emily Dickinson: Letters from the World* is a collection of forty-five poems on Dickinson written by contemporary poets, including Gregory Corso, Richard Eberhart, and William Stafford.[74]

Clark Griffith in *The Long Shadow: Emily Dickinson's Tragic Poetry* perceptively analyzed some fifty of her best poems for their "*angst, dread, and terror*."[75] In contrast, Thomas W. Ford, *Heaven Beguiles the Tired: Death in the Poetry of Emily Dickinson*, offered unsatisfactory explications for many of her death poems, and failed to relate the subject to her work as a whole.[76] Martha Winburn England's "Emily Dickinson and Isaac Watts: Puritan Hymnodists," is a thorough analysis of Dickinson's use of the metrical conventions of the hymn.[77]

David T. Porter's *The Art of Emily Dickinson's Early Poetry* examines her apprenticeship as a poet in some 300 early poems.[78] Albert J. Gelpi, *Emily Dickinson: The Mind of the Poet*, and William R. Sherwood, *Circumference and Circumstance: Stages in the Mind and Art of Emily Dickinson*, approach the same territory with differing results.[79] Gelpi describes her adjustment to contrary cultural influences, while Sherwood emphasizes to an extreme the singular importance of

Puritanism in the development of her mind. Hyatt H. Waggoner's "Emily Dickinson: The Transcendent Self," emphasized the importance of the Emersonian influence in the development of her mind.[80]

Brita Lindberg-Seyersted, *The Voice of the Poet: Aspects of Style in the Poetry of Emily Dickinson* applied linguistic theory to analyze Dickinson's language and language habits.[81] She focused on Dickinson's stylistic uses of colloquialness, slantness, and privateness, and investigated them on the levels of diction, metrics, and syntatic structures. Dolores Dyer Lucas argued that Dickinson exploited the technique of the literary and folk riddle in her poetry in *Emily Dickinson and Riddle*.[82] Denis Donoghue's *Emily Dickinson* is a useful forty-seven page introductory pamphlet for the undergraduate on her life and work.[83]

Scholars in India have shown much interest in Emily Dickinson, and one of the first major studies written in that country is Salamatullah Khan's *Emily Dickinson's Poetry; The Flood Subjects*.[84] In addition to analyzing her major themes, Kahn notes likeness with major Indian poems such as the *Rig Veda*.

Richard Howard's article "A Consideration of the Writings of Emily Dickinson," has implications for future editors of Dickinson's manuscripts.[85] He argues that the profusion of variants and the untamed quality of her grammar and punctuation is part of her "process" phenomenology. He urges that such improvisational qualities need to be preserved for the reader to understand the poet's intentions.

Inder Nath Kher's *The Landscape of Absence* is a major effort at understanding the numerous primary patterns that appear in Dickinson's poetry, e.g., the myth of the eternal return, and the quest for indentity.[86] Kher treats the poetry without reference at all to biography, consequently the study fails to indicate a sense of artistic growth or change in the poet.

Albert Gelpi's chapter on Dickinson in *The Tenth Muse* tries to delineate the psychological sources of her poetry.[87] Using a Jungian framework Frederick L. Morey attempts a classification of her best poems according to the themes of ascension, descension, or stasis in "Jungian Dickinson."[88] Jean McClure Mudge's phenomenological study, *Emily Dickinson and the Image of Home* is a sustained effort to define the poet's consciousness by a variety of physical, psychic, and cultural images.[89] Of utmost significance is her "creative inner space," the poet's true home. Robert Weisbuch's *Emily Dickinson's Poetry* is an intense effort at exploring the underlying assumptions of the poetry through style and theme.[90] He argues that she is best understood as using archtypal situations with multiple meanings in her poetry, than actual life experiences with limited or assigned meanings.

Paul J. Ferlazzo's *Emily Dickinson* is an overall introduction to the life and work of the poet, and a survey of the major scholarship to that time.[91] Offering explications of many key poems the book is arranged thematically (faith, mortality, love, sanity, nature) with additional chapters on the legends and life of the poet, and on her prose.

The methods of literary analysis devised by phenomenological and structuralist critics offer a provocative and useful understanding of Dickinson's craftmanship. This is a relatively new approach to her work, and though impressive achievements have already been realized, a good deal remains to be done. Elizabeth F. Perlmutter's "Hide and Seek: Emily Dickinson's Use of the Existential Sentence," is a skillful examination of Dickinson's strategy of transforming subjective phenomena, such as fear and hope, into animate entities thus vivifying their certainty and effect.[92] Suzanne Juhasz, " 'I Dwell in Possibility,' Emily Dickinson in the Subjunctive Mood," notes that the subjunctive verb form is used not to express wish fulfillment, but to articulate extravagant emotional activity.[93] In two 1978 essays and a 1979 book by Sharon Cameron, the phenomenalist approach is significantly advanced. In "Naming as History: Dickinson's Poems of Definition," Cameron examines the psychic equilibrium strived for by the persona in the poetry when faced with overwhelming realities such as death or despair.[94] In contrast, her article " 'A Loaded Gun': Dickinson and the Dialectic of Rage," identifies those poetic persona that respond in an angry, eruptive voice to the necessities of temporality and sacrifice.[95] In her book, *Lyric Time*, Cameron applies the speech act theory to Dickinson's use of the lyric, and discusses the poems as acts of consciousness.[96] She analyzes clusters of poems and points out Dickinson's skillful work at the boundaries of lyric structure.

The women's studies perspective on the poetry has also yielded significant and sound judgments, with much important work remaining to be done. Joanne Feit Diehl's " 'Come Slowly—Eden': An Exploration of Women Poets and Their Muse," uses Dickinson as a principal example to examine how women poets perceive themselves in relation to a male-dominated tradition.[97] Barbara J. Williams's "A Room of Her Own: Emily Dickinson as Woman Artist" in *Feminist Criticism* examines through poetic images of diminution and disenfranchisement Dickinson's perception of herself as economically and physically dependent on others.[98] The concluding chapter of Sandra M. Gilbert and Susan Gubar's *Madwoman in the Attic* analyzes the fictional lives described in the poems as typical of the submissive female trapped in a relationship with a dominating male.[99]

A posthumous assembly of Rebecca Patterson's essays appeared in 1979 as *Emily Dickinson's Imagery*.[100] Weaving throughout essays on colors, gems, places, and science, Patterson stresses sexual implications at the expense of other possible meanings.

Karl Keller's *The Only Kangaroo Among the Beauty* is a panoramic view of Dickinson's relation with other American poets.[101] He shows how Dickinson is like or unlike a vast number of other American writers from Anne Bradstreet to Robert Frost. As intellectual history the volume is a comprehensive analysis of Puritan esthetics, and a thoughtful examination of her influence upon twentieth century writers.

Paul J. Ferlazzo

Montana State University

Notes

1. Willis J. Buckingham, *Emily Dickinson: An Annotated Bibliography—Writings, Scholarship, Criticism, and Ana, 1850–1968* (Bloomington, Ind.: Indiana University Press, 1970).

2. Willis J. Buckingham, "1880–1968 Addenda to the Buckingham Bibliography," *EDB*, 26 (1974), 103–28; and Willis J. Buckingham, "Second Addendum to the Buckingham Bibliography," *EDB* 33 (1978), 61–75.

3. Sheila Clendenning, *Emily Dickinson, A Bibliography: 1850–1966* (Kent, Oh.: Kent State University Press, 1968).

4. Susan Freis, *Emily Dickinson: A Checklist of Criticism, 1930–1966, PBSA*, 61 (1967), 359–385.

5. William White, "Emily Dickinsoniana: An Annotated Checklist of Books About the Poet," *BB*, 26 (1969), 100–104.

6. James Woodress, "Emily Dickinson," in *Fifteen American Authors Before 1900: Bibliographic Essays on Research and Criticism*, ed. Robert A. Rees and Earl N. Harbert (Madison: University of Wisconsin Press, 1971), pp. 139–168.

7. Alfred Leete Hampson, *Emily Dickinson: A Bibliography* (Northampton, Mass.: Hampshire Bookshop, 1930).

8. *Emily Dickinson, December 10, 1830–May 15, 1886: A Bibliography* (Amherst, Mass.: Jones Library, 1930).

9. Willis J. Buckingham, "The Bibliographical Study of Emily Dickinson," *RALS*, 4 (1974), 57–71.

10. S. P. Rosenbaum, *A Concordance to the Poems of Emily Dickinson* (Ithaca, N.Y.: Cornell University Press, 1964).

11. Joseph Duchac, *The Poems of Emily Dickinson: An Annotated Guide to Commentary Published in English, 1890–1977* (Boston: G.K. Hall, 1979).

12. Millicent Todd Bingham, *Ancestors' Brocades: The Literary Debut of Emily Dickinson* (New York and London: Harper, 1945); R.W. Franklin, *The Editing of Emily Dickinson: A Reconsideration* (Madison: University of Wisconsin Press, 1967); John S. van E. Kohn, "Giving Emily Dickinson to the World," *PULC*, 31 (1969), 47–54; Robert B. Laurence, "The Mind Alone," *EDB*, 15 (1970), 94–102.

13. *Poems by Emily Dickinson*, eds. Mabel Loomis Todd and T.W. Higginson (Boston: Roberts Brothers, 1890); and *Poems by Emily Dickinson, Second Series*, ed. Mabel Loomis Todd and T.W. Higginson (Boston: Roberts Brothers, 1891).

14. *Poems by Emily Dickinson, Third Series*, ed. Mabel Loomis Todd (Boston: Roberts Brothers, 1896).

15. *Letters of Emily Dickinson*, 2 vols., ed. Mabel Loomis Todd (Boston: Roberts Brothers, 1894).

16. *The Single Hound, Poems of a Lifetime by Emily Dickinson*, ed. Martha Dickinson Bianchi (Boston: Little, Brown, 1914).

17. *The Complete Poems of Emily Dickinson*, ed. Martha Dickinson Bianchi (Boston: Little, Brown; Toronto: McClelland, 1924); *Further Poems of Emily Dickinson*, ed. Martha

Dickinson Bianchi and Alfred Leete Hampson (Boston: Little, Brown, 1929); *The Poems of Emily Dickinson: Centenary Edition*, ed. Martha Dickinson Bianchi and Alfred Leete Hampson (Boston: Little, Brown, 1930); and *Unpublished Poems by Emily Dickinson*, ed. Martha Dickinson Bianchi and Alfred Leete Hampson (Boston: Little, Brown, 1935).

18. Martha Dickinson Bianchi, *The Life and Letters of Emily Dickinson* (Boston and New York: Houghton Mifflin; London: Cape, 1924); and Martha Dickinson Bianchi, *Emily Dickinson Face to Face: Unpublished Letters with Notes and Reminiscences* (Boston and New York: Houghton Mifflin, 1932).

19. *Selected Poems of Emily Dickinson*, ed. Conrad Aiken (London: Cape, 1924).

20. Conrad Aiken, "Emily Dickinson and Her Editors," *Yale Review*, 18 (1929), 796–98.

21. *Bolts of Melody: New Poems of Emily Dickinson*, ed. Mabel Loomis Todd and Millicent Todd Bingham (New York and London: Harper, 1945); Millicent Todd Bingham, *Emily Dickinson: A Revelation* (New York: Harper; Toronto: Musson, 1954); and Millicent Todd Bingham, *Emily Dickinson's Home: Letters of Edward Dickinson and His Family* (New York: Harper; Toronto: Musson, 1955).

22. *The Poems of Emily Dickinson, Including Variant Readings Critically Compared With All Known Manuscripts*, 3 vols., ed. Thomas H. Johnson (Cambridge, Mass.: Belknap Press of Harvard University Press, 1955).

23. *The Complete Poems of Emily Dickinson*, ed. Thomas H. Johnson (Boston: Little, Brown, 1960); and *Final Harvest: Emily Dickinson's Poems*, ed. Thomas H. Johnson (Boston: Little, Brown, 1962).

24. R. W. Franklin, *The Editing of Emily Dickinson: A Reconsideration* (Madison: University of Wisconsin Press, 1967).

25. Edith Wylder, *The Last Face: Emily Dickinson's Manuscripts* (Albuquerque: University of New Mexico Press, 1971).

26. Edith Perry Stamm, "Emily Dickinson: Poetry and Punctuation," *Sat R*, 46 (March 30, 1963), 26–27, 74.

27. Brita Lindberg, "Emily Dickinson's Punctuation," *SN*, 38 (1965), 327–359.

28. *The Letters of Emily Dickinson*, 3 vols. ed. Thomas H. Johnson and Theodora Ward (Cambridge, Mass.: Belknap Press of Harvard University Press; Toronto: S. J. R. Saunders; London: Oxford University Press, 1958).

29. R. W. Franklin, *The Editing of Emily Dickinson: A Reconsideration* (Madison: University of Wisconsin Press, 1967).

30. *The Manuscript Books of Emily Dickinson*, ed. R. W. Franklin (Cambridge, Mass.: Belknap Press of Harvard University Press, 1981).

31. *The Single Hound, Poems of a Lifetime by Emily Dickinson*, ed. Martha Dickinson Bianchi (Boston: Little, Brown, 1914), p. xviii.

32. Martha Dickinson Bianchi, *The Life and Letters of Emily Dickinson* (Boston and New York: Houghton Mifflin; London: Cape, 1924).

33. Josephine Pollitt, *Emily Dickinson: The Human Background of Her Poetry* (New York: Harper, 1930).

34. Genevieve Taggard, *The Life and Mind of Emily Dickinson* (New York: Knopf; London: G. Allen, 1930).

35. George Frisbie Whicher, *This Was a Poet: A Critical Biography of Emily Dickinson* (New York: Scribners, 1938).

36. Winfield Townley Scott, "Emily Dickinson and Samuel Bowles," *Fresco*, 10 (1959), 7–17; David Higgins, *Portrait of Emily Dickinson: The Poet and Her Prose* (New Brunswick, N.J.: Rutgers University Press, 1967); and Ruth Miller, *The Poetry of Emily Dickinson* (Middletown, Conn.: Wesleyan University Press, 1968).

37. Rebecca Patterson, *The Riddle of Emily Dickinson* (Boston: Houghton Mifflin; Toronto: Thomas Allen, 1951; London: Gollancz, 1953).

38. Lillian Faderman, "Emily Dickinson's Homoerotic Poetry," *HJ*, 18 (1978), 19–27.

39. Frederick L. Morey, "ED's Elusive Lover," *HJ*, 18 (1978), 28–34.

40. Dorothy Waugh, *Emily Dickinson's Beloved: A Surmise* (New York: Vantage Press, 1976).

41. David Higgins, *Portrait of Emily Dickinson: The Poet and Her Prose* (New Brunswick, N.J.: Rutgers University Press, 1967); and Ruth Miller, *The Poetry of Emily Dickinson* (Middletown, Conn.: Wesleyan University Press, 1968).

42. Millicent Todd Bingham, *Emily Dickinson: A Revelation* (New York: Harper; Toronto: Musson, 1954).

43. Richard Chase, *Emily Dickinson* (New York: William Sloane Associates, 1951); and Thomas H. Johnson, *Emily Dickinson: An Interpretive Biography* (Cambridge, Mass.: Belknap Press of Harvard University Press; London: Oxford University Press; Toronto: S. J. R. Saunders, 1955).

44. Jay Leyda, *The Years and Hours of Emily Dickinson*, 2 vols. (New Haven: Yale University Press; London: Oxford University Press; Toronto: Burns and MacEachern, 1960).

45. Theodora Ward, *The Capsule of the Mind: Chapters in the Life of Emily Dickinson* (Cambridge, Mass.: Harvard University Press; London: Oxford University Press, 1961); and Jack L. Capps, *Emily Dickinson's Reading 1836–1886* (Cambridge, Mass.: Harvard University Press; London: Oxford University Press, 1966).

46. Richard B. Sewall, *The Life of Emily Dickinson* 2 vols. (New York: Farrar, Strauss, and Giroux, 1974).

47. John Cody, *After Great Pain: The Inner Life of Emily Dickinson* (Cambridge, Mass.: Belknap Press of Harvard University Press, 1971).

48. Eleanor Lyons, "A Psychiatric Look at Emily Dickinson," *HSL*, 4 (1972), 174–79.

49. Cynthia Chaliff, "*After Great Pain: The Inner Life of Emily Dickinson*," *L&P*, 22 (1972), 45–47.

50. Adrienne Rich, "Vesuvius at Home: The Power of Emily Dickinson," *Parnassus*, 5 (1976), 49–74.

51. Suzanne Juhasz, " 'A Privilege So Awful': Emily Dickinson as Woman Poet," *SJS*, 2 (1976), 94–107.

52. Barbara Welter, *Dimity Convictions: The American Woman in the Nineteenth Century* (Athens: Ohio University Press, 1976).

53. Ellen Moers, *Literary Women* (Garden City, N.Y.: Doubleday, 1976).

54. Martin Wand and Richard B. Sewall, " 'Eyes Be Blind, Heart Be Still': A New Perspective on Emily Dickinson's Eye Problem," *NEQ*, 52 (1979), 400–06.

55. Jerry Ferris Reynolds, " 'Banishment from Native Eyes': The Reason for Emily Dickinson's Seclusion Reconsidered," *Markham R*, 8 (1979), 41–48.

56. Klaus Lubbers, *Emily Dickinson: The Critical Revolution* (Ann Arbor: University of Michigan Press, 1968).

57. Thomas Wentworth Higginson, "An Open Portfolio," *Christian Union*, 42 (September 25, 1890), 392–93; and *Poems by Emily Dickinson*, ed. Mabel Loomis Todd and T. W. Higginson (Boston: Roberts Brothers, 1890), pp. iii–vi.

58. William Dean Howells, "The Poems of Emily Dickinson," *Harper's Magazine*, 82 (January 1891), 318–21.

59. Andrew Lang, "Some American Poets," *Illustrated London News*, 98 (March 7, 1891), 307.

60. Bliss Carmen, "A Note on Emily Dickinson," *Boston Evening Transcript*, November

21, 1896, p. 15; Harry Lyman Koopman, "Emily Dickinson," *Brown Magazine*, 8 (December 1896), 82–92; and Rupert Hughes, "The Ideas of Emily Dickinson," *Godey's Magazine*, 133 (November 1896), 541–43.

61. Elizabeth Shepley Sergeant, "An Early Imagist," *New Republic*, 4 (August 14, 1915), 52–54.

62. Amy Lowell, *A Critical Fable* (Boston: Houghton Mifflin, 1922).

63. *Selected Poems of Emily Dickinson*, ed. Conrad Aiken (London: Cape, 1924), pp. 5–22.

64. Norman Foerster, "Later Poets: Emily Dickinson" in *Cambridge History of American Literature*, ed. W. P. Trent, S. P. Sherman, and C. Van Doren (New York: Macmillan, 1921), III, pp. 31–34.

65. Allen Tate, "New England Culture and Emily Dickinson," *Symposium*, 3 (April 1932), 206–26.

66. Yvor Winters, "Emily Dickinson and the Limits of Judgment," in *Maule's Curse: Seven Studies in the History of American Obscurantism* (Norfolk, Conn.: New Directions, 1938), pp. 149–65; and R. P. Blackmur, "Emily Dickinson: Notes on Prejudice and Fact," *Southern Review*, 3 (Autumn 1937), 323–47.

67. Sister Mary James Power, *In the Name of the Bee: The Significance of Emily Dickinson* (New York: Sheed and Ward, 1943); and Henry W. Wells, *Introduction to Emily Dickinson* (Chicago: Hendricks House, 1947).

68. Clement Wood, *Emily Dickinson: The Volcanic Heart* (n.p., 1945).

69. Sister Mary Humiliata, "Emily Dickinson—Mystic Poet?" *College English*, 12 (December 1950), 144–49.

70. Richard Chase, *Emily Dickinson* (New York: William Sloane Associates, 1951); and Donald E. Thackrey, *Emily Dickinson's Approach to Poetry* (Lincoln: University of Nebraska Press, 1954).

71. Thomas H. Johnson, *Emily Dickinson: An Interpretive Biography* (Cambridge, Mass.: Belknap Press of Harvard University Press; London: Oxford University Press; Toronto: S. J. R. Saunders, 1955).

72. Charles R. Anderson, *Emily Dickinson's Poetry: Stairway of Surprise* (New York: Holt Rinehart and Winston; London: Heinemann, 1960).

73. Archibald MacLeish, Louise Bogan, and Richard Wilbur, *Emily Dickinson: Three Views* (Amherst, Mass.: Amherst College Press, 1960).

74. Marguerite Harris, *Emily Dickinson: Letters from the World* (n.p., 1970).

75. Clark Griffith, *The Long Shadow: Emily Dickinson's Tragic Poetry* (Princeton: Princeton University Press, 1964).

76. Thomas W. Ford, *Heaven Beguiles the Tired: Death in the Poetry of Emily Dickinson* (University, Ala.: University of Alabama Press, 1966).

77. Martha Winburn England, "Emily Dickinson and Isaac Watts: Puritan Hymnodists," *Bulletin of the New York Public Library*, 69 (February 1965), 83–116.

78. David T. Porter, *The Art of Emily Dickinson's Early Poetry* (Cambridge, Mass.: Harvard University Press, 1966).

79. Albert J. Gelpi, *Emily Dickinson: The Mind of the Poet* (Cambridge, Mass.: Harvard University Press; London: Oxford University Press, 1965); and William R. Sherwood, *Circumference and Circumstance: Stages in the Mind and Art of Emily Dickinson* (New York: Columbia University Press, 1968).

80. Hyatt H. Waggoner, "Emily Dickinson: The Transcendent Self," *Criticism*, 7 (Fall 1965), 297–334.

81. Brita Lindberg-Seyersted, *The Voice of the Poet: Aspects of Style in the Poetry of Emily Dickinson* (Cambridge, Mass.: Harvard University Press, 1968).

82. Dolores Dyer Lucas, *Emily Dickinson and Riddle* (DeKalb, Ill.: Northern Illinois University Press, 1969).

83. Denis Donoghue, *Emily Dickinson* (Minneapolis: University of Minnesota Press, 1969).

84. Salamatullah Khan, *Emily Dickinson's Poetry: The Flood Subjects* (New Delhi: Aarti Book Centre, 1969).

85. Richard Howard, "A Consideration of the Writings of Emily Dickinson," *Prose*, 6 (1973), 67–97.

86. Inder Nath Kher, *The Landscape of Absence: Emily Dickinson's Poetry* (New Haven: Yale University Press, 1974).

87. Albert Gelpi, *The Tenth Muse: The Psyche of the American Poet* (Cambridge, Mass.: Harvard University Press, 1975), pp. 219–99.

88. Frederick L. Morey, "Jungian Dickinson," *EDB*, 27 (1975), 4–72.

89. Jean McClure Mudge, *Emily Dickinson and the Image of Home* (Amherst: University of Massachusetts Press, 1975).

90. Robert Weisbuch, *Emily Dickinson's Poetry* (Chicago: University of Chicago Press, 1975).

91. Paul J. Ferlazzo, *Emily Dickinson* (Boston: Twayne Publishers, 1976).

92. Elizabeth F. Perlmutter, "Hide and Seek: Emily Dickinson's Use of the Existential Sentence," *Lang & S*, 10 (1977), 109–19.

93. Suzanne Juhasz, " 'I Dwell in Possibility,' Emily Dickinson in the Subjunctive Mood," *EDB*, 32 (1977), 105–9.

94. Sharon Cameron, "Naming as History: Dickinson's Poems of Definition," *Crit I*, 5 (1978), 223–51.

95. Sharon Cameron, " 'A Loaded Gun': Dickinson and the Dialectic of Rage," *PMLA*, 93 (1978), 423–37.

96. Sharon Cameron, *Lyric Time: Dickinson and the Limits of Genre* (Baltimore: Johns Hopkins University Press, 1979).

97. Joanne Feit Diehl, " 'Come Slowly—Eden': An Exploration of Women Poets and Their Muse," *Signs*, 3 (1978), 572–87.

98. Barbara J. Williams, "A Room of Her Own: Emily Dickinson as Woman Artist" in *Feminist Criticism: Essays on Theory, Poetry and Prose*, ed. Cheryl L. Brown and Karen Olson (Metuchen, N.J.: Scarecrow, 1978), pp. 69–91.

99. Sandra M. Gilbert and Susan Gubar, *Madwoman in the Attic: The Woman Writer and the Nineteenth-Century Literary Imagination* (New Haven: Yale University Press, 1979), pp. 581–650.

100. Rebecca Patterson, *Emily Dickinson's Imagery* ed. Margaret H. Freeman (Amherst: University of Massachusetts Press, 1979).

101. Karl Keller, *The Only Kangaroo Among the Beauty: Emily Dickinson and America* (Baltimore: Johns Hopkins University Press, 1979).

An Open Portfolio
Thomas Wentworth Higginson[*]

Emerson said, many years since in the *Dial*, that the most interesting department of poetry would hereafter be found in what might be called "The Poetry of the Portfolio"; the work, that is, of persons who wrote for the relief of their own minds, and without thought of publication. Such poetry, when accumulated for years, will have at least the merit of perfect freedom; accompanied, of course, by whatever drawback follows from the habitual absence of criticism. Thought will have its full strength and uplifting, but without the proper control and chastening of literary expression; there will be wonderful strokes and felicities, and yet an incomplete and unsatisfactory whole. If we believe, with Ruskin, that "no beauty of execution can outweigh one grain or fragment of thought," then we may often gain by the seclusion of the portfolio, which rests content with a first stroke and does not over-refine and prune away afterwards. Such a sheaf of unpublished verse lies before me, the life-work of a woman so secluded that she lived literally indoors by choice for many years, and within the limits of her father's estate for many more—who shrank even from the tranquil society of a New England college town, and yet loved her few friends with profound devotedness, and divided her life between them and her flowers. It absolutely startles one to find among the memorials of this secluded inland life a picture so vividly objective as this:

BY THE SEA

Glee! the great storm is over!
 Four have recovered the land;
Forty gone down together
 Into the boiling sand.

Ring! for the scant salvation!
 Toll! for the bonnie souls
Neighbor and friend and bridegroom,
 Spinning upon the shoals.

[*]From the *Christian Union*, 42 (Sept. 25, 1890), 392–93.

How they will tell the shipwreck
    When winter shakes the door,
Till the children ask, "But the forty?
    Did they come back no more?"

Then a silence suffuses the story
    And a softness the teller's eye,
And the children no further question;
    And only the waves reply.

Celia Thaxter on her rocky island, Jean Ingelow by her English cliffs, never drew a sea picture in stronger lines than this secluded woman in her inland village, who writes elsewhere, as tersely:

I never saw a moor,
    I never saw the sea,
Yet know I how the heather looks
    And what the billows be.

I never spoke with God
    Nor visited in heaven,
Yet certain am I of the spot,
    As if the chart were given.

See now with what corresponding vigor she draws the mightier storms and shipwrecks of the soul; the title being here, as elsewhere, my own, for she herself never prefixes any:

ROUGE ET NOIR

Soul, wilt thou toss again?
By just such a hazard
Hundreds have lost, indeed,
But tens have won an all.

Angels' breathless ballot
Lingers to record thee;
Imps in eager caucus
Raffle for my soul!

Was ever the concentrated contest of a lifetime, the very issue between good and evil, put into fewer words? Then comes another, which might fairly be linked with it, and might be called

ROUGE GAGNE!

'Tis so much joy! 'Tis so much joy!
If I should fail, what poverty!
    And yet as poor as I
Have ventured all upon a throw;
Have gained! Yes! Hesitated so
    This side the victory.

Life is but life, and death but death!
Bliss is but bliss, and breath but breath!
    And if indeed I fail,
At least, to know the worst is sweet!
Defeat means nothing but defeat,
    No drearier can prevail.

And if I gain! O sun at sea!
O bells! that in the steeple be,
    At first, repeat it slow!
For heaven is a different thing
Conjectured and waked sudden in,
    And might o'erwhelm me so.

Many of these poems are, as might be expected, drawn from the aspects of Nature, but always with some insight or image of their own; as in the following, which might be called

THE SEA OF SUNSET

This is the land the sunset washes,
    These are the banks of the yellow sea;
Where it rose, or whither it rushes,
    These are the western mystery.

Night after night, her purple traffic
    Strews the landing with opal bales,
Merchantmen poise upon horizons,
    Dip and vanish with airy sails.

Or this:

THE WIND

Of all the sounds despatched abroad
    There's not a charge to me
Like that old measure in the boughs,
    That phraseless melody
The wind makes, working like a hand
    Whose fingers brush the sky,
Then quiver down, with tufts of tune,
    Permitted gods—and me.

I crave him grace of summer boughs
    If such an outcast be
Who never heard that fleshless chant
    Rise solemn in the tree;
As if some caravan of sound
    On deserts in the sky
Had broken rank, then knit, and passed
    In seamless company.

This last image needs no praise, and in dealing with Nature she often seems to possess—as was said of her fellow-townswoman, Helen Jackson ("H. H.")—a sixth sense. But most of her poems grapple at first hand—the more audaciously the better—with the very mysteries of life and death, as in the following:

TWO KINSMEN

I died for Beauty, but was scarce
Adjusted in the tomb
When one who died for Truth was lain
In an adjoining room.

He questioned softly, why I failed?
"For Beauty," I replied;
"And I for Truth—the two are one—
We brethren are," he said.

And so, as kinsmen, met a night,
We talked between the rooms
Until the moss had reached our lips
And covered up our names.

The conception is weird enough for William Blake, and one can no more criticise a faulty rhyme here and there than a defect of drawing in one of Blake's pictures. When a thought takes one's breath away, who cares to count the syllables? The same iron strength shows itself, merging into tenderness, in this brief dirge for one of the nameless Marthas, cumbered about many things:

REQUIESCAT

How many times these low feet staggered
    Only the soldered mouth can tell;
Try! can you stir the awful rivet?
    Try! can you lift the hasps of steel?

Stroke the cool forehead, hot so often;
    Lift, if you can, the listless hair;
Handle the adamantine fingers
    Never a thimble more shall wear.

Buzz the dull flies on the chamber window;
    Brave shines the sun through the freckled pane;
Fearless the cobweb swings from the ceiling;
    Indolent housewife! in daisies lain.

The unutterable dignity of death seems to have forced itself again and again upon this lonely woman, and she has several times touched it with her accustomed terse strength, as in these verses:

One dignity delays for all,
     One mitred afternoon.
None can avoid this purple;
     None can evade this crown.

Coach it insures, and footmen,
     Chamber and state and throng,
Bells also, in the village,
     As we ride grand along.

What dignified attendants!
     What service when we pause!
How loyally, at parting,
     Their hundred hats they raise!

What pomp surpassing ermine
     When simple you and I
Present our meek escutcheon
     And claim the rank to die!

Then, approaching the great change from time to eternity at a different angle, she gives two verses of superb concentration, like the following, which might be christened, after the mediaeval motto,

ASTRA CASTRA
Departed to the Judgment
     A mighty afternoon;
Great clouds, like ushers, leaning,
     Creation looking on.

The flesh surrendered, canceled,
     The bodiless begun;
Two worlds, like audiences, disperse,
     And leave the soul alone.

She shrinks from no concomitant of death; all is ennobled in her imagination:

Safe in their alabaster chambers,
     Untouched by morning and untouched by noon,
Sleep the meek members of the resurrection;
     Rafter of satin and roof of stone.

Light laughs the breeze in her castle above them;
     Babbles the bee in a stolid ear;
Pipe the sweet birds in ignorant cadence—
     Ah! what sagacity perished here!

This is the form in which she finally left these lines, but as she sent them to me, years ago, the following took the place of the second verse, and it seems to me that, with all its too daring condensation, it strikes a note too fine to be lost:

> Grand go the years in the crescent above them,
>   Worlds scoop their arcs, and firmaments row;
> Diadems drop, and Doges surrender,
>   Soundless as dots on a disk of snow.

But with these mighty visions of death and eternity, there are such touches of tender individual sympathy as we find in this, which may be called

TOO LATE

> Delayed till she had ceased to know!
> Delayed till in its vest of snow
>   Her loving bosom lay.
> An hour behind the fleeting breath!
> Later by just an hour than Death!
>   O! lagging yesterday!
>
> Could she have guessed that it would be;
> Could but a crier of the glee
>   Have climbed the distant hill;
> Had not the bliss so slow a pace,
> Who knows but this surrendered face
>   Were undefeated still?
>
> O! if there may departing be
> Any forgot by victory
>   In her imperial sound,
> Show them this meek-appareled thing,
> That could not stop to be a king,
>   Doubtful if it be crowned!

Almost all these poems are strangely impersonal, but here and there we have a glimpse of experiences too intense to be more plainly intimated, as in the following:

> I shall know why, when time is over
>   And I have ceased to wonder why;
> Christ will explain each separate anguish
>   In the fair schoolroom of the sky.
>
> He will tell me what Peter promised,
>   And I, for wonder at his woe,
> I shall forget the drop of anguish
>   That scalds me now—that scalds me now!

Surely this is as if woven out of the heart's own atoms, and will endear the name of Emily Dickinson, in some hour of trial, to those who never before encountered that name, and who will seek it vainly in the cyclopaedias. Her verses are in most cases like poetry plucked up by the roots; we have them with earth, stones, and dew adhering, and must accept them as they are. Wayward and unconventional in the last degree; defiant of form, measure, rhyme, and even grammar; she yet had an exacting standard of her own, and would wait many days for a word that satisfied. Asked again and again for verses to be published, she scarcely ever yielded, even to a friend so tried and dear as the late Mr. Bowles, of the Springfield *Republican*; but she sent her poems with gifts of flowers or—as in my own case—to correspondents whom she had never seen. It is with some misgiving, and almost with a sense of questionable publicity, that it has at last been decided by her surviving sister and her friends to print a small selection from these poems, which will be issued by Roberts Brothers, Boston. The only hint found among her papers of any possible contact with a wider public is found in these few lines, which—although probably the utterance of a passing mood only—have been selected as the prelude to the forthcoming volume:

> This is my letter to the world
>   That never wrote to me;
> The simple news that nature told
>   With tender majesty.
>
> Her message is committed
>   To hands I cannot see;
> For love of her, sweet countrymen,
>   Judge tenderly of me!

[Preface to *Poems by Emily Dickinson*]
Thomas Wentworth Higginson*

The verses of Emily Dickinson belong emphatically to what Emerson long since called "the Poetry of the Portfolio,"—something produced absolutely without the thought of publication, and solely by way of expression of the writer's own mind. Such verse must inevitably forfeit whatever advantage lies in the discipline of public criticism and the enforced conformity to accepted ways. On the other hand, it may often gain something through the habit of freedom and the unconventional utterance of daring thoughts. In the case of the present author, there was absolutely no choice in the matter; she must write thus, or not at all. A recluse by temperament and habit, literally spending years without setting her foot beyond the doorstep, and many more years during which her walks were strictly

*From *Poems by Emily Dickinson*, ed. Mabel Loomis Todd and T. W. Higginson (Boston: Roberts Brothers, 1890), pp. [iii]–vi.

limited to her father's grounds, she habitually concealed her mind, like her person, from all but a very few friends; and it was with great difficulty that she was persuaded to print, during her lifetime, three or four poems. Yet she wrote verses in great abundance; and though curiously indifferent to all conventional rules, had yet a rigorous literary standard of her own, and often altered a word many times to suit an ear which had its own tenacious fastidiousness.

Miss Dickinson was born in Amherst, Mass., Dec. 10, 1830, and died there May 15, 1886. Her father, Hon. Edward Dickinson, was the leading lawyer of Amherst, and was treasurer of the well-known college there situated. It was his custom once a year to hold a large reception at his house, attended by all the families connected with the institution and by the leading people of the town. On these occasions his daughter Emily emerged from her wonted retirement and did her part as gracious hostess; nor would any one have known from her manner, I have been told, that this was not a daily occurrence. The annual occasion once past, she withdrew again into her seclusion, and except for a very few friends was as invisible to the world as if she had dwelt in a nunnery. For myself, although I had corresponded with her for many years, I saw her but twice face to face, and brought away the impression of something as unique and remote as Undine or Mignon or Thekla.

This selection from her poems is published to meet the desire of her personal friends, and especially of her surviving sister. It is believed that the thoughtful reader will find in these pages a quality more suggestive of the poetry of William Blake than of anything to be elsewhere found,—flashes of wholly original and profound insight into nature and life; words and phrases exhibiting an extraordinary vividness of descriptive and imaginative power, yet often set in a seemingly whimsical or even rugged frame. They are here published as they were written, with very few and superficial changes, although it is fair to say that the titles have been assigned, almost invariably, by the editors. In many cases these verses will seem to the reader like poetry torn up by the roots, with rain and dew and earth still clinging to them, giving a freshness and a fragrance not otherwise to be conveyed. In other cases, as in a few poems of shipwreck or of mental conflict, we can only wonder at the gift of vivid imagination by which this recluse woman can delineate, by a few touches, the very crises of physical or mental struggle. And sometimes again we catch glimpses of a lyric strain, sustained perhaps but for a line or two at a time, and making the reader regret its sudden cessation. But the main quality of these poems is that of extraordinary grasp and insight, uttered with an uneven vigor sometimes exasperating, seemingly wayward, but really unsought and inevitable. After all, when a thought takes one's breath away, a lesson on grammar seems an impertinence. As Ruskin wrote in his earlier and better days, "No weight nor mass nor beauty of execution can outweigh one grain or fragment of thought."

[Review of *Poems* (1890)]

Anonymous*

The poems of Emily Dickinson are not so seriously weighed down by their editors—Mrs. Mabel Loomis Todd and Mr. T. W. Higginson—since they leave her mainly to speak for herself. We learn that she was born in 1830 and died in 1886, living almost always in extreme seclusion in the college town of Amherst, Mass., where her father, a lawyer, held also the responsible position of college treasurer. She resolutely refused to publish her verses, showing them only to a very few friends. As a consequence, she had almost no criticism, and was absolutely untrammelled: so that the verses are sometimes almost formless, while at other times they show great capacity for delicate and sweet melody, suggesting the chance strains of an Aeolian harp. But in compass of thought, grasp of feeling, and vigor of epithet, they are simply extraordinary, and strike notes, very often, like those of some deep-toned organ. Take, for instance, this, which fully sustains the Blake-like quality suggested by the editors in their preface:

> "I died for beauty, but was scarce
> Adjusted in the tomb.
> When one who died for truth was lain
> In an adjoining room.
>
> "He questioned softly why I failed?
> 'For beauty,' I replied.
> 'And I for truth—the two are one;
> We brethren are,' he said.
>
> "And so, as kinsmen met a night,
> We talked between the rooms,
> Until the moss had reached our lips
> And covered up our names."

The extraordinary terseness and vigor of that weird conclusion runs through all the poems; in this case it so grasps the ear that you hardly notice the defect in the rhyme. Little cared she for that, provided she uttered her thought. Yet at times she reached with the same sudden grasp a completeness of utterance that was nothing less than lyric—as in the two verses on the opposite page to the above:

> "A train went through a burial gate;
>   A bird broke forth and sang,
> And trilled, and quivered, and shook his throat
>   Till all the churchyard rang;
>
> "And then adjusted his little notes
>   And bowed and sang again,

*From the *Nation*, 51 (November 1890), 423.

> Doubtless he thought it meet of him
> To say good-bye to men."

With all its inequalities and even oddities on its face, there is power enough on many a page of this little book to set up whole volumes of average poetry; and the public will inevitably demand to know more of the thoughts and mental processes of Emily Dickinson.

[Review of *Poems* (1890)]   Anonymous*

Here is a volume of striking and original poems by a writer who, during the fifty years of her life, wrote much and published almost nothing. The name of Emily Dickinson is a new name in our literature, but whoever reads the striking verses in this book which her two friends, Mabel Loomis Todd and Col. T. W. Higginson, have edited, will agree that its place is established and sure to remain, associated with a collection of poems whose main quality, as is pointed out in an admirable preface, is an extraordinary grasp and insight. So clearly are the characteristics of these verses defined and so exactly does our opinion of them agree with the writer's, that we are almost tempted to quote him literally; but there are some features which he has left for others to describe—namely, the similarity between these poems and some of Emerson's (a similarity both of thought and manner of expression), and, in the poems of love, the absence of much that is essential to poems of this kind—sensuousness and symmetry and melody. It is in the other poems that the rare genius of Miss Dickinson is best seen—in those of Life, Nature, Time and Eternity. Here, for instance, is an example chosen from the verses on Life, which will show, too, what we call the Emersonian influence. The poem appeared first in 'A Masque of Poets,' published at the request of the author's friend 'H.H.,' who had often urged her to print a volume. It is called 'Success.'

> Success is counted sweetest
> By those who ne'er succeed.
> To comprehend a nectar
> Requires sorest need.
>
> Not one of all the purple host
> Who took the flag to-day
> Can tell the definition,
> So clear, of victory,

*From the *Critic*, 17 (Dec. 13, 1890), 305–306.

As he, defeated, dying,
On whose forbidden ear
The distant strains of triumph
Break, agonized and clear.

We venture to give some of the things which have most impressed us. Many of the poems are untitled, but the first of the following is called 'The Secret':—

Some things that fly there be,—
Birds, hours, the bumble-bee:
Of these no elegy.

Some things that stay there be,—
Grief, hills, eternity:
Not this behooveth me.

There are, that resting, rise.
Can I expound the skies?
How still the riddle lies!

It is of Nature that the poet writes best. Of the thirty-one poems under this heading, it is hard to find favorites, they are all so fine. We select the two following:—

New feet within my garden go,
New fingers stir the sod;
A troubadour upon the elm
Betrays the solitude.

New children play upon the green,
New weary sleep below;
And still the pensive spring returns,
And still the punctual snow!

———

Like trains of cars on tracks of plush
I hear the level bee:
A jar across the flower goes,
Their velvet masonry
Withstands until the sweet assault
Their chivalry consumes,
While he, victorious, tilts away
To vanquish other blooms.
*   *   *   *   *
His labor is a chant,
His idleness a tune;
Oh, for a bee's experience
Of clovers and of noon!

We must make room for this one of the poems on Life and Eternity:—

If I shouldn't be alive
When the robins come,
Give the one in red cravat
A memorial crumb.

If I couldn't thank you,
Being just asleep,
You will know I'm trying
With my granite lip!

Miss Dickinson's poems, though rough and rugged, are surprisingly individual and genuinely inspired.

The Poems of Emily Dickinson   William Dean Howells*

The strange *Poems of Emily Dickinson* we think will form something like an intrinsic experience with the understanding reader of them. They have been edited by Mrs. Mabel Loomis Todd, who was a personal friend of the poet, and by Colonel T. W. Higginson, who was long her epistolary and literary acquaintance, but only met her twice. Few people met her so often, as the reader will learn from Colonel Higginson's interesting preface, for her life was mainly spent in her father's house at Amherst, Massachusetts; she seldom passed its doors, and never, for many years, passed the gates of its grounds. There is no hint of what turned her life in upon itself, and probably this was its natural evolution, or involution, from tendencies inherent in the New England, or the Puritan, spirit. We are told that once a year she met the local world at a reception in her father's house; we do not know that there is any harm in adding, that she did not always literally meet it, but sometimes sat with her face averted from the company in another room. One of her few friends was Helen Hunt Jackson, whom she suffered to send one of her poems to be included in the volume of anonymous pieces which Messrs. Roberts Brothers once published with the title of *A Masque of Poets*. Whether the anonymity flattered her love of obscurity or not, it is certain that her darkling presence in this book was the occasion of her holding for many years a correspondence with its publishers. She wrote them, as the fancy took her, comments on their new books, and always enclosed a scrap of her verse, though without making any reference to it. She never intended or allowed anything more from her pen to be printed in her lifetime; but it was evident that she wished her poetry finally to meet the eyes of that world which she had herself always shrunk from. She could not have made such poetry without knowing its rarity, its singular worth; and no doubt it was a radiant happiness in the twilight of her hidden, silent life.

*From *Harper's Magazine*, 82 (Jan., 1891), 318–21.

The editors have discharged their delicate duty toward it with unimpeachable discretion, and Colonel Higginson has said so many apt things of her work in his introduction, that one who cannot differ with him must be vexed a little to be left so little to say. He speaks of her "curious indifference to all conventional rules of verse," but he adds that "when a thought takes one's breath away, a lesson on grammar seems an impertinence." He notes "the quality suggestive of the poetry of William Blake" in her, but he leaves us the chance to say that it is a Blake who had read Emerson who had read Blake. The fantasy is as often Blakian as the philosophy is Emersonian; but after feeling this again and again, one is ready to declare that the utterance of this most singular and authentic spirit would have been the same if there had never been an Emerson or a Blake in the world. She sometimes suggests Heine as much as either of these; all three in fact are spiritually present in some of the pieces; yet it is hardly probable that she read Heine, or if she had, would not have abhorred him.

Here is something that seems compact of both Emerson and Blake, with a touch of Heine too:

> I taste a liquor never brewed,
> From tankards scooped in pearl;
> Not all the vats upon the Rhine
> Yield such an alcohol!
>
> Inebriate of air am I,
> And debauchee of dew,
> Reeling, through endless summer days,
> From inns of molten blue.
>
> When landlords turn the drunken bee
> Out of the foxglove's door,
> When butterflies renounce their drams,
> I shall but drink the more!
>
> Till seraphs swing their snowy hats,
> And saints to windows run,
> To see the little tippler
> Leaning against the sun!

But we believe it is only seeming; we believe these things are as wholly her own as this:

> The bustle in a house
> The morning after death
> Is solemnest of industries
> Enacted upon earth,—

The sweeping up the heart,
And putting love away
We shall not want to use again
Until eternity.

Such things could have come only from a woman's heart to which the experiences in a New England town have brought more knowledge of death than of life. Terribly unsparing many of these strange poems are, but true as the grave and certain as mortality. The associations of housekeeping in the following poem have a force that drags us almost into the presence of the poor, cold quiet thing:

TROUBLED ABOUT MANY THINGS

How many times these low feet staggered,
Only the soldered mouth can tell:
Try! Can you stir the awful rivet?
Try! Can you lift the hasps of steel?

Stroke the cool forehead, hot so often,
Lift, if you can, the listless hair;
Handle the adamantine fingers
Never a thimble more shall wear.

Buzz the dull flies on the chamber window;
Brave shines the sun through the freckled pane;
Fearless the cobweb swings from the ceiling—
Indolent housewife, in daisies lain!

Then in this, which has no name—how could any phrase nominate its weird witchery aright?—there is the flight of an eerie fancy that leaves all experience behind:

I died for beauty, but was scarce
Adjusted in the tomb,
When one who died for truth was lain
In an adjoining room.

He questioned softly why I failed.
"For beauty," I replied.
"And I for truth,—the two are one;
We brethren are," he said.

And so, as kinsmen met a night,
We talked between the rooms,
Until the moss had reached our lips,
And covered up our names.

All the Puritan longing for sincerity, for veracious conduct, which in some good New England women's natures is almost a hysterical shriek, makes its exultant grim assertion in these lines:

REAL

I like a look of agony,
Because I know it's true;
Men do not sham convulsion,
Nor simulate a throe.

The eyes glaze once, and that is death.
Impossible to feign
The beads upon the forehead
By homely anguish strung.

These mortuary pieces have a fascination above any others in the book; but in the stanzas below there is a still, solemn, rapt movement of the thought and music together that is of exquisite charm:

New feet within my garden go,
New fingers stir the sod;
A troubadour upon the elm
Betrays the solitude.

New children play upon the green,
New weary sleep below;
And still the pensive spring returns,
And still the punctual snow!

This is a song that sings itself; and this is another such, but thrilling with the music of a different passion:

SUSPENSE

Elysium is as far as to
The very nearest room,
If in that room a friend await
Felicity or doom.

What fortitude the soul contains,
That it can so endure
The accent of a coming foot,
The opening of a door!

The last poem is from the group which the editors have named "Love"; the other groups from which we have been quoting are "Nature," and "Time and Eternity"; but the love poems are of the same piercingly introspective cast as those differently named. The same force of imagination is in them; in them, as in the rest, touch often becomes clutch. In them love walks on heights he seldom treads, and it is the heart of full womanhood that speaks in the words of this nun-like New England life.

Few of the poems in the book are long, but none of the short, quick impulses of intense feeling or poignant thought can be called fragments. They are each a compassed whole, a sharply finished point, and there is evidence, circumstantial and direct, that the author spared no pains in the perfect expression of her ideals. Nothing, for example, could be added that would say more than she has said in four lines:

> Presentiment is that long shadow on the lawn
> Indicative that suns go down;
> The notice to the startled grass
> That darkness is about to pass.

Occasionally, the outside of the poem, so to speak, is left so rough, so rude, that the art seems to have faltered. But there is apparent to reflection the fact that the artist meant just this harsh exterior to remain, and that no grace of smoothness could have imparted her intention as it does. It is the soul of an abrupt, exalted New England woman that speaks in such brokenness. The range of all the poems is of the loftiest; and sometimes there is a kind of swelling lift, an almost boastful rise of feeling, which is really the spring of faith in them:

> I never saw a moor,
> I never saw the sea;
> Yet know I how the heather looks,
> And what a wave must be.
>
> I never spoke with God,
> Nor visited in heaven;
> Yet certain am I of the spot
> As if the chart were given.

There is a noble tenderness, too, in some of the pieces; a quaintness that does not discord with the highest solemnity:

> I shall know why, when time is over,
> And I have ceased to wonder why;
> Christ will explain each separate anguish
> In the fair school-room of the sky,
>
> He will tell me what Peter promised,
> And I, for wonder at his woe,
> I shall forget the drop of anguish
> That scalds me now, that scalds me now.

The companionship of human nature with inanimate nature is very close in certain of the poems; and we have never known the invisible and intangible ties binding all creation in one, so nearly touched as in them.

If nothing else had come out of our life but this strange poetry we should feel that in the work of Emily Dickinson, America, or New England rather, had made a distinctive addition to the literature of the world, and could not be left out of any record of it; and the interesting and important thing is that this poetry is as characteristic of our life as our business enterprise, our political turmoil, our demagogism, our millionairism. "Listen!" says Mr. James McNeill Whistler in that "Ten o'Clock" lecture of his which must have made his hearers feel very much lectured indeed, not to say browbeaten,—"Listen! There never was an artistic period. There never was an art-loving nation." But there were moments and there were persons to whom art was dear, and Emily Dickinson was one of these persons, one of these moments in a national life, and she could as well happen in Amherst, Mass., as in Athens, Att.

Some American Poets   Andrew Lang[*]

I read somewhere, lately, that the Americans possess, at present, more minor poets, and better minor poets, than we can boast in England. The phrase "minor poet" is disliked by minstrels, and here let it be taken to denote merely poets who have not yet a recognized national fame, like Lord Tennyson with us and Mr. Whittier in America. Whether, in the larger and less recognized class, we have not at least as many poets to show as the States is a question of statistics. But it is very probable that the Western singers, whether better than ours or not, are, at all events, different from ours, and therefore, so far, interesting.

The works of four new Transatlantic poets lie beside me. *Place aux dames*. Let us take, first, "Poems" by the late Miss Emily Dickinson. This is certainly a very curious little book. It has already reached its fourth edition, partly, no doubt, because Mr. Howells praised it very highly. I cannot go nearly so far as Mr. Howells, because, if poetry is to exist at all, it really must have form and grammar, and must rhyme when it professes to rhyme. The wisdom of the ages and the nature of man insist on so much. We may be told that Democracy does not care, any more than the Emperor did, for grammar. But even if Democracy overleaps itself and lands in savagery again, I believe that our savage successors will, though unconsciously, make their poems grammatical. Savages do not use bad grammar in their own conversation or in their artless compositions. That is a fault of defective civilizations. Miss Dickinson, who died lately at the age of fifty-six, was a recluse, dwelling in Amherst, a town of Massachusetts. She did not write for publication. Her friends have produced her work. Sometimes it is as bad as this—

> Angels' breathless ballot
> Lingers to record thee;
> Imps in eager caucus
> Raffle for my soul.

This, of course, is mere nonsense. What is a "breathless ballot"? How can a ballot record anything, and how can it "linger" in recording, especially

*From *Illustrated London News*, 98 (Mar. 7, 1891), 307.

if it is in such a hurry as to be breathless? Indeed, one turns over Miss Dickinson's book with a puzzled feeling that there was poetry in her subconscious, but that it never became explicit. One might as well seek for an air in the notes of a bird as for articulate and sustained poetry here. One piece begins—

> This is the land the sunset washes
> These are the banks of the Yellow Sea.

And here is rhythm and the large sense of evening air—

> Where it rose, or whither it rushes,
> These are the Western mystery.
>
> Night after night her purple traffic
> Strews the landing with opal bales;
> Merchantmen poise upon horizons,
> Dip and vanish with fairy sails.

The second verse is not very easy to construe, but there was poetry in the writer. This, again, has the true lyrical note—

> I never saw a moor,
> I never saw the sea,
> Yet know I how the heather looks,
> And what a wave must be.

There is not much else that can be quoted without bringing in the fantastic, irresponsible note of a poet who has her own audience, and had constructed her own individual "Ars Poetica." The words of Mr. Aldrich in "The Sister's Tragedy" (Macmillan) might have been written about Miss Dickinson—

> A twilight poet groping quite alone,
> Belated in a sphere where every nest
> Is emptied of its music and its wings.

In Re Emily Dickinson   Thomas Bailey Aldrich*

The English critic who said of Miss Emily Dickinson that she might have become a fifth-rate poet "if she had only mastered the rudiments of grammar and gone into metrical training for about fifteen years,"—the rather candid English critic who said this somewhat overstated his case. If Miss Dickinson had undergone the austere curriculum indicated, she would, I am sure, have become an admirable lyric poet of the second magnitude. In the first volume of her poetical chaos is a little poem which

*From *Atlantic Monthly*, 69 (Jan. 1892), 143–44. Reprinted by permission of the *Atlantic Monthly*.

needs only slight revision in the initial stanza in order to make it worthy of ranking with some of the odd swallow flights in Heine's lyrical *intermezzo*. I have ventured to desecrate this stanza by tossing a rhyme into it, as the other stanzas happened to rhyme, and here print the lyric, hoping the reader will not accuse me of overvaluing it:

> I taste a liquor never brewed
> In vats upon the Rhine;
> No tankard ever held a draught '
> Of alcohol like mine.
>
> Inebriate of air am I,
> And debauchee of dew,
> Reeling, through endless summer days,
> From inns of molten blue.
>
> When landlords turn the drunken bee
> Out of the Foxglove's door,
> When butterflies renounce their drams,
> I shall but drink the more!
>
> Till seraphs swing their snowy caps
> And saints to windows run,
> To see the little tippler
> Leaning against the sun!

Certainly those inns of molten blue, and that disreputable honey-gatherer who got himself turned out-of-doors at the sign of the Foxglove, are very taking matters. I know of more important things that interest me less. There are three or four bits of this kind in Miss Dickinson's book; but for the most part the ideas totter and toddle, not having learned to walk. In spite of this, several of the quatrains are curiously touching, they have such a pathetic air of yearning to be poems.

It is plain that Miss Dickinson possessed an extremely unconventional and grotesque fancy. She was deeply tinged by the mysticism of Blake, and strongly influenced by the mannerism of Emerson. The very way she tied her bonnetstrings, preparatory to one of her nunlike walks in her claustral garden, must have been Emersonian. She had much fancy of a queer sort, but only, as it appears to me, intermittent flashes of imagination. I fail to detect in her work any of that profound thought which her editor professes to discover in it. The phenomenal insight, I am inclined to believe, exists only in his partiality; for whenever a woman poet is in question Mr. Higginson always puts on his rose-colored spectacles. This is being chivalrous; but the invariable result is not clear vision. That Miss Dickinson's whimsical memoranda have a certain something which, for want of a more precise name, we term *quality* is not to be denied except by the unconvertible heathen who are not worth conversion. But the incoherence and formlessness of her—I don't know how to designate them—versicles are fatal. Sydney Smith, or some other humorist, mentions a person whose bump of veneration was so inadequately developed as to permit him to damn the equator if he wanted to. This certainly established a precedent for independence; but an eccentric, dreamy, half-educated recluse in an out-of-the-way New England village (or anywhere else) cannot with impunity set at defiance the laws of gravitation and grammar. In his charming preface to Miss Dickinson's collection, Mr. Higginson insidiously remarks: "After all, when a thought takes one's breath away, a lesson on grammar seems an impertinence." But an ungrammatical thought does not, as a general thing, take one's breath away, except in a sense the reverse of flattering. Touching this matter of mere technique Mr. Ruskin has a word to say (it appears that he said it "In his earlier and better days"), and Mr. Higginson quotes it: "No weight, nor mass, nor beauty of execution can outweigh one grain or fragment of thought." This is a proposition to which one would cordially subscribe, if it were not so intemperately stated. A suggestive commentary on Mr. Ruskin's impressive dictum is furnished by the fact that Mr. Ruskin has lately published a volume of the most tedious verse that has been printed in this century. The substance of it is weighty enough, but the workmanship lacks just that touch which distinguishes the artist from the bungler,—the touch which Mr. Ruskin seems not to have much regarded either in his later or "in his earlier and better days."

If Miss Dickinson's *disjecta membra* are poems, then Shakespeare's prolonged imposition should be exposed without further loss of time, and Lord Tennyson ought to be advised of the error of his ways before it is too late. But I do not hold the situation to be so desperate. Miss Dickinson's versicles have a queerness and a quaintness that have stirred a momentary curiosity in emotional bosoms. Oblivion lingers in the immediate neighborhood.

[Review of *Letters* (1894)]   Anonymous*

In publishing the letters of that remarkable woman Emily Dickinson, Mrs. Todd has not merely performed a labor of love, but has given to American literature a unique book. To review Miss Dickinson's letters is like reviewing her poetry: the critic instantly sees that here is something of unquestionable power that may not be labeled off-hand with any of the well-worn formulas that fit most books. In the conventional sense of the word, artist is not the term that one thinks of applying to Miss Dickinson. She had the Emersonic habit of trying to express her meaning poignantly

*From the *Critic*, 23 (Feb. 16, 1895), 119.

and letting the rest go. This trait becomes a confused and irritating abruptness in writers whose meaning is of little worth: in writers of genius it is the startling abruptness of the seer. Men of the one class are ignorant of the value of art, and men of the other class deem their unrestrained utterance more precious than artistic success. But having something to say, and saying it in the way that most perfectly expresses the speaker's personality—this is after all the supreme, though not the only, element of art. Beyond any doubt, to Miss Dickinson must be ascribed this cardinal literary virtue. Spontaneity—the birth-right gift of the lyric poet and of woman—was hers also. Poetic spontaneity means not merely the desire to speak, but the need to speak. Miss Dickinson's reluctance to publish (it need only be recalled that her two volumes of poetry are posthumous) and her constant literary activity confirm, if confirmation be needed, her possession of the poetic instinct, which seeks utterance for the sake of utterance, because silence is impossible. "And when," she says, "a sudden light on orchards, or a new fashion in the wind troubled my attention, I felt a palsy, here, the verses just relieve." Herein is the note of every line that she penned—sincerity. Her letters, not a few of which are poems in everything but the conventional typographical arrangement in verses, help to make evident this vital characteristic of her poetry. And they bring to our knowledge the woman as well as the poet.

These letters reveal the inner life of their writer, and the editor accompanies them with a running commentary on such of the outward events of Miss Dickinson's retired existence as give a key to them. It is to be regretted that the comments are so brief, and that Mrs. Todd has not given us the life as well as the letters of her friend. In the early part of the book many will feel disappointed, now and then, after being brought to an interesting point, to find that the next letter bears date of a year or two later. The letters are grouped, all those addressed to one person being printed together. This prevents chronological sequence, but gives an air of unity to each friendship. Some of the earliest are written by the boarding-school girl of sixteen to her brother. They show the simplicity of unaffected girlhood, touched here and there by the promise of thoughtful maturity, and sparkling with sunny humor. Girlish jokes are followed, to be sure, by girlish explanations of the same, and the letters are not extraordinarily precocious. But their independence and originality and their spirit of family affection prelude the life that followed, foreshadowing especially the pathetic intensity with which the poet clung to her friends. "Pardon my sanity in a world insane," she wrote, "and love me if you will, for I had rather be loved than to be called a king in earth, or a lord in Heaven." "My friends are my estate. Forgive me, then, the avarice to hoard them." As the years go on, there are flashes of spontaneous phrasing, which become more and more frequent, until to that buoyancy of spirit which so often marks the writing of a shy and sensitive person there is added the radiancy of literary power.

Miss Dickinson's letters lend themselves to quotation, but merely to quote the epigrams with which her pages are strewn would give an unfair idea of her writing. It is the farthest possible remove from the delightfully diffuse correspondence of some of the famous letter writers of her sex, to the condensed, sublimated missives of Emily Dickinson: and for this reason the letters should be quoted in full. Quotation must be confined to a few extracts, however, of those "thoughts like daisies and sentences [that] could hold the bees." A letter written in response to some inquiries from Col. Higginson (she had just sent to him, a stranger, four of her poems for criticism) contains some characteristic sentences:—

"You asked how old I was? I made no verse, but one or two until this winter, sir. . . . You inquire my books. For poets, I have Keats, and Mr. and Mrs. Browning. For prose, Mr. Ruskin, Sir Thomas Browne, and the Revelations. I went to school, but in your manner of the phrase, had no education. When a little girl, I had a friend who taught me immortality; but, venturing too near, himself, he never returned. . . . . You ask of my companions. Hills, sir, and the sundown, and a dog, large as myself, that my father bought me. They are better than beings because they know, but do not tell; and the noise in the pool at noon excels my piano."

Without further comment, here are some extracts from very diverse letters:—

"I am glad my little girl is at peace. Peace is a deep place. Some, too faint to push, are assisted by angels." "Men and women,—they talk of hallowed things, aloud, and embarrass my dog." "Home is the definition of God." [On the death of a child.] " 'Come unto me' could not alarm those minute feet—how sweet to remember. . . . The little creature must have been priceless—yours and not yours—how hallowed. . . . The little furniture of loss has lips of dirks to stab us. I hope Heaven is warm, there are so many barefoot ones. I hope it is near—the little tourist was so small. I hope it is not so unlike earth that we shall miss the peculiar form—the mould of the bird." "How strange that nature does not knock, and yet does not intrude."

> "There is no frigate like a book
>   To take us lands away,
> Nor any coursers like a page
>   Of prancing poetry.
> This traverse may the poorest take
>   Without oppress of toil;
> How frugal is the chariot
>   That bears the human soul!"

"Mother went rambling, and came in with a burdock on her shawl, so we know that the snow has perished from the earth."

A genuinely heroic spirit is in the noble description of the death in battle and the burial of her young townsman, Frazer Stearns. It is too long to quote, but it is impossible not to refer to it. The dignity of this passage speaks for itself:—"He went to sleep from the village church. Crowds came to tell him good-night, choirs sang to him, pastors told how brave he was—early-soldier heart. And the family bowed their heads, as the reeds the wind shakes." The hand that could write such a requiem needs no further praise.

A New England Nun   Louis J. Block*

The conscience of New England a half century ago demanded much of its votaries and adherents. The limitations which it set about human intelligence and activity were many and certain. Its intense assurance of its own completeness and rectitude had its incommodities as well as its insights and rewards. To those who could acquiesce in its demands, it opened avenues to spiritual heights whence the outlook was large and superb, though the air might be somewhat thin for the health of daily life. At last, however, the burdens it imposed became too severe for a generation alive to much that was outside of its enclosed space, and the revolt began.

It seems that valuable literatures usually begin with such revolts, and the stronger spirits, after considerable effort and some suffering, throw off the fetters no longer endurable, and rejoice in the larger freedom which they have won. There are always, however, sensitive souls who feel that they must break with the traditions, but cannot find themselves wholly at home in the new and strange. Among the latter must be counted such writers as Emily Dickinson, as well as the Concord recluse, William Ellery Channing, whose poems, when again and properly presented to the world, will doubtless receive a recognition which has thus far been denied them. What has been done for Emily Dickinson will assuredly be done for him, and the result is no more doubtful in his case than it has proved in hers.

Miss Dickinson's letters make an admirable complement to her poems. In her early years she was a copious correspondent, and during her school-days she had a great reputation as a writer of long, and, as we can readily surmise, singularly original compositions. The change in her epistolary style, with her growth in years and experience, is worthy of notice. The diffuse and minute letter-writing becomes condensed to a remarkable degree, epigrammatic, and mystical. Her correspondents were many, and include such names as Dr. Holland, Samuel Bowles, Helen Hunt Jackson, and, of course, Mrs. Todd, the devoted editor of these "Letters," and her guide and mentor, Colonel Higginson.

Not quite able to avail herself of the wider scope which the New

*From the *Dial*, 18 (Mar. 1, 1895), 146–47.

England revolt was disclosing to her, and incapable of satisfaction with the creeds and moods in which she had been brought up, Emily Dickinson retired into herself, and found solace and serenity in her vivid apprehensions of the truth, and the manifestations of that truth in Nature, which became to her a symbol easily read and transparent to the meaning which it contained. Her correspondence is replete with a gay and delicate humor; the recluse was full of wit and of gentle happiness with her friends. Perhaps she did not take herself and her abandonment of the world with too much seriousness; probably she saw something of its humorous aspect, and would gladly enough have had the strength to share the generous life outside; the effort, doubtless, was too great, and the sympathetic appreciation not sufficiently vigorous and insistent. The letters are free from that strain of morbidness which we sometimes find in her poems, especially in those dealing with the subject of death and its dark accompaniments. Here we have such exquisite passages as this:

> "The bed on which he came was enclosed in a large casket, shut entirely, and covered from head to foot with the sweetest flowers. He went to sleep from the village church. Crowds came to tell him good night, choirs sang to him, pastors told how brave he was—early-soldier heart. And the family lowered their heads, as the reeds the wind shakes."

As the introspective habit grew upon her, every incident of a life simple and unvarying in the extreme became touched with an illumination that her thoughts and mood poured forth. "A letter," she says, "always feels to me like immortality, because it is the mind alone without corporeal friend." A burst of severe weather in the spring gives rise to this: "The apple blossoms were slightly disheartened, yesterday, by a snowstorm, but the birds encouraged them all that they could—and how fortunate that the little ones had come to cheer their damask brethren." Here is a letter entire:

> "The little package of Ceylon arrived in fragrant safety, and Caliban's 'clust'ring filberds' were not so luscious nor so brown. Honey in March is blissful as inopportune, and to caress the bee a severe temptation, but was not temptation the first zest? We shall seek to be frugal with our sweet possessions, though their enticingness quite leads us astray, and shall endow Austin [Emily Dickinson's brother], as we often do, after a parched day. For how much we thank you. Dear arrears of tenderness we can never repay till the will's great ores are finally sifted; but bullion is better than minted things, for it has no alloy. Thinking of you with fresher love, as the Bible boyishly says, 'New every morning and fresh every evening.' "

The unexpected abounds in these letters, as the reader of the poems will anticipate. "To make even Heaven more heavenly is within the aim of us all." "I shall bring you a handful of Lotus next, but do not tell the Nile." "Not what the stars have done, but what they are to do, is what detains the sky." "Changelessness is Nature's change." She lavishes her verse upon her correspondents.

> "Take all away from me
> But leave me ecstasy,
> And I am richer then
> Than all my fellow-men.
> Is it becoming me
> To dwell so wealthily,
> When at my very door
> Are those possessing more,
> In boundless poverty?"

Mrs. Todd says: "It is impossible to conceive that any sense of personal isolation, or real loneliness of spirit, because of the absence of humanity from her daily life, could have oppressed a nature so richly endowed." And again: "Emily Dickinson's method of living was so simple and natural an outcome of her increasingly shy nature, a development so perfectly in the line of her whole constitution, that no far-away and dramatic explanation of her quiet life is necessary to those who are capable of apprehending her." Notwithstanding the authoritative source from which this statement comes, many readers will hold a different opinion. No doubt the adjustment of Emily Dickinson to her environment grew in difficulty, and, as often happens in such cases, the effective help was not at hand. The extent of her correspondence, and the character of much of it, indicate how deeply she felt the need and how warmly she would have welcomed the possibility of closer relations with her fellows. The nun and the saint make a figure delicate and unique; but the poet with something real to say to mankind deserves our larger appreciation.

A Note on Emily Dickinson

Bliss Carmen*

Pending the coming in of [Kipling's] "The Seven Seas," it is safe to say that the publication of a new volume of poems by Emily Dickinson is the literary event of the season. Six years ago when her first book was given to the public, it ran through several editions, achieving a larger sale, I believe, than any other first volume ever printed at the University Press, and that is saying a good deal, when one recalls the distinguished works that have issued from that excellent printing shop. Its author's name was entirely unknown, and she herself already passed beyond the confusion of renown; yet so distinctive was her note, so spiritual and intense and absolutely sincere, that she sprang at once into a posthumous fame, unadulterated and almost splendid. It was one more tribute to the

*From *Boston Evening Transcript*, Nov. 21, 1896, p. 15.

New England ideal, the American interest in morality, the bent for transcendentalism inherited from Emerson; and, by the way, it was at the same time another evidence of the alertness of the American reading public, and its sensitiveness to excellent originality. For while there was novelty in the verse of Emily Dickinson, there was nothing sensational, hardly anything strange; no peculiarity on which a cult could batten. Those who admired her verse must admire it for its poetry alone.

I have just said that there is nothing sensational in Emily Dickinson's poetry; and yet there was, in a small way, a genuine sensation in the editorial rooms of one of the oldest journals in New York when our chief, with that tireless and impetuous enthusiasm of his, came rushing in with his bright discovery—like a whirl of October leaves. He is one of the two American editors who have the superfluous faculty of knowing poetry when they see it; he had fallen upon the immortal maid's first book, and the slumbering poet in him was awake. Nothing would suffice but we must share his youthful elation, listen to the strains of this original and accredited singer. The heat of New York, the routine of an office, the jaded mind of a reviewer, the vitiated habit of the professional manuscript-taster—it was not easy to shake off these at once; we were somewhat cold, perhaps, and a little sceptical of the chief's discovery. Still, we must listen. Hear this—

> Belshazzar had a letter—
> He never had but one;
> Belshazzar's correspondent
> Concluded and begun
> In that immortal copy
> The conscience of us all
> Can read without its glasses
> On revelation's wall.

Why, yes, certainly that is original enough. But can your wonderful prodigy turn off another verse like it?

"Can she? To be sure! Listen again!"

> I taste a liquor never brewed.
>   From tankards scooped in pearl;
> Not all the vats upon the Rhine
>   Yield such an alcohol!
>
> Inebriate of air am I,
>   And debauchee of dew,
> Reeling, through endless summer days,
>   From inns of molten blue.
>
> When landlords turn the drunken bee
>   Out of the foxglove's door,
> When butterflies renounce their drams,
>   I shall but drink the more!

Till seraphs swing their snowy hats,
  And saints to windows run,
To see the little tippler
  Leaning against the sun.

Well, we are convinced, indeed. There can be no doubt of the genuineness of this writer. Such work is fresh from the mint; not immediately current without some scrutiny; yet stamped plainly enough with the hallmark of genius. We could but give unqualified assent; put the new book on the old shelf at once, with its peers, the acknowledged classics of American literature.

Following this first venture, there has been a second collection of poems, two volumes of letters and now this third book of verse. And allowing one's judgment time to cool, I must say the conviction remains that Emily Dickinson's contribution to English poetry (or American poetry, if you prefer to say so) is by far the most important made by any woman west of the Atlantic. It is so by reason of its thought, its piquancy, its untarnished expression. She borrowed from no one; she was never commonplace; always imaginative and stimulating; and finally, the region of her brooding was that sequestered domain where our profoundest convictions have origin, and whence we trace the Puritan strain within us.

For this New England woman was a type of her race. A life-long recluse, musing on the mysteries of life and death, she yet had that stability of character, that strong sanity of mind, which could hold out against the perils of seclusion, unshaken by solitude, undethroned by doubt. The very fibre of New England must have been there, founded of granite, nourished by an exhilarating air. We are permitted, through Colonel Higginson's introduction to the first series of poems, the merest glimpse into the story of her life in that beautiful college town in the lovely valley of the Connecticut. We imagine her in the old-fashioned house with its stately decency, its air of breeding and reserve, set a little back from the street, ambushed behind a generous hedge, and flanked by an ample garden on the side—a garden full of roses and tall elms and the scent of new-mown hay. There among her own, she chose an unaustere and voluntary monasticism for her daily course, far indeed removed from the average life of our towns, yet not so untypical of that strain of Puritan blood which besets us all. It would never, I feel sure, occur to anyone with the least insight into the New England character, or the remotest inheritance of the New England conscience (with its capacity for abstemiousness, its instinct for being always aloof and restrained, rather than social and blithe), to think of Emily Dickinson as peculiar, or her mode of life as queer. Somewhat strange as the record of it may show to foreign eyes, it was natural enough in its own time and place, though sufficiently unusual to claim something of distinction even of itself. Illumined and revealed in her poems, the life and character of this original nature makes a fit study for the subtlest criticism—such a criticism, indeed, as I know not where they will receive. And all the while, as we speak of Emily Dickinson's secluded life, and her individual habit of isolation, her parsimony in friendship and human intercourse, I have a conviction that we should guard against the fancy that she was tinged with any shadow of sadness, or any touch of misanthropy or gloom. It seems rather that she must have had the sunniest of dispositions, as she certainly had the most sensitive and exquisite organization. It was not that the persons or fellows seemed to her superfluous or harsh or unnecessary, but rather that in one so finely organized as she must have been, the event of meeting another was too exquisite and portentous to be borne. For there are some natures so shy and quick, so undulled by the life of the senses, that they never quite acquire the easy part of the world. You will hear of them shunning the most delightful acquaintance, turning a corner sharply to avoid an encounter, hesitating at the very threshold of welcome, out of some dim inherited, instinctive dread of casual intercourse. They are like timorous elusive spirits, gone astray, perhaps, and landed on the rough planet Earth by a slight mischance; and when they are compelled by circumstance to share in the world's work, their part in it is likely to be an unhappy one. Theirs is the bent for solitude, the custom of silence. And once that fleeing sense of self-protection arises within them, the chances are they will indulge it to the end. And fortunate, indeed, it is, if that end be not disaster. But in Emily Dickinson's case, the stray health of genius came to the support of this hermit's instinct, and preserved her to the end of life sweet and blithe and contented in that innocent nun-like existence in which she chose to be immured. Her own room served her for native land, and in the painted garden beyond her window-sill was foreign travel enough for her. For that frugal soul, the universe of experience was bounded by the blue hills of a New England valley.

It was, of course, part of the inheritance of such a woman to have the religious sense strongly marked. She came of a race that never was at ease in Zion, yet never was content out of sight of the promised land. It best suited their strenuous and warlike nature always to be looking down on the delectable Canaan from the Pisgah of their own unworthiness. Yet, however severe a face life wore to them, and unlovely as their asperity often was, they were still making, though unwittingly, for the liberation of humanity. They were laying a sub-structure of honesty and seriousness, on which their intellectual inheritors might build, whether in art or politics. And their occupation with religion, with the affairs of the inward life and all its needs, has left an impress on ourselves, given us a trend from which we swerve in vain. And on every page of Emily Dickinson's poetry this ethical tendency, this awful environment of spirituality, is evident. Meditations of Psyche in the House of Clay; epigrams of an immortal guest, left behind on the chamber wall on the eve of silent departure, these brief lyrics seem:

This world is not conclusion;
    A sequel stands beyond,
Invisible as music,
    But positive as sound.

It beckons and it baffles;
    Philosophies don't know,
And through a riddle, at the last,
    Sagacity must go.

To guess it puzzles scholars;
    To gain it, men have shown
Contempt of generations,
    And crucifixion known.

That is an orphic utterance, no doubt; and such is all of this poet's work. She is, like Emerson, a companion for solitude, a stimulating comrade in the arduous intellectual ways. A symbolist of the symbolists, she is with them a reviver and establisher of the religious sentiment. Full of scepticism and the gentle irony of formal unbelief, putting aside the accepted and narrowing creed, she brings us, as Emerson did, face to face with new objects of worship. In their guidance we come a step nearer the great veil. For it is quite true that he who was hailed as a sceptic and destroyer in his early career, was in reality a prophet and a founder.

And it was inevitable, too, that one so much at home in spiritual matters should be deeply versed in nature—should be on intimate terms of friendship with all Nature's creatures.

Not that her knowledge of them was wide; it could hardly be that. But her sympathy with them was deep. She had ever a word of interpretation for the humblest of the mute dwellers in her garden world, clover or bee or blade. Often in these verses on the natural world there is a touch of whimsical humor that shows her character in very delightful color; as, for instance, in the lines on cobwebs:

The spider as an artist
    Has never been employed,
Though his surpassing merit
    Is freely certified

By every broom and Bridget
    Throughout a Christian land.
Neglected son of genius,
    I take thee by the hand.

There is the touch of intimacy, of fellowship, of kinship with all creation, which is so characteristic of modern poetry, and which is to become characteristic of modern religion. It is the tolerant, gay, debonair note of blameless joy which has been banished so long from the world, coming back to claim its own again.

Did I say that Emily Dickinson's contribution to poetry was more important than that of any other woman in America? Perhaps it is. Yet it has its faults, so hard a thing is perfection in any art, and so perfect the balance of fine qualities necessary to attain it. For while this poet was so eminent in wit, so keen in epigram, so rare and startling in phrase, the extended laborious architecture of an impressive poetic creation was beyond her. So that one has to keep her at hand as a stimulus and refreshment rather than as a solace. She must not be read long at a sitting. She will not bear that sort of treatment any more than Mr. Swinburne will; and for the very opposite reason. In Swinburne there is such a richness of sound, and often such a paucity of thought that one's even mental poise is sadly strained in trying to keep an equilibrium. He is like those garrulous persons, enamored of their own voice, who talk one to death so pleasingly. While in Emily Dickinson there is a lack of sensuousness, just as there was in Emerson. So that, like him, she never could have risen into the first rank of poets. And it was a sure critical instinct that led her never to venture beyond the range where her success was sure.

There is one thing to be remembered in considering her poetry, if we are to allow ourselves the full enjoyment of it; and that is her peculiar rhymes. As Colonel Higginson well remarks, "Though curiously indifferent to all conventional rules, she had a rigorous literary standard of her own, and often altered a word many times to suit an ear which had its own tenacious fastidiousness."

It is usual in verse to call those sounds perfect rhymes in which the final consonants (if there be any) and the final vowels are identical, but the consonants preceding these final vowels, different. So that we call "hand" and "land" perfect rhymes. But this is only a conventional custom among poets. It is consonant with laws of poetry, of course; but it is not in itself a law. It is merely one means at the writer's disposal for marking off his lines for the reader's ear. And when Emily Dickinson chose to use in her own work another slightly different convention, she was at perfect liberty to do so. She violated no law of poetry. The laws of art are as inviolable as the laws of nature.

> Who never wanted—maddest joy
> Remains to him unknown;
> The banquet of abstemiousness
> Surpasses that of wine.

"Wine" and "unknown" are not perfect rhymes. No more are "ground" and "mind," "done" and "man"; yet they serve to mark her lines for her reader quite well. Why? Because she has made a new rule for herself, and has followed it carefully. It is simply this—that the final vowels need not be identical; only the final consonants need be identical.

The vowels may vary. It is wrong to say that she disregarded any law here. The question is rather: Did her new usage tend to beautiful results? For my part I confess that I like that falling rhyme very much. There is a haunting gypsy accent about it, quite in keeping with the tenor of that wilding music. What a strange and gnomelike presence lurks in all her lines!

[Review of *Poems* (British edition, 1904)]

Anonymous*

In editing Miss Dickinson's *Poems*, Mr. T. W. Higginson claims for them "a quality more suggestive of the poetry of William Blake than of anything to be elsewhere found." This faith is justified to a point, but one might add that the influence of Browning is very marked, as witness the poem entitled 'The Lonely House.' Where else does this echo come from?

> Day rattles, too,
>   Stealth's slow;
> The sun has got as far
> As the third sycamore.
>   Screams chanticleer,
>   "Who's there?"
> And echoes, trains away,
> Sneer—"Where?"
> While the old couple, just astir,
> Fancy the sunrise left the door ajar!

Mr. Higginson very justly describes these verses as "poetry of the portfolio"; they were, he tells us, produced absolutely without thought of publication, and the author was only induced to publish a few in her lifetime. The result is, as the editor remarks, that though the verses gain sometimes "through the habit of freedom and the unconventional utterance of daring thoughts," they lose "whatever advantage lies in the discipline of public criticism and the enforced conformity to accepted ways."

Miss Dickinson was born in 1830, and died in 1886, and this book has found considerable favour in America since her death. It is not likely to secure a great vogue in this country, but certainly those who are genuinely interested in poetry will like to possess this specimen of the genuine thing. Miss Dickinson was absolutely indifferent to form and rule. She used rhyme when it came handy, and she ruthlessly abandoned it when it did not. She fell back on assonance, and often very indifferent assonance. Blake had far more form than she; yet is not this like Blake?

*From the *Anthenaeum*, No. 4036 (Mar. 4, 1905), 269–70.

Apparently with no surprise
To any happy flower,
The frost beheads it at its play
In accidental power.
The bland assassin passes on,
The sun proceeds unmoved
To measure off another day
For an approving God.

Indeed, one feels at times disposed to echo Miss Dickinson's verses:—

Much madness is divinest sense
To a discerning eye;
Much sense the starkest madness.

Does divine sense, then, lie in such madness as this?—

I asked no other thing,
No other was denied.
I offered Being for it;
The mighty merchant smiled.

Brazil? He twirled a button,
Without a glance my way:
"But, madam, is there nothing else
That we can show to-day?"

Yet while one is being brought up by these inexplicable eccentricities one
comes upon such a lyrical gem as

New feet within my garden go,
New fingers stir the sod;
A troubadour upon the elm
Betrays the solitude.

New children play upon the green,
New weary sleep below;
And still the pensive spring returns,
And still the punctual snow!

Miss Dickinson rushed at her meanings blindly and recklessly. Very
often she reached them, and expressed them often in her uncouth mannerisms, and sometimes with sweetness and dignity. But, as often as not,
her wild career merely issues in vagueness, in helplessness, in a mist in
which she gropes hopelessly after a lost and intangible significance. How
simple and how real she can be is seen in such verses as 'The First Lesson';
how bizarre and how much divorced from equable emotion is visible in a
poem which, nevertheless, clings to the reluctant memory:

I died for beauty, but was scarce
Adjusted in the tomb,

When one who died for truth was lain
    In an adjoining room.

He questioned softly why I failed?
    "For beauty," I replied.
"And I for truth,—the two are one;
    We brethren are," he said.

And so, as kinsmen met a night,
    We talked between the rooms,
Until the moss had reached our lips,
    And covered up our names.

An Early Imagist   Elizabeth Shepley Sergeant*

"Criticism is timid," writes Emerson. "When shall we dare to say only that is poetry which cleanses and mans me?" "The Single Hound" is poetry of this tonic sort, and—though the lifetime it records ended nearly thirty years ago—throws a searching light on the revolutionary volumes of 1915. For starkness of vision, "quintessentialness" of expression, boldness and solidity of thought, and freedom of form, a New England spinster who flourished between 1830 and 1886 in an elm-shaded college town above the Connecticut valley, might give the imagists "pointers": here is a discovery to quicken the modern New England heart. To this day in western Massachusetts Sundays are almost Sabbaths, "ministers" almost men of awe, and Longfellow is almost a great poet. Where, then, in the golden age of "Evangeline" and the Congregational Church, did Emily Dickinson get her daring inspiration?

Certainly she did not go abroad for it, but dug it out of her native granite. To me she is one of the rarest flowers the sterner New England ever bore, and justifies, as Carlyle justified his narrow Scotch inheritance—there is a curious analogy between his prose and her nubbly, elliptical verse—the stiff-necked Puritan elders from whom we all sprang. For without those elders and their family Bibles, and the mystical marriage of the absolute and the homely which was the very essence of their minds and hours, Emily Dickinson could never have been on such friendly, not to say familiar terms with God, or sported so whimsically and so stupendously with the mysteries of living and dying. The peculiar quality of her short concentrated poems is that they bring infinity and eternity within a village hedge; and to her, as to the early Puritan, the great earthly experience was poignantly individual:

*From *New Republic*, 4 (Aug. 14, 1915), 52–54. Reprinted by permission of the *New Republic*.

> Adventure most unto itself
> The Soul condemned to be;
> Attended by a Single Hound—
> Its own Identity.

For Emily Dickinson—of how few, even among "strong-minded" women, can it be said—was a genuine solitary.

> There is a solitude of space,
> A solitude of sea,
> A solitude of death, but these
> Society shall be,
> Compared with that profounder site,
> That polar privacy,
> A Soul admitted to Itself:
> Finite Infinity.

The theme finds many variations in "The Single Hound":

> The Soul that hath a Guest
> Doth seldom go abroad.
> Diviner Crowd at home
> Obliterate the need, . . .

and it was probably this "other loneliness," not occasioned by "want, or friend, or circumstances, or lot," in which she felt herself so richly companioned by her own spirit, that led her to keep her verse out of print during her life.

The poems collected in the present volume—the fourth to be published since her death—were all addressed, "on any chance slip of paper," during many years of "romantic friendship," to a sister-in-law who lived the width of a green lawn away. Yet "days, and even weeks, slipped by sometimes without their actual meeting." Mrs. Martha Dickinson Bianchi, deciding at last to publish her mother's treasury, adds a suggestive preface of anecdote and reminiscence to prove how little the aunt she loved resembled the poetess as she is "taught in colleges"—"a weird recluse eating her heart out in morbid or unhappy longing, or a victim of unsatisfied passion."

Emily Dickinson, to her nieces and nephews, was "of fairy lineage"—"the confederate in every contraband desire," ready to start with horse and buggy for the moon at a moment's notice. "Fascination was her element." She was "lightning and fragrance in one." Mrs. Bianchi's delicate phrases give one hints of it: "her way of flitting, like a shadow upon the hillside, a motion known to no other mortal"; the way "her spirit seemed merely playing through her body as the aurora borealis through darkness"; her revelling "in the wings of her mind—I had almost said the fins, too—so universal was her identification with every form of life and element of being." We read of her wiles and ruses for escaping dull society: "He has the facts, but not the phosphorescence of learning";

of her respect for her father, the august leading lawyer of Amherst: "If Father is asleep on the sofa the house is full, though it were empty otherwise."

We learn, too, of the many lovers who attended her elusive and skittish path, and who were on the whole—though men were more stimulating to her than the gentlewomen of her day, whom she once set down in verse as "soft cherubic creatures" of "dimity convictions"—well lost as husbands. For "she was not daily bread. She was stardust." As Emily Dickinson herself puts it:

> The missing All prevented me
> From missing minor things—

The colleges must be losing their sense of humor. For what thwarted old maid could write:

> To this apartment deep
> No ribaldry may creep.
> Untroubled this abode
> By any man but God.

Or say so perfectly:

> That Love is all there is,
> Is all we know of Love.
> It is enough: the freight should be
> Proportioned to the groove.

There is, I think, less of human passion in this collection than in the earlier ones; and somewhat less, perhaps, of that so exquisite and intense identification with nature which Mrs. Bianchi mentions. Yet what a skipping sense—one feels it in one's very heels—of the life of bee, bird, flower, hill, cloud, wind and sun is here.

> Beauty crowds me till I die,

she cries. There are also nature poems, as the one that begins:

> The winds drew off
> Like hungry dogs
> Defeated of a bone—

which for sheer "decorative" quality might go into an imagist anthology. The following is typical of the more resonant and abstruse Dickinsonian manner:

> The long sigh of the Frog
> Upon a Summer's day,
> Enacts intoxication
> Upon the revery.
> But his receding swell

> Substantiates a peace,
> That makes the ear inordinate
> For corporal release.

For the "phosphorescence" of poetry, however, give me:

> A little madness in the Spring
> Is wholesome even for the King,
> But God be with the Clown,
> Who ponders this tremendous scene—
> This whole experiment of green,
> As if it were his own!

"Pondering" kept Emily Dickinson face to face with the other side of the visible world. Half her impatience with her kind was that they prated of "charming April Day"; mistook "the outside for the in"; talked, as she says in a letter, "of sacred things aloud and embarrass my dog." Her own curious imagination sought the "area superior" beyond each day and life. Death was her constant preoccupation; the "overtakelessness" of those who had accomplished it was more majestic than the majesties of earth. Sometimes she wrote of it with utter simplicity:

> To-day or this noon,
> She dwelt so close,
> I almost touched her;
> To-night she lies
> Past neighborhood—
> And bough and steeple—
> Now past surmise.

Again, inquisitively sybilline:

> How went the agile kernel out—
> Contusion of the husk,
> Nor rip nor wrinkle indicate,—
> But just an Asterisk.

There are poems, too, where lovers of literary "influence" might find echoes of Donne's rhetoric and abstract vocabulary:

> Eternity will be
>   Velocity, or pause,
> At fundamental signals
>   From fundamental laws.
> To die, is not to go—
>   On doom's consummate chart
> No territory new is staked,
>   Remain thou as thou art.

Donne may well have been in the Hon. Mr. Dickinson's library. But provincial New England kept, well through the nineteenth century, much of the seventeenth century tradition; and transcendentalism was, of course, in Emily Dickinson's air—the academic-minded should take these facts to heart before assuming that either her ideas or her quaint expression were borrowed. They should read Emerson's Journals and compare Emily with his "Cousin Margaret." Her letters show that she thought obliquely, yet unflinchingly, as Meredith did; if ever his "Comic Spirit" found personification, it was in this woman, with her wit, her glancing mind, her range from the sublime to the ridiculous. The difficulties of syntax, the obscurities and abstractions which mark her verse were no more derived than her Amherst realisms, but a very part of her. So were her impertinencies towards her Creator and his prophets.

> Papa above!
> Regard a Mouse
> O'erpowered by the Cat—

"To live," she once wrote, "is so startling it leaves but little room for other occupations"; and I believe it is her deeply "startled" sense of man and the universe that keeps her terse and pregnant yet thistle-down verse from archaism, though it sometimes has a jingle, sometimes no rhyme at all. "The Single Hound" is as surprising as a cold douche, as acute as the edge of a precipice, as lambent as a meteor cleaving the night. "If I feel physically as if the top of my head were taken off," she said, "I know that is poetry." To those who like to find their brains exposed to the illimitable I recommend this white and fearless New England spinster.

> Except the smaller size, no Lives are round.
> These hurry to a sphere, and show, and end.
> The larger, slower grow, and later hang—
> The Summers of Hesperides are long.

Emily Dickinson
Norman Foerster[*]

In the expanding, heterogeneous America of the second half of the nineteenth century, poetry lost its clearly defined tendencies and became various and experimental. It did not cease to be provincial; for although no one region dominated as New England had dominated in the first half of the century, the provincial accent was as unmistakable, and the purely national accent as rare, as before. The East, rapidly becoming the so-called "effete East," produced a poetry to which the West was indifferent;

[*]From *The Cambridge History of American Literature*, ed. W. P. Trent, J. Erskine, S. P. Sherman, and C. Van Doren (New York: Macmillan Publishing Co., 1921), III, pp. 31–34. Copyright 1921, renewed 1948 by Macmillan Publishing Co., Inc. Reprinted with permission of Macmillan Publishing Co., Inc.

the West, still the West of "carnivorous animals of a superior rank," produced a poetry that the cultivated classes of the East regarded as vulgar.
In a broad way it may perhaps be said that the poetry of this period was
dedicated either to beauty or to "life"; to a revered past, or to the present
and the future; to the civilization of Asia and Europe, or to the ideals and
manners of America, at least the West of America. The virtue of the
poetry of beauty was its fidelity to a noble tradition, its repetition, with a
difference, of familiar and justly approved types of beauty; its defect was
mechanical repetition, petty embellishment. The virtue of the poetry of
"life" was fidelity to experience, vitality of utterance; its defect, crudity,
meanness, insensitiveness to fineness of feeling and beauty of expression.
Where the poets are many and all are minor it is difficult to make a
choice, but on the whole it seems that the outstanding poets of the East
were Emily Dickinson, Aldrich, Bayard Taylor, R. H. Stoddard, Stedman, Gilder, and Hovey; and of the West, Bret Harte, Joaquin Miller,
Sill, Riley, and Moody.

None of these has gained more with time than has Emily Dickinson.
Despite her defective sense of form, which makes her a better New
Englander than Easterner, she has acquired a permanent following of
discriminating readers through her extraordinary insight into the life of
the mind and the soul. This insight is that of a latter-day Puritan, completely divorced from the outward stir of life, retiring, by preference,
deeper and deeper within. Born in 1830 at Amherst, Massachusetts, she
lived there all her life, and in 1886 died there. The inwardness and moral
ruggedness of Puritanism she inherited mainly through her father, Edward Dickinson, lawyer and treasurer of Amherst College, a Puritan of
the old type, whose heart, according to his daughter, was "pure and terrible." Her affection for him was so largely compounded with awe that in
a sense they were strangers. "I have a brother and sister," she wrote to her
poetical preceptor, Thomas Wentworth Higginson; "my mother does not
care for thought, and father, too busy with his briefs to notice what we
do. He buys me many books, but begs me not to read them, because he
fears they jiggle the mind. They are religious, except me." Of course, she
too was religious, and intensely so, breathing as she did the intoxicating
air of Transcendentalism. In person she described herself as "small, like
the wren; and my hair is bold like the chestnut burr; and my eyes, like the
sherry in the glass that the guest leaves." "You ask of my companions.
Hills, sir, and the sundown, and a dog large as myself." These, and not
her family, were actually her companions, together with a few books and
her own soul. She had an alert introspection that brought her more than
the wealth of the Indies. There is no better example of the New England
tendency to moral revery than this last pale Indian-summer flower of
Puritanism. She is said literally to have spent years without passing the
doorstep, and many more years without leaving her father's grounds.
After the death of her parents, not to mention her dog Carlo, she retired

still further within herself, till the sounds of the everyday world must have come to her as from a previous state of existence.

"I find ecstasy in living," she said to Higginson, and spoke truly, as her poems show. In an unexpected light on orchards, in a wistful mood of meadow or wood-border held secure for a moment before it vanished; in the few books that she read—her Keats, her Shakespeare, her *Revelation*; in the echoes, obscure in origin, that stirred within her own mind and soul, now a tenuous melody, now a deep harmony, a haunting question, or a memorable affirmation;—everywhere she displayed something of the mystic's insight and joy. And she expressed her experience in her poems, forgetting the world altogether, intent only on the satisfaction of giving her fluid life lasting form, her verse being her journal. Yet the impulse to expression was probably not strong, because she wrote no poems, save one or two, as she herself asserts, until the winter 1861–62, when she was over thirty years old. In the spring of 1862 she wrote a letter to Higginson beginning, "Are you too deeply occupied to say if my verse is alive? The mind is so near itself it cannot see distinctly, and I have none to ask." Discerning the divine spark in her shapeless verse, he welcomed her advances, and became her "preceptor," loyally listened to but, as was inevitable, mainly unheeded. Soon perceiving this, Higginson continued to encourage her, for many years, without trying to divert her lightning-flashes. In "H.H."—Helen Hunt Jackson, herself a poetess of some distinction, and her early schoolmate at Amherst—she had another sympathetic friend, who, suspecting the extent of her production, asked for the post of literary executor. At length, in 1890, a volume edited by Higginson and Mabel Loomis Todd was published, *Poems by Emily Dickinson*, arranged under various heads according to subject. The book succeeded at once, six editions being sold in the first six months; so that a second series, and later a third, seemed to be justified. From the first selection to the third, however, there is a perceptible declension.

The subject division adopted by her editors serves well enough: Life, Love, Nature, Time and Eternity. A mystical poetess sequestered in a Berkshire village, she naturally concerned herself with neither past nor present, but with the things that are timeless. Apparently deriving no inspiration from the war to which Massachusetts, including her preceptorial colonel, gave itself so freely, she spent her days in brooding over the mystery of pain, the true nature of success, the refuge of the tomb, the witchcraft of the bee's murmur, the election of love, the relation of deed to thought and will. On such subjects she jotted down hundreds of little poems.

Though she had an Emersonian faith that fame, if it belonged to her, could not escape her, she cared nothing at all about having it; like not a few Transcendentalists, she might have written on the lintels of her doorpost, *Whim*. That was her guiding divinity. Whim in a high sense: not unruliness, for all her impishness, but complete subjection to the inner dictate. She obeyed it in her mode of life, in her friendships, in her letters, in her poems. It makes her poetry eminently spontaneous—as fresh and artless as experience itself—in spite of the fact that she was not a spontaneous singer. The ringing bursts of melody that are characteristic of the born lyrical poet, such as Burns, she was incapable of; but she had insight, and intense, or rather tense, emotion, and expressed herself with an eye single to the truth. Something she derived from her reading, no doubt, from Emerson, the Brownings, Sir Thomas Browne; but rarely was poet less indebted. From her silent thought she derived what is essential in her work, and her whole effort was to state her findings precisely. She could not deliberately arrange her thoughts; "when I try to organize," she said, "my little force explodes and leaves me bare and charred." If she revised her work, as she did industriously, it was to render it not more attractive but truer.

Her poems are remarkable for their condensation, their vividness of image, their delicate or pungent satire and irony, their childlike responsiveness to experience, their subtle feeling for nature, their startling abruptness in dealing with themes commonly regarded as trite, their excellence in imaginative insight and still greater excellence in fancy. Typical is such a poem as that in which she celebrates the happiness of a little stone on the road, or that in which she remarks with gleeful irony upon the dignity that burial has in store for each of us—coach and footmen, bells in the village, "as we ride grand along." Emily Dickinson takes us to strange places; one never knows what is in store. But always she is penetrating and dainty, both intimate and aloof, challenging lively thought on our part while remaining, herself, a charmingly elfish mystery. Her place in American letters will be inconspicuous but secure.

Emily Dickinson   Conrad Aiken*

Emily Dickinson was born in Amherst, Massachusetts, on December 10th, 1830. She died there, after a life perfectly devoid of outward event, in 1886. She was thus an exact contemporary of Christina Rossetti, who was born five days earlier than she, and outlived her by eight years. Of her life we know little. Her father, Edward Dickinson, was a lawyer, and the Treasurer of Amherst College; and it is clear that what social or intellectual life was in that bleak era available, was available for her. That she did not choose to avail herself of it, except in very slight degree, is also clear; and that this choice, which was gradually to make of her life an almost inviolable solitude, was made early, is evident from her Letters. In

*From *Selected Poems of Emily Dickinson*, edited by Conrad Aiken (London: Cape, 1924), pp. 5–22. Reprinted by permission of Brandt and Brandt Literary Agents. Copyright 1935, 1939, 1940, 1942, 1951, © 1958 by Conrad Aiken.

a letter dated 1853, when she was twenty-three years old, she remarked, "I do not go from home." By the time she was thirty, the habit of sequestration had become distinct, a subject on which she was explicit and emphatic in her letters to T. W. Higginson—editor of the *Atlantic Monthly* at that time. She made it clear that if there was to be any question of a meeting between them, he would have to come to Amherst—she would not go to Boston. Higginson, as a matter of fact, saw her twice, and his record of the encounter is practically the only record we have of her from any "literary" personage of her lifetime. Even this is meagre—Higginson saw her superficially, as was inevitable. Brave soldier, courtly gentleman, able editor, he was too much of the old school not to be a little puzzled by her poetry; and if he was fine enough to guess the fineness, he was not quite fine enough wholly to understand it. The brief correspondence between these two is an extraordinary document of unconscious irony—the urbanely academic editor reproaching his wayward pupil for her literary insubordination, her false quantities, and reckless liberties with rhyme; the wayward pupil replying with a humility, beautiful and pathetic, but remaining singularly, with unmalleable obstinacy, herself. "I saw her," wrote Higginson, "but twice, face to face, and brought away the impression of something as unique and remote as Undine or Mignon or Thekla." When, thirty years after the acquaintance had begun, and four after Emily Dickinson's death, he was called upon to edit a selection from her poetry, practically none of which had been published during her lifetime, his scruples were less severe, and he spoke of her with generosity and insight. "After all," he then wrote, "when a thought takes one's breath away, a lesson on grammar seems an impertinence." Again, "In many cases these verses will seem to the reader like poetry torn up by the roots." And again, "a quality more suggestive of the poetry of Blake than of anything to be elsewhere found—flashes of wholly original and profound insight into nature and life."

Thus began and ended Emily Dickinson's only important connexion with the literary life of her time. She knew, it is true, Helen Hunt Jackson, a poetess, for whose anthology, *A Masque of Poets*, she gave the poem "Success," one of the few poems she allowed publication during her life. And she knew the Bowles family, owners and editors of the *Springfield Republican*, at that time the *Manchester Guardian* of New England— which, as she put it mischievously, was one of "such papers . . . as have nothing carnal in them." But these she seldom saw; and aside from these she had few intimates outside of her family; the circle of her world grew steadily smaller. This is a point of cardinal importance, but unfortunately no light has been thrown upon it. It is apparent that Miss Dickinson became a hermit by deliberate and conscious choice. "A recluse," wrote Higginson, "by temperament and habit, literally spending years without setting her foot beyond the doorstep, and many more years during which her walks were strictly limited to her father's grounds, she habitually concealed her mind, like her person, from all but a very few friends; and it was with great difficulty that she was persuaded to print, during her lifetime, three or four poems." One of the co-editors of *Poems: Second Series* assures us that this voluntary hermitage was not due to any "love-disappointment," and that she was "not an invalid." "She had tried society and the world, and had found them lacking." But this, of course, tells us nothing. Her letters show us convincingly that her girlhood was a normally "social" one—she was active, high-spirited, and endowed with a considerable gift for extravagant humour. As a young woman she had, so Mrs. Bianchi, a niece, informs us in the preface to *The Single Hound*, several love-affairs. But we have no right, without other testimony, to assume here any ground for the singular psychological change that came over her. The only other clue we have, of any sort, is the hint from one of her girlhood friends, that perhaps, *"she was longing for poetic sympathy."* Perhaps! But we must hope that her relatives and literary executors will eventually see fit to publish *all* her literary remains, verse and prose, and to give us thus, perhaps, a good deal more light on the nature of her life. Anecdotes relating to her mischievousness, her wit, her waywardness, are not enough. It is amusing, if horrifying, to know that once, being anxious to dispose of some kittens, she put them on a shovel, carried them into the cellar, and dropped them into the nearest jar—which, subsequently, on the occasion of the visit of a distinguished judge, turned out to have been the pickle-jar. We like to know too, that even when her solitude was most remote she was in the habit of lowering from her window, by a string, small baskets of fruit or confectionery for children. But there are other things we should like to know more.

There seems, however, little likelihood of our being told, by her family, anything more; and if we seek for the causes of the psychic injury which so sharply turned her in upon herself, we can only speculate. Her letters, in this regard, give little light, only showing us again and again that the injury was deep. Of the fact that she suffered acutely from intellectual drought, there is evidence enough. One sees her vividly here—but one sees her, as it were, perpetually in retreat; always discovering anew, with dismay, the intellectual limitations of her correspondents; she is discreet, pathetic, baffled, a little humbled, and draws in her horns; takes sometimes a perverse pleasure in indulging more than ever, on the occasion of such a disappointment, in her love of a cryptic style—a delicate bombardment of parable and whim which she perfectly knows will stagger; and then again retreats to the safe ground of the superficial. It is perhaps for this reason that the letters give us so remarkably little information about her literary interests. The meagreness of literary allusion is astounding. The Brontës and the Brownings are referred to—she thought Alexander Smith "not very coherent"—Joaquin Miller she "could not care about." Of her own work she speaks only in the brief unsatisfactory correspondence with Higginson. To him she wrote in 1862, "I wrote no verse, but one or two, until this winter." Otherwise, no scrap of her own literary history: she appears to have existed in a vacuum. Of the literary events, tremendous for America, which were taking place during her most impressionable years, there is hardly a mention. Emerson was at the height of his career, and living only sixty miles away: his poems came out when she was seventeen. When she was twenty, Hawthorne published *The Scarlet Letter*; and *The House of the Seven Gables* the year after. The same year, 1851, brought out Melville's *Moby Dick*. The death of Poe took place in 1849—in 1850 was published the first collected edition of his poems. When she was twenty-four, Thoreau's *Walden* appeared; when she was twenty-five, *Leaves of Grass*. One can say with justice that she came to full "consciousness" at the very moment when American literature came to flower. That she knew this, there cannot be any question; nor that she was stimulated and influenced by it. One must assume that she found in her immediate environment no one of her own stature, with whom she could admit or discuss such things; that she lacked the energy or effrontery to voyage out into the unknown in search of such companionship; and that lacking this courage, and wanting this help, she became easily a prey to the then current Emersonian doctrine of mystical Individualism. In this connexion it is permissible to suggest that her extreme self-seclusion and secrecy was both a protest and a display—a kind of vanity masquerading as modesty. She became increasingly precious, of her person as of her thought. Vanity is in her letters—at the last an unhealthy vanity. She believes that anything she says, however brief, will be of importance; however cryptic, will be deciphered. She enjoys being something of a mystery, and she sometimes deliberately and awkwardly exaggerates it. Even in notes of condolence—for which she had a morbid passion—she is vain enough to indulge in sententiousness: as when she wrote, to a friend whose father had died on her wedding-day, "Few daughters have the immortality of a father for a bridal gift."

When we come to Emily Dickinson's poetry, we find the Emersonian individualism clear enough, but perfectly Miss Dickinson's. Henry James observed of Emerson:

> The doctrine of the supremacy of the individual to himself, of his originality and, as regards his own character, *unique* quality, must have had a great charm for people living in a society in which introspection, thanks to the want of other entertainment, played almost the part of a social resource. . . . There was . . . much relish for the utterances of a writer who would help one to take a picturesque view of one's internal possibilities, and to find in the landscape of the soul all sorts of fine sunrise and moonlight effects.

This sums up admirably the social "case" of Miss Dickinson—it gives us a shrewd picture of the causes of her singular introversion, and it suggests that we are perhaps justified in considering her the most perfect flower of New England Transcendentalism. In her mode of life she carried the doctrine of self-sufficient individualism farther than Thoreau carried it, or the naïve zealots of Brook Farm. In her poetry she carried it, with its complement of passionate moral mysticism, farther than Emerson: which is to say that as a poet she had more genius than he. Like Emerson, whose essays must greatly have influenced her, and whose poetry, especially his gnomic poems, only a little less, she was from the outset, and remained all her life, a singular mixture of Puritan and freethinker. The problems of good and evil, of life and death, obsessed her; the nature and destiny of the human soul; and Emerson's theory of compensation. Towards God, as one of her earliest critics is reported to have said, "she exhibited an Emersonian self-possession." Indeed, she did not, and could not, accept the Puritan God at all. She was frankly irreverent, on occasion, a fact which seems to have made her editors a little uneasy—one hopes that it has not resulted in the suppression of any of her work. What she was irreverent to, of course, was the Puritan conception of God, the Puritan attitude toward him.

> Heavenly father, take to thee
> The supreme iniquity,
> Fashioned by thy candid hand
> In a moment contraband.
> Though to trust us seems to us
> More respectful,—we are dust,
> We apologize to thee
> For thine own Duplicity.

This, it must be repeated, is Emily Dickinson's opinion of the traditional and anthropomorphic "God," who was still, in her day, a portentous Victorian gentleman. Her real reverence, the reverence that made her a mystic poet of the finest sort, was reserved for Nature, which seemed to her a more manifest and beautiful evidence of Divine Will than creeds and churches. This she saw, observed, loved, with a burning simplicity and passion which nevertheless did not exclude her very agile sense of humour. Her Nature poems, however, are not the most secretly revelatory or dramatically compulsive of her poems, nor, on the whole, the best. They are often of extraordinary delicacy—nearly always give us, with deft brevity, the exact in terms of the quaint. But, also, they are often superficial, a mere affectionate playing with the smaller things that give her delight; and to see her at her best and most characteristic and most profound, one must turn to the remarkable range of metaphysical speculation and ironic introspection which is displayed in those sections of her posthumous books which her editors have captioned Life, and Time and Eternity. In the former sections are the greater number of her set "meditations" on the nature of things. For some critics they will always appear too bare, bleak and fragmentary. They have no trappings, only here and there a shred of purple. It is as if Miss Dickinson who, in one of her letters uttered her contempt for the "obtrusive body," had wanted to make them, as nearly as possible, disembodied thought. The thought is there, at all events, hard, bright, and clear; and her symbols, her metaphors, of which she could be prodigal, have an analogous clarity and translucency. What is also there is a downright homeliness which is a perpetual surprise and delight. Emerson's gnomic style she tunes up to the epigrammatic—the epigrammatic she often carries to the point of the cryptic; she becomes what one might call an epigrammatic symbolist.

> Lay this laurel on the one
> Too intrinsic for renown.
> Laurel! veil your deathless tree,—
> Him you chasten, that is he!

This, from *Poems: Second Series*, verges perilously on the riddle. And it often happens that her passionate devotion to concise statement in terms of metaphor left for her readers a small rich emblem of which the colours tease, the thought entices, but the meaning escapes. Against this, however, should be set her capacity, when occasion came, for a granite simplicity, any parallel to which one must seek in the Seventeenth Century. This, for example, called Parting.

> My life closed twice before its close;
> It yet remains to see
> If Immortality unveil
> A third event to me,
>
> So huge, so hopeless to conceive,
> As these that twice befell.
> Parting is all we know of heaven
> And all we need of hell.

Or this, from *The Single Hound:*

> Not any sunny tone
> From any fervent zone
> Finds entrance there.
> Better a grave of Balm
> Toward human nature's home,
> And Robins near,
> Than a stupendous Tomb
> Proclaiming to the gloom
> How dead we are.

Both these poems, it will be noted, deal with death; and it must be observed that the number of poems by Miss Dickinson on this subject is one of the most remarkable things about her. Death, and the problem of life after death, obsessed her. She seems to have thought of it constantly—she died all her life, she probed death daily. "That bareheaded life under grass worries one like a wasp," she wrote. Ultimately, the obsession became morbid, and her eagerness for details, after the death of a friend—the hungry desire to know *how* she died—became almost vulture-like. But the preoccupation, with its horrible uncertainties—its doubts about immortality, its hatred of the flesh, and its many reversals of both positions—gave us her sharpest work. The theme was inexhaustible for her. If her poetry seldom became "lyrical," seldom departed from the colourless sobriety of its bare iambics and toneless assonance, it did so most of all when the subject was death. Death profoundly and cruelly invited her. It was most of all when she tried "to touch the smile," and dipped her "fingers in the frost," that she took full possession of her genius.

Her genius was, it remains to say, as erratic as it was brilliant. Her disregard for accepted forms or for regularities was incorrigible. Grammar, rhyme, metre—anything went by the board if it stood in the way of thought or freedom of utterance. Sometimes this arrogance was justified; sometimes not. She did not care in the least for variety of effect—of her six hundred-odd poems practically all are in octosyllabic quatrains or couplets, sometimes with rhyme, sometimes with assonance, sometimes with neither. Everywhere, when one first comes to these poems, one seems to see nothing but a colourless dry monotony. How deceptive a monotony, concealing what reserves of depth and splendour; what subtleties of mood and tone! Once adjust oneself to the spinsterly angularity of the mode, its lack of eloquence or rhetorical speed, its naïve and often prosaic directness, one discovers felicities of thought and phrase on every page. The magic is terse and sure. And ultimately one simply sighs at Miss Dickinson's singular perversity, her lapses and tyrannies, and accepts them as an inevitable part of the strange and original genius she was. The lapses and tyrannies become a positive charm—one even suspects they were deliberate. They satisfied her—therefore they satisfy us. This marks, of course, our complete surrender to her highly individual gift, and to the singular sharp beauty, present everywhere, of her personality. The two things cannot be separated; and together, one must suppose, they suffice to put her among the finest poets in the language.

The Irregularities of Emily Dickinson

Susan Miles*

Emily Dickinson's rhymes are from the conventional point of view so hopeless that it appears to me incredible that they should be due to incompetence. There is, however, wide divergence of opinion as to the

*From *London Mercury*, 13 (Dec. 1925), 145–50, 157–58.

significance which should be attached to her irregularities. Mr. Harold Monro, in the January issue of *The Criterion*, writes with extreme severity. "At a first impression," he begins, "Emily Dickinson's tiny lyrics appear more like the jottings of a half-idiotic schoolgirl than the grave musings of a fully educated woman. . . . Her style is clumsy; her language is poor; her technique is appalling." But after sending in this apparently unsatisfactory report, Mr. Monro half-withdraws his first impression, surprising us by a sentence which, if it means anything, means that he puts her best work on a level with that of Keats. Must we then understand that had it been *Hyperion* that Mr. Monro was introducing today to a public ignorant for the most part even of the author's name, it too would have been dismissed with a curt notice wholly derogatory save for three or four phrases of grudging commendation? Mr. Monro tells us that "Emily Dickinson has been over-rated, but not so far over-rated as a first survey of her selected poems might indicate," and that "as we progress in the art of understanding her we find in many of her flaws a kind of large splendid awkwardness, something innocently audacious, grotesque and abnormal." He then goes on to quote a lyric which he describes as "clumsy enough, but redeemed entirely by a magic of pathos and loveliness." After a final rebuke, to which I shall revert at the close of this article, Mr. Monro turns to *The Thirteenth Caesar*, regretting that "justice cannot be done to Mr. Sitwell in a short notice of this kind." It is a short notice; but it is considerably longer than that allotted to Emily Dickinson.

Others among Emily Dickinson's critics consistently make light of her irregularities, deliberately disregarding them as a mother might the lisp of a precocious child, or a legatee a sprinkle of misspellings in a will that made him rich. "It would be ungracious to carp when given a good gift," these critics seem to exclaim, "even if the bearer, large and flat of foot, has trodden on our toes," adding perhaps, "especially if she apologises as meekly as Emily Dickinson to the editor of *The Atlantic Monthly*."

But most of the critics who refuse to scold, sigh. Few seem prepared to go so far as the writer in *The Times Literary Supplement*, who asserts that "in a great deal of her work there is a kind of perfection in imperfection which, if it sometimes reveals the limits of her technical resources, does honor to her judgment," and who speaks of her use in one poem of a "rhyme which is not a rhyme" as "a kind of imaginative triumph."

Yet even this critic writes grudgingly. He admits by implication that the rhyme in defeating the ear's expectation fulfills the imagination's need—why then assert that "if perfection was unattainable it is the right kind of imperfection"? If a full rhyme would have been less expressive, wherein lies the imperfection of the Dickinsonian rhyme? Why speak of the Dickinsonian technique as "*almost* a device"? Why "*a kind* of imaginative triumph"?

My aim in writing this article is to claim quite explicitly, and without any apology, that Emily Dickinson's irregularities have a definite artistic significance. I believe that could we—*per impossibile*—without altering her vocabulary, substitute full rhymes for Dickinsonian, nothing would be gained by the substitution and, in many cases, much would be lost.

I do not, of course, intend to suggest that there is any intrinsic merit in a rhyme-scheme which arouses expectation and then defeats it. The device is a piece of technique which may be justified or may not. It is wholly a question of what it is that the artist using it wishes to express. If he wishes to give expression to a consistent belief in a world where not a worm is cloven in vain and not a moth with vain desire is shrivelled in a fruitless fire, he does artistically well to construct a volume of neat stanzas where "sin" rhymes with "in," "fall" with "all," "night" with "light," and "ill" with "will." If he has had an impression of a universe where all discord is harmony not understood, all partial ill is universal good, he will adequately express that impression in trim heroic couplets, rhyming "be" with "me" and "curse" with "worse" in undeviating regularity. As a matter of fact, neither Pope nor Tennyson nor any other poet ever had a wholly consistent impression of such a world. And when these poets were not actively believing in a dove-tailed universe their rhymes ceased to resemble a game of ping-pong played by expert and cautious children. When his impressions demanded such expression, Tennyson rhymed "death" with "faith," "home" with "masterdom," "move" with "love," "wood" with "blood," and "heath" with "death"; Pope rhymed "food" with "blood," "mourns" with "burns," and "rest" with "beast." These are not full rhymes; but critics pass them without question, partly perhaps because they find them in the work of poets with an established reputation for orthodoxy, partly, no doubt, because they have some sense of what is artistically seemly. Ping-pong rhyming is consistently practiced only by such writers as Ella Wheeler Wilcox, who labels her verses *Poems of Optimism* and plasters her pages with the tags "Ignore Misfortune" and "Be indifferent to evil."

But the universe as Emily Dickinson envisaged it was very different from the universe as pictured by Ella Wheeler Wilcox. Emily Dickinson viewed a world made up of pieces which often did not dove-tail, and it was her impression of this world that she sought to express in her poetry. The annual resurrection in field and forest was to her extremely odd. Experience for her was a precarious gait. A splinter very often seemed to swerve in her brain while the brains of other people ran evenly and true within their grooves. She pondered a tremendous scene, and a little madness in her rhymes was part of her expression of it. Sometimes that expression demanded a three-quarters rhyme, that is, an echo of the final consonant (if any), and the substitution of a long for a corresponding short vowel, or of a short for a corresponding long; sometimes the expression demanded a half-rhyme, that is, an echoing vowel and a contrasting consonant, or an echoing consonant and a contrasting vowel; sometimes a non-rhyme, that is, a sound which echoes neither final consonant nor vowel, but which clangs out its contrast to both. . . .

I do not wish to labor my thesis in detail; it may easily be tested by reference to such poems as: "He dropped so low in my regard," "I never hear the word 'escape,' " "I know that he exists," "The heart asks pleasure first," "Pain has an element of blank," "The brain within its groove," "She rose to his requirement," and "The sun kept setting, setting still."

As we might expect, the irregularities of rhyme are less frequent in the poems that deal with inanimate nature than in those concerned with humanity.

> It makes no difference abroad,
> The seasons fit the same,
> The mornings blossom into noons,
> And split their pods of flame.
>
> Wild-flowers kindle in the woods,
> The brooks brag all the day;
> No blackbird bates his jargoning
> For passing Calvary.

Here the significance of the part-rhyme in the second stanza is as obvious as is that of the full rhyme in the first.

And consider "A lady red upon the hill." Here in the first three stanzas which describe the imminence of spring, the rhymes come pat as Pope's. It is only in the last stanza that an irregularity of rhyme is called for by the thought:

> A lady red upon the hill
>   Her annual secret keeps;
> A lady white within the field
>   In placid lily sleeps!
>
> The tidy breezes with their brooms
>   Sweep vale, and hill, and tree!
> Prithee, my pretty housewives!
>   Who may expected be?
>
> The neighbours do not yet suspect!
>   The woods exchange a smile—
> Orchard, and buttercup, and bird—
>   In such a little while!
>
> And yet how still the landscape stands,
>   How nonchalant the wood,
> As if the resurrection
>   Were nothing very odd!

We have only to substitute the following to see by contrast how far from clumsy is the poet's technique.

> And yet how still the landscape stands,
>   How nonchalant the vale,
> As if the resurrection
>   Were commonplace and stale.

If we seek to enrich what Mr. Monro regards as the poverty of Emily Dickinson's language by substituting, let us say, "silent lies" for "nonchalant" and "coming of the spring" for "resurrection," the ruin will be completed.

> And yet how still the landscape stands,
>   How silent lies the vale,
> As if the coming of the spring
>   Were commonplace and stale.

Let us turn to "The sky is low," another nature poem which includes a rhyme that, in defeating the ear, echoes the implication of defeat in the thought.

> The sky is low, the clouds are mean,
> A travelling flake of snow
> Across a barn or through a rut
> Debates if it will go.
>
> A narrow wind complains all day
> How some one treated him;
> Nature, like us, is sometimes caught
> Without her diadem.

Here again, it is a flash of the human that cleaves the thought and leaves a pair of ragged edges demanding representation in the rhyme. "Nature, like us. . . ." Change the second stanza to:

> An icy wind complains all day
> Like angry men who frown,
> Nature like us is sometimes caught
> Without her golden crown.

and it is evident that the virtue has departed almost as obviously through the patness of the substituted rhyme as through the flatness of the substituted words.

It would be interesting, by the way, to know how "again" was pronounced in Amherst by Emily Dickinson's circle. To pronounce it "agen," in the following poem is to end on a more harmonious and a less wistful note than that given us by "agane."

> A train went through a burial gate,
> A bird broke forth and sang,
> And trilled, and quivered, and shook his throat
> Till all the churchyard rang;
>
> And then adjusted his little notes,
> And bowed and sang again.
> Doubtless, he thought it meet of him
> To say good-bye to men.

For that reason "agane" is the pronunciation I should favor; the more so, perhaps, in view of this couplet from "An altered look about the hills":

> A flippant fly upon the pane;
> A spider at his trade again,

where the sense seems to demand a full rhyme.

I have said that there is obviously no intrinsic merit in rhymes which defeat the ear. It is equally obvious, of course, that no system of consistently irregular rhymes is possible. There must be expectation to be defeated. Except in the nonsense verses written for her brother's children, in which she seems to be writing quite carelessly, I cannot recall any instances in Emily Dickinson's poems of irregular rhymes which have no artistic significance. . . .

In conclusion, I should like to turn to the final paragraph of Mr. Monro's criticism: "She seems," he writes, "to have been afraid. She dwelt in seclusion; social, physical and psychological. She gives the impression of wanting to keep some secret. Clarity of thought is constantly veiled in obscurity of expression. She was not candid; she does not seem to have been moved by any over-ruling instinct for truth. And we compare her unavoidably with her contemporary, Emily Brontë, whose infatuated desire to be faithful to her every aspect of truth overcame all timidity."

But Emily Dickinson is surely one of the comparatively few poets—Thomas Hardy is another—who have achieved an aesthetic impression of a cleft and unmatching world. Artistic necessity is too often confused with logical necessity—surely Mr. Abercrombie is, at any rate verbally, guilty of this confusion in the final chapter of his *Theory of Poetry*—and I can see no reason for assuming that the artistic necessity which compelled the "perfection in imperfection" of Emily Dickinson's technique had any connection with a wish-fulfilment for a logical necessity such as might compel the existence of a universe spiritually coordinated in spite of apparent inco-ordination. I do not agree with Mr. Abercrombie that "every poem is an ideal version of the world we most profoundly desire; and that by virtue of its form." His is an ingenious, and an intriguing theory, but I doubt whether it is more than plausible. It seems to me to be the case that whereas aesthetic activity purges us of desire, in the case of artistic activity desire is irrelevant. It does not appear to me that Emily Dickinson was using her art as a means of escape from life; but that on the other hand art such as Emily Dickinson's must necessarily involve preliminary courage in the envisaging of life. In the eyes of many who are not poets the world fails to fit, but in most the emotion of fear, or bewilderment, or pity, or disgust is too devastating for the detachment of an artist to be possible. To achieve detachment when envisaging a fissure on the edge of which we ourselves are clinging needs surely a supreme courage. Had Emily Dickinson become a social worker, or even a journalist, in Boston, would she have been credited with more independence and fortitude? A leisured life at Amherst could call for courage from the woman who wrote "that bareheaded life under grass worries one like a wasp."

Emily Dickinson   Amy Lowell*

I wonder what made Emily Dickinson as she was. She cannot be accounted for by any trick of ancestry or early influence. She was the daughter of a long line of worthy people; her father, who was the leading lawyer of Amherst, Massachusetts, and the treasurer of Amherst College, is typical of the aims and accomplishments of the race. Into this well-ordered, high-minded, average, and rather sombre milieu, swept Emily Dickinson like a beautiful, stray butterfly, 'beating in the void her luminous wings in vain.' She knew no different life; and yet she certainly did not belong to the one in which she found herself. She may have felt this in some obscure fashion; for, little by little, she withdrew from the world about her, and shut herself up in a cocoon of her own spinning. She had no heart to fight; she never knew that a battle was on and that she had been selected for a place in the vanguard; all she could do was to retire, to hide her wounds, to carry out her little skirmishings and advances in byways and side-tracks, slowly winning a territory which the enemy took no trouble to dispute. What she did seemed insignificant and individual, but thirty years after her death the flag under which she fought had become a great banner, the symbol of a militant revolt. It is an odd story, this history of Imagism, and perhaps the oddest and saddest moment in it is comprised in the struggle of this one brave, fearful, and unflinching woman.

There is very little to tell about Emily Dickinson's life. In a sense, she had no life except that of the imagination. Born in Amherst in December, 1830, she died there in May, 1886. Her travels consisted of occasional trips to Boston, and one short sojourn in Washington during her father's term

*From Amy Lowell, *Poetry and Poets* (Boston: Houghton Mifflin Co., 1930), pp. 88–108. Copyright 1930 by Houghton Mifflin Co. © renewed 1958 by Harvey H. Bundy and G. d'Andelot Belin. Reprinted by permission of Houghton Mifflin Co.

in Congress. As the years went on, she could scarcely be induced to leave her own threshold; what she saw from her window, what she read in her books, were her only external *stimuli*. Those few people whom she admitted to her friendship were loved with the terrible and morbid exaggeration of the profoundly lonely. In this isolation, all resilience to the blows of illness and death was atrophied. She could not take up her life again because there was no life to take. Her thoughts came to be more and more preoccupied with the grave. Her letters were painful reading indeed to the normal-minded. Here was a woman with a nice wit, a sparkling sense of humour, sinking under the weight of an introverted imagination to a state bordering upon neurasthenia; for her horror of publicity would not certainly be classed as a 'phobia.' The ignorance and unwisdom of her friends confused illness with genius, and, reversing the usual experience in such cases, they saw in the morbidness of hysteria, the sensitiveness of a peculiarly artistic nature. In the introduction to the collection of her letters, the editor, Mrs. Mabel Loomis Todd, says, 'In her later years, Emily Dickinson rarely addressed the envelopes; it seemed as if her sensitive nature shrank from the publicity which even her handwriting would undergo, in the observation of indifferent eyes. Various expedients were resorted to—obliging friends frequently performed this office for her; sometimes a printed newspaper label was pasted upon the envelope; but the actual strokes of her own pencil were, so far as possible, reserved exclusively for friendly eyes.'

That is no matter for laughter, but for weeping. What loneliness, disappointment, misunderstanding must have preceded it! What unwise protection against the clear, buffeting winds of life must have been exerted to shut the poor soul into her stifling hot-house! The times were out of joint for Emily Dickinson. Her circle loved her, but utterly failed to comprehend. Her daring utterances shocked; her whimsicality dazed. The account of this narrow life is heart-rending. Think of Charles Lamb joking a New England deacon; imagine Keats's letters read aloud to a Dorcas Society; conceive of William Blake sending the 'Songs of Experience' to the 'Springfield Republican'! Emily Dickinson lived in an atmosphere of sermons, church sociables, and county newspapers. It is ghastly, the terrible, inexorable waste of Nature, but it is a fact. The direct descendant of Blake (although she probably never heard of him) lived in this surrounding. The marvel is that her mind did not give way. It did not; except in so far as her increasing shrinking from society and her preoccupation with death may be considered giving way. She lived on; she never ceased to write; and the torture which she suffered must have been exquisite indeed.

Whenever a little door opened, some kind friend immediately slammed it to. Her old school companion Mrs. Jackson, better known as H.H., the author of 'Ramona,' repeatedly begged her to write for the 'No Name Series,' then just starting. And the poet whom everybody deemed so retiring was half inclined to accept. She needed to be pushed into the healthy arena of publicity, a little assistance over the bump of her own shyness and a new, bright, and vigorous life would have lain before her. In an evil moment she asked the advice of Mr. Thomas Wentworth Higginson. The very words of her letter show her half pleading to be urged on:

> Dear Friend:
>   Are you willing to tell me what is right? Mrs. Jackson, of Colorado, was with me a few moments this week, and wished me to write for this. I told her I was unwilling, and she asked me why? I said I was incapable, and she seemed not to believe me and asked me not to decide for a few days. Meantime she would write to me. . . . I would regret to estrange her, and if you would be willing to give me a note saying you disapproved it and thought me unfit, she would believe you.

The disapproval was cordially given; the door shut again upon the prisoner, who thanks her jailor with the least hint of regret between the lines:

> Dear Friend:
>   . . . I am glad I did as you would like. The degradation to displease you, I hope I may never incur.

Mild, sweet-tempered, sympathetic, and stupid Mr. Higginson! It was an evil moment when Emily chose him for the arbiter of her fate. And yet who, at the time, would have done better? Certainly not Longfellow, nor Lowell, nor Emerson. Poe? But Emily could not write to a man like Poe. Whitman? She herself says in another letter to her mentor, 'You speak of Mr. Whitman. I never read his book, but was told that it was disgraceful.'

No, there was no hope. All her friends were in the conspiracy of silence. They could not believe that the public was made up of many people as sensitive as themselves. Mrs. Gordon L. Ford has related an interesting anecdote illustrative of this point of view. I will give it in her own words:

> Dr. Holland once said to me, 'Her poems are too ethereal for publication.' I replied. 'They are beautiful—so concentrated—but they remind me of air-plants that have no roots in earth.' 'That is true,' he said, 'a perfect description;' and I think these lyrical ejaculations, these breathed-out projectiles, sharp as lances, would at that time have fallen into idle ears.

And yet when her first volume was published posthumously, it went through six editions in as many months.

The truth is that, as some one once said to me, the average man is a good deal above the average. A fact which the newly awakened interest in poetry is proving every day. This same first edition was published in 1890, more than twenty years before Imagism as a distinct school was heard of, but its reception shows that the soil was already ripe for sowing.

They bothered the critics dreadfully, these original, impossible poems, where form (conventional form) was utterly disregarded, but where somehow effects were got surprisingly well without it. Mr. Higginson shuddered and admired in about equal proportions, but he comes out nobly in praise (with reservations) in the preface to the first edition. His praise shows more discrimination than one would expect; his reservations are those proper to the time and the person. Addressing the 'thoughtful reader' (O, age of apologies and bombast!) he trusts that this judicious person 'will find in these pages a quality more suggestive of the poetry of William Blake than of anything to be elsewhere found—flashes of wholly original and profound insight into nature and life; words and phrases exhibiting an extraordinary vividness of descriptive and imaginative power, yet often set in a seemingly whimsical or rugged frame.'

The 'ruggedness' consists in the rhymes being frequently ignored. Mr. Higginson has himself told us how stiff in her own convictions the docile Emily became when he tried to improve the technique of her poems. To him, her practice was a lapse from the only true way, and he wondered at the firmness with which she held to her own method:

> Though curiously indifferent to all conventional rules, [she] had a rigorous literary standard of her own, and often altered a word many times to suit an ear which had its own tenacious fastidiousness.

Mrs. Todd is more understanding. She probably had had a less exacting classical education, and possessed a less prejudiced and more musical ear. In an explanatory passage in the volume of letters, she says: 'They [her verses] are pervaded by a singular cadence of hidden rhythmical music, which becomes sympathetically familiar upon intimate acquaintance.' And again in the preface to the second series of poems: 'In Emily Dickinson's exacting hands, the especial, intrinsic fitness of a particular order of words might not be sacrificed to anything virtually extrinsic; and her verses all show a strange cadence of inner rhythmical music. Lines are always daringly constructed, and the "thought-rhyme" appears frequently—appealing, indeed, to an unrecognized sense more elusive than hearing.'

Exactly what Mrs. Todd means by 'thought-rhyme,' I do not know. Perhaps she means a return of the idea, perhaps she merely means assonance, a compromise which Emily often substituted for true rhyme.

Thanks to Mr. Higginson, some of my work has already been done for me. He has told us that this is a poetry of 'flashes,' therefore it must be extremely concentrated; he says that it is wholly original, so it must give free rein to individualistic freedom of idea; he thinks that it exhibits 'an extraordinary vividness of description and imaginative power,' which is merely to restate the third and fourth Imagist canons in other words. His

very objection to its rugged character proves that it occupies itself with
new rhythms. What else is left? Simplicity and directness of speech,
perhaps. For that, we had better seek our answer in the poems
themselves, remembering that Mrs. Todd specifically says that 'a particular order of words might not be sacrificed to anything virtually
extrinsic.'

In 'The Single Hound,' the fourth volume of her work, issued in 1914
by her niece, is this poem, No. LXVI. Emily seldom gave her poems titles.
Most of the titles in the first three volumes were added by Mr. Higginson
and Mrs. Todd.

LXVI

A prompt, executive Bird is the Jay,
Bold as a Bailiff's hymn,
Brittle and brief in quality—
Warrant in every line;
Sitting a bough like a Brigadier,
Confident and straight,
Much is the mien
Of him in March
As a Magistrate.

I can easily imagine that the language in that poem might have
struck Mr. Higginson as 'rugged.' Anything more racy and forthright it
would be hard to conceive. The speech of her letters is often sentimental
and effeminate; the speech of her poems is almost without exception
strong, direct, and almost masculine in its vigour. This, No. XLII, in 'The
Single Hound,' has that acid quality of biting satire which we remarked in
Blake's 'Songs of Experience':

XLII

The butterfly obtains
But little sympathy,
Though favourably mentioned
In Entomology.
Because he travels freely
And wears a proper coat,
The circumspect are certain
That he is dissolute.
Had he the homely scutcheon of modest Industry.
'Twere fitter certifying for Immortality.

Emily Dickinson had the divine gift of startlingly original expression.
Her letters are full of such 'flashes' as:

> I love those little green ones [snakes] that slide around by your shoes in the
> grass, and make it rustle with their elbows.

> The wind blows gay to-day and the jays bark like blue terriers.

The lawn is full of south and the odours tangle, and I hear to-day for the first the river in the tree.

The moon rides like a girl through a topaz town.

And, in a description of a thunderstorm:

> The leaves unhooked themselves from trees
> And started all abroad;
> The dust did scoop itself like hands
> And throw away the road.

Her sense of sound was extraordinarily acute, for instance the droning of this:

> Like trains of cars on tracks of plush
> I hear the level bee:
> A jar across the flower goes.

The following might be said to be the inaudible but realized sound of an overwhelming burst of bright light:

> . . . mornings blossom into noons
> And split their pods of flame.

She has something of Coleridge's feeling for the sound connotations of words, in one place she says:

> An awful tempest mashed the air.

Down from Blake through Coleridge, that is Emily Dickinson's line of descent. Here is something of the fantastic quality of 'The Ancient Mariner,' and the true Coleridge use of colour:

> VII
> When Etna basks and purrs,
> Naples is more afraid
> Than when she shows her Garnet Tooth;
> Security is loud.

No poet ever revelled more in his own imagination than did this one. She flies her kite with infinite satisfaction to herself and to us. Over poor little Amherst it goes, tipping and veering, and her friends, intrigued but not wholly at ease in the sight, beg her not to let the neighbours see. This poem was sent with a nosegay of brilliant flowers:

> LV
> I send two Sunsets—
> Day and I in competition ran,
> I finished two, and several stars,
> While He was making one.

His own is ampler—
But, as I was saying to a friend,
Mine is the more convenient
To carry in the hand.

Here is one in which she half piteously, half bitterly refers to her own obsession by the thought of death:

LIII
The long sigh of the Frog
Upon a Summer's day,
Enacts intoxication
Upon the revery.
But his receding swell
Substantiates a peace,
That makes the ear inordinate
For corporal release.

Religion is an attitude of the spirit, and no one was ever more innately, positively religious than Emily Dickinson. But the cramped religion of orthodox New England repelled her in spite of her training. Her family and friends recognized this dimly, but too dimly not to feel that the point of view needed a kindly cloak. In the Preface to the 'Letters,' Mrs. Todd explains and explains: 'To her, God was not a far-away and dreary Power to be daily addressed—the great "Eclipse" of which she wrote—but He was near and familiar and pervasive. Her garden was full of His brightness and glory; the birds sang and the sky glowed because of Him. To shut herself out of the sunshine in a church, dark, chilly, restricted, was rather to shut herself away from Him; almost pathetically she wrote, "I believe the love of God may be taught not to seem like bears." In essence, no real irreverence mars her poems or her letters.'

Was that necessary? Perhaps it was at the time, although I hardly think so; it certainly is not now. And for that very reason this little volume, 'The Single Hound,' is worth the other three volumes put together. One cannot help feeling that the editors of the first three series compiled the books with an eye to conciliating criticism. The whole of Emily is not in them, as it is in 'The Single Hound'; in fact, the most interesting part of her genius suffers eclipse at the hands of her timorous interpreters. Yet even in the first collection there are poems which reveal the whole tragedy of her life, poems which must have wounded her survivors if they really understood them, which must have shocked some sensibilities by the sheer brutality of their truth.

Book IV
X
I died for beauty, but was scarce
Adjusted in the tomb,
When one who died for truth was lain
In an adjoining room.

He questioned softly why I failed.
'For beauty,' I replied.
'And I for truth,—the two are one;
We brethren are,' he said.

And so, as kinsmen met a night,
We talked between the rooms,
Until the moss had reached our lips,
And covered up our names.

Her whimsicality is very refreshing. It is not only in thought, but in expression:

XXX
I bet with every Wind that blew, till Nature in chagrin
Employed a *Fact* to visit me and scuttle my Balloon!

Now notice the next to last line of this poem, and see if it is not complete Imagism:

XXXVIII
A little madness in the Spring
Is wholesome even for the King,
But God be with the Clown,
Who ponders this tremendous scene—
This whole experiment of green,
As if it were his own!

'This whole experiment of green!' Why, to read that is to see the little-leaved May world, all broken out in light, jocund verdure, such as happens at no other time of the year!

The exact word, the perfect image, that is what makes these short poems so telling. Take this picture:

LXVII
Like brooms of steel
The Snow and Wind
Had swept the Winter Street,
The House was hooked,
The Sun sent out
Faint Deputies of heat—
Where rode the Bird
The Silence tied
His ample, plodding Steed,
The Apple in the cellar snug
Was all the one that played.

Here is a stanza describing the wriggling forward of a snake. Forget the involutions of the words, and notice only the movement contained in them:

> Then, to a rhythm slim
> Secreted in his form,
> As patterns swim,
> Projected him.

If we were to arrange those words in a more usual order, should we get the sinuosity of the snake's advance? I doubt it.

Emily Dickinson is a master in the art of presenting movement. In another poem, she gives all the collateral effects of a snake squirming through grass so poignantly that, as one reads it, one involuntarily looks down at one's feet with a shudder:

> The grass divides as with a comb,
> A spotted shaft is seen;
> And then it closes at your feet
> And opens further on.

Those lines illustrate very aptly the 'ruggedness' which so troubled Mr. Higginson. 'Seen' does not rhyme with 'on,' the two words do not even make an assonance; we have only the two *n*'s and the long *e* against the *o* to help the ear to a kind of return. Yet return is here; and that the poet sought for it is quite evident. She would not sacrifice the *exact* word for a rhyme, but she must round her circle somehow.

Emily Dickinson was not one of those poets who rhyme by nature. The necessity for rhyming evidently bothered her. She had no conscious idea of any form of verse not built upon metre. All the poetry with which she was familiar was metrical and rhymed. She tried to tie her genius down to the pattern and signally failed. But she was too much of an artist to cramp herself beyond a certain point. When what she wanted to say clashed with her ability to rhyme, the rhymes went to the wall. In the following poem, she evidently intended to rhyme the second and fourth lines of each stanza, but the words were stubborn, the idea exacting; the result is that there is not a single rhyme throughout, only so many subterfuges, ingenious enough, but a begging of the issue after all.

> The Saints' Rest
> Of tribulation these are they,
>   Denoted by the white;
> The spangled gowns, a lesser rank
>   Of victors designate.
>
> All these did conquer; but the ones
>   Who overcame most times,
> Wear nothing commoner than snow,
>   No ornaments but palms.
>
> 'Surrender' is a sort unknown
>   On this superior soil;

'Defeat,' an outgrown anguish,
Remembered as the mile

Our panting ankle barely gained
When night devoured the road;
But we stood whispering in the house,
And all we said was 'Saved!'

I have said that Emily Dickinson had no conscious idea of any form of verse other than the metrical. She does not seem to have known Blake at all, and if she read Matthew Arnold, or Henley, she made no happy discovery of their use of *vers libre*. The poetry she knew was in metre, and she did her best to cram her subtle rhythmic sense into a figure of even feet and lines. But it would not do. Her genius revolted, and again and again carried her over into cadence in spite of herself. Here is a poem, part metre, part cadence:

VI

Peril as a possession
'Tis good to bear,
Danger disintegrates satiety;
There's Basis there
Begets an awe,
That searches Human Nature's creases
As clean as Fire.

The first two lines are perfect metre, the third is cadence, the fourth and fifth again are metre, while cadence returns in the sixth and seventh.

A knowledge of the principles of unitary verse (that is, verse based upon a unit of time instead of a unit of accent) would have liberated Emily Dickinson from the bonds against which she chafed. But she was of too unanalytical a nature to find this for herself, consciously; that she found it subconsciously this poem proves:

XXVI

Victory comes late,
And is held low to freezing lips
Too rapt with frost
To take it.
How sweet it would have tasted,
Just a drop!
Was God so economical?
His table's spread too high for us
Unless we dine on tip-toe.
Crumbs fit such little mouths,
Cherries suit robins;
The eagle's golden breakfast
Strangles them.
God keeps his oath to sparrows,

> Who of little love
> Know how to starve!

There is one other way in which Emily Dickinson was a precursor of the Imagists. She, first of all in English I believe, made use of what I have called elsewhere the 'unrelated' method. That is, the describing of a thing by its appearance only, without regard to its entity in any other way. Even to-day, the Imagists are, so far as I know, the only poets to employ this device. Mr. Fletcher constantly uses it in his 'Symphonies,' but they are too long to quote. This little poem, however, will serve as an example of the *genre*:

THE SKATERS

TO A. D. R.

> Black swallows swooping or gliding
> In a flurry of entangled loops and curves;
> The skaters skim over the frozen river.
> And the grinding click of their skates as they impinge
>   upon the surface,
> Is like the brushing together of thin wing-tips of silver.

Now hear Emily Dickinson on a humming-bird:

THE HUMMING-BIRD

> A route of evanescence
> With a revolving wheel;
> A resonance of emerald;
> A rush of cochineal;
> And every blossom on the bush
> Adjusts its tumbled head,—
> The mail from Tunis, probably,
> An easy morning's ride.

'She was not daily-bread,' says her niece, 'she was star-dust.' Do we eat stars more readily than we did, then? I think we do, and if so, it is she who has taught us to appreciate them.

New England Culture
and Emily Dickinson
Allen Tate*

I

Great poetry needs no special features of difficulty to make it mysterious. When it has them, the reputation of the poet is likely to re-

*From Allen Tate, *Collected Essays* (Denver: Swallow Press, 1959), pp. 197–211.
Reprinted by permission of Ohio University Press/Swallow Press.

main uncertain. This is still true of Donne, and it is true of Emily Dickinson, whose verse appeared in an age unfavorable to the use of intelligence in poetry. Her poetry is not like any other poetry of her time; it is not like any of the innumerable kinds of verse written today. In still another respect it is far removed from us. It is a poetry of ideas, and it demands of the reader a point of view—not an opinion of the New Deal or of the League of Nations, but an ingrained philosophy that is fundamental, a settled attitude that is almost extinct in this eclectic age. Yet it is not the sort of poetry of ideas which, like Pope's, requires a point of view only. It requires also, for the deepest understanding, which must go beneath the verbal excitement of the style, a highly developed sense of the specific quality of poetry—a quality that most persons accept as the accidental feature of something else that the poet thinks he has to say. This is one reason why Miss Dickinson's poetry has not been widely read.

There is another reason, and it is a part of the problem peculiar to a poetry that comes out of fundamental ideas. We lack a tradition of criticism. There were no points of critical reference passed on to us from a preceding generation. I am not upholding here the so-called dead hand of tradition, but rather a rational insight into the meaning of the present in terms of some imaginable past implicit in our own lives: we need a body of ideas that can bear upon the course of the spirit and yet remain coherent as a rational instrument. We ignore the present, which is momently translated into the past, and derive our standards from imaginative constructions of the future. The hard contingency of fact invariably breaks these standards down, leaving us the intellectual chaos which is the sore distress of American criticism. Marxian criticism has become the latest disguise of this heresy.

Still another difficulty stands between us and Miss Dickinson. It is the failure of the scholars to feel more than biographical curiosity about her. We have scholarship, but that is no substitute for a critical tradition. Miss Dickinson's value to the research scholar, who likes historical difficulty for its own sake, is slight; she is too near to possess the remoteness of literature. Perhaps her appropriate setting would be the age of Cowley or of Donne. Yet in her own historical setting she is, nevertheless, remarkable and special.

Although the intellectual climate into which she was born, in 1830, had, as all times have, the features of a transition, the period was also a major crisis culminating in the war between the States. After that war, in New England as well as in the South, spiritual crises were definitely minor until the First World War.

Yet, a generation before the war of 1861–65, the transformation of New England had begun. When Samuel Slater in 1790 thwarted the British embargo on mill machinery by committing to memory the whole design of a cotton spinner and bringing it to Massachusetts, he planted the seed of the "Western spirit." By 1825 its growth in the East was rank enough to begin choking out the ideas and habits of living that New England along with Virginia had kept in unconscious allegiance to Europe. To the casual observer, perhaps, the New England character of 1830 was largely an eighteenth-century character. But theocracy was on the decline, and industrialism was rising—as Emerson, in an unusually lucid moment, put it, "Things are in the saddle." The energy that had built the meeting-house ran the factory.

Now the idea that moved the theocratic state is the most interesting historically of all American ideas. It was, of course, powerful in seventeenth-century England, but in America, where the long arm of Laud could not reach, it acquired an unchecked social and political influence. The important thing to remember about the puritan theocracy is that it permeated, as it could never have done in England, a whole society. It gave final, definite meaning to life, the life of pious and impious, of learned and vulgar alike. It gave—and this is its significance for Emily Dickinson, and in only slightly lesser degree for Melville and Hawthorne—it gave an heroic proportion and a tragic mode to the experience of the individual. The history of the New England theocracy, from Apostle Eliot to Cotton Mather, is rich in gigantic intellects that broke down—or so it must appear to an outsider—in a kind of moral decadence and depravity. Socially we may not like the New England idea. Yet it had an immense, incalculable value for literature: it dramatized the human soul.

But by 1850 the great fortunes had been made (in the rum, slave, and milling industries), and New England became a museum. The what-nots groaned under the load of knickknacks, the fine china dogs and cats, the pieces of Oriental jade, the chips off the leaning tower of Pisa. There were the rare books and the cosmopolitan learning. It was all equally displayed as the evidence of a superior culture. The Gilded Age had already begun. But culture, in the true sense, was disappearing. Where the old order, formidable as it was, had held all this personal experience, this eclectic excitement, in a comprehensible whole, the new order tended to flatten it out in a common experience that was not quite in common; it exalted more and more the personal and the unique in the interior sense. Where the old-fashioned puritans got together on a rigid doctrine, and could thus be individualists in manners, the nineteenth-century New Englander, lacking a genuine religious center, began to be a social conformist. The common idea of the Redemption, for example, was replaced by the conformist idea of respectability among neighbors whose spiritual disorder, not very evident at the surface, was becoming acute. A great idea was breaking up, and society was moving towards external uniformity, which is usually the measure of the spiritual sterility inside.

At this juncture Emerson came upon the scene: the Lucifer of Concord, he had better be called hereafter, for he was the light-bearer who could see nothing but light, and was fearfully blind. He looked around and saw the uniformity of life, and called it the routine of tradition, the tyranny of the theological idea. The death of Priam put an end to the hope of Troy, but it was a slight feat of arms for the doughty Pyrrhus; Priam was an old gentleman and almost dead. So was theocracy; and Emerson killed it. In this way he accelerated a tendency that he disliked. It was a great intellectual mistake. By it Emerson unwittingly became the prophet of a piratical industrialism, a consequence of his own transcendental individualism that he could not foresee. He was hoist with his own petard.

He discredited more than any other man the puritan drama of the soul. The age that followed, from 1865 on, expired in a genteel secularism, a mildly didactic order of feeling whose ornaments were Lowell, Longfellow, and Holmes. "After Emerson had done his work," says Mr. Robert Penn Warren, "any tragic possibilities in that culture were dissipated." Hawthorne alone in his time kept pure, in the primitive terms, the primitive vision; he brings the puritan tragedy to its climax. Man, measured by a great idea outside himself, is found wanting. But for Emerson man is greater than any idea and, being himself the Over-Soul, is innately perfect; there is no struggle because—I state the Emersonian doctrine, which is very slippery, in its extreme terms—because there is no possibility of error. There is no drama in human character because there is no tragic fault. It is not surprising, then, that after Emerson New England literature tastes like a sip of cambric tea. Its center of vision has disappeared. There is Hawthorne looking back, there is Emerson looking not too clearly at anything ahead: Emily Dickinson, who has in her something of both, comes in somewhere between.

With the exception of Poe there is no other American poet whose work so steadily emerges, under pressure of certain disintegrating obsessions, from the framework of moral character. There is none of whom it is truer to say that the poet *is* the poetry. Perhaps this explains the zeal of her admirers for her biography; it explains, in part at least, the gratuitous mystery that Mrs. Bianchi, a niece of the poet and her official biographer, has made of her life. The devoted controversy that Miss Josephine Pollitt and Miss Genevieve Taggard started a few years ago with their excellent books shows the extent to which the critics feel the intimate connection of her life and work. Admiration and affection are pleased to linger over the tokens of a great life; but the solution to the Dickinson enigma is peculiarly superior to fact.

The meaning of the identity—which we merely feel—of character and poetry would be exceedingly obscure, even if we could draw up a kind of Binet correlation between the two sets of "facts." Miss Dickinson was a recluse; but her poetry is rich with a profound and varied experience. Where did she get it? Now some of the biographers, nervous in the presence of this discrepancy, are eager to find her a love affair, and I think this search is due to a modern prejudice: we believe that no virgin can know enough to write poetry. We shall never learn where she got the rich quality of her mind. The moral image that we have of Miss Dickinson stands out in every poem; it is that of a dominating spinster whose very sweetness must have been formidable. Yet her poetry constantly moves within an absolute order of truths that overwhelmed her simply because to her they were unalterably fixed. It is dangerous to assume that her "life," which to the biographers means the thwarted love affair she is supposed to have had, gave to her poetry a decisive direction. It is even more dangerous to suppose that it made her a poet.

Poets are mysterious, but a poet, when all is said, is not much more mysterious than a banker. The critics remain spellbound by the technical license of her verse and by the puzzle of her personal life. Personality is a legitimate interest because it is an incurable interest, but legitimate as a personal interest only; it will never give up the key to anyone's verse. Used to that end, the interest is false. "It is apparent," writes Mr. Conrad Aiken, "that Miss Dickinson became a hermit by deliberate and conscious choice"—a sensible remark that we cannot repeat too often. If it were necessary to explain her seclusion with disappointment in love, there would remain the discrepancy between what the seclusion produced and the seclusion looked at as a cause. The effect, which is her poetry, would imply the whole complex of anterior fact, which was the social and religious structure of New England.

The problem to be kept in mind is thus the meaning of her "deliberate and conscious" decision to withdraw from life to her upstairs room. This simple fact is not very important. But that it must have been her sole way of acting out her part in the history of her culture, which made, with the variations of circumstance, a single demand upon all its representatives—this is of the greatest consequence. All pity for Miss Dickinson's "starved life" is misdirected. Her life was one of the richest and deepest ever lived on this continent.

When she went upstairs and closed the door, she mastered life by rejecting it. Others in their way had done it before; still others did it later. If we suppose—which is to suppose the improbable—that the love affair precipitated the seclusion, it was only a pretext; she would have found another. Mastery of the world by rejecting the world was the doctrine, even if it was not always the practice, of Jonathan Edwards and Cotton Mather. It is the meaning of fate in Hawthorne: his people are fated to withdraw from the world and to be destroyed. And it is one of the great themes of Henry James.

There is a moral emphasis that connects Hawthorne, James, and Miss Dickinson, and I think it is instructive. Between Hawthorne and James lies an epoch. The temptation to sin, in Hawthorne, is, in James, transformed into the temptation not to do the "decent thing." A whole world-scheme, a complete cosmic background, has shrunk to the dimensions of the individual conscience. This epoch between Hawthorne and

James lies in Emerson. James found himself in the post-Emersonian world, and he could not, without violating the detachment proper to an artist, undo Emerson's work; he had that kind of intelligence which refuses to break its head against history. There was left to him only the value, the historic role, of rejection. He could merely escape from the physical presence of that world which, for convenience, we may call Emerson's world: he could only take his Americans to Europe upon the vain quest of something that they had lost at home. His characters, fleeing the wreckage of the puritan culture, preserved only their honor. Honor became a sort of forlorn hope struggling against the forces of "pure fact" that had got loose in the middle of the century. Honor alone is a poor weapon against nature, being too personal, finical, and proud, and James achieved a victory by refusing to engage the whole force of the enemy.

In Emily Dickinson the conflict takes place on a vaster field. The enemy to all those New Englanders was Nature, and Miss Dickinson saw into the character of this enemy more deeply than any of the others. The general symbol of Nature, for her, is Death, and her weapon against Death is the entire powerful dumb-show of the puritan theology led by Redemption and Immortality. Morally speaking, the problem for James and Miss Dickinson is similar. But her advantages were greater than his. The advantages lay in the availability to her of the puritan ideas on the theological plane.

These ideas, in her poetry, are momently assailed by the disintegrating force of Nature (appearing as Death) which, while constantly breaking them down, constantly redefines and strengthens them. The values are purified by the triumphant withdrawal from Nature, by their power to recover from Nature. The poet attains to a mastery over experience by facing its utmost implications. There is the clash of powerful opposites, and in all great poetry—for Emily Dickinson is a great poet—it issues in a tension between abstraction and sensation in which the two elements may be, of course, distinguished logically, but not really. We are shown our roots in Nature by examining our differences with Nature; we are renewed by Nature without being delivered into her hands. When it is possible for a poet to do this for us with the greatest imaginative comprehension, a possibility that the poet cannot himself create, we have the perfect literary situation. Only a few times in the history of English poetry has this situation come about: notably, the period between about 1580 and the Restoration. There was a similar age in New England from which emerged two talents of the first order—Hawthorne and Emily Dickinson.

There is an epoch between James and Miss Dickinson. But between her and Hawthorne there exists a difference of intellectual quality. She lacks almost radically the power to seize upon and understand abstractions for their own sake; she does not separate them from the sensuous illuminations that she is so marvelously adept at; like Donne, she *perceives abstraction* and *thinks sensation*. But Hawthorne was a master of ideas, within a limited range; this narrowness confined him to his own kind of life, his own society, and out of it grew his typical forms of experience, his steady, almost obsessed vision of man; it explains his depth and intensity. Yet he is always conscious of the abstract, doctrinal aspect of his mind, and when his vision of action and emotion is weak, his work becomes didactic. Now Miss Dickinson's poetry often runs into quasi-homiletic forms, but it is never didactic. Her very ignorance, her lack of formal intellectual training, preserved her from the risk that imperiled Hawthorne. She cannot reason at all. She can only *see*. It is impossible to imagine what she might have done with drama or fiction; for, not approaching the puritan temper and through it the puritan myth, through human action, she is able to grasp the terms of the myth directly and by a feat that amounts almost to anthropomorphism, to give them a luminous tension, a kind of drama, among themselves.

One of the perfect poems in English is "The Chariot," and it illustrates better than anything else she wrote the special quality of her mind. I think it will illuminate the tendency of this discussion:

> Because I could not stop for death,
> He kindly stopped for me;
> The carriage held but just ourselves
> And immortality.
>
> We slowly drove, he knew no haste,
> And I had put away
> My labor, and my leisure too,
> For his civility.
>
> We passed the school where children played,
> Their lessons scarcely done;
> We passed the fields of gazing grain,
> We passed the setting sun.
>
> We paused before a house that seemed
> A swelling of the ground;
> The roof was scarcely visible,
> The cornice but a mound.
>
> Since then 'tis centuries, but each
> Feels shorter than the day
> I first surmised the horses' heads
> Were toward eternity.

If the word "great" means anything in poetry, this poem is one of the greatest in the English language. The rhythm charges with movement the pattern of suspended action back of the poem. Every image is precise and, moreover, not merely beautiful, but fused with the central idea. Every image extends and intensifies every other. The third stanza especially shows Miss Dickinson's power to fuse, into a single order of perception, a heterogeneous series: the children, the grain, and the setting sun (time) have the same degree of credibility; the first subtly preparing for the last. The sharp *gazing* before *grain* instills into nature a cold vitality of which the qualitative richness has infinite depth. The content of death in the poem eludes explicit definition. He is a gentleman taking a lady out for a drive. But note the restraint that keeps the poet from carrying this so far that it becomes ludicrous and incredible; and note the subtly interfused erotic motive, which the idea of death has presented to most romantic poets, love being a symbol interchangeable with death. The terror of death is objectified through this figure of the genteel driver, who is made ironically to serve the end of Immortality. This is the heart of the poem: she has presented a typical Christian theme in its final irresolution, without making any final statements about it. There is no solution to the problem; there can be only a presentation of it in the full context of intellect and feeling. A construction of the human will, elaborated with all the abstracting powers of the mind, is put to the concrete test of experience: the idea of immortality is confronted with the fact of physical disintegration. We are not told what to think; we are told to look at the situation.

The framework of the poem is, in fact, the two abstractions, mortality and eternity, which are made to associate in equality with the images: she sees the ideas, and thinks the perceptions. She did, of course, nothing of the sort; but we must use the logical distinctions, even to the extent of paradox, if we are to form any notion of this rare quality of mind. She could not in the proper sense think at all, and unless we prefer the feeble poetry of moral ideas that flourished in New England in the eighties, we must conclude that her intellectual deficiency contributed at least negatively to her great distinction. Miss Dickinson is probably the only Anglo-American poet of her century whose work exhibits the perfect literary situation—in which is possible the fusion of sensibility and thought. Unlike her contemporaries, she never succumbed to her ideas, to easy solutions, to her private desires.

Philosophers must deal with ideas, but the trouble with most nineteenth-century poets is too much philosophy; they are nearer to being philosophers than poets, without being in the true sense either. Tennyson is a good example of this; so is Arnold in his weak moments. There have been poets like Milton and Donne, who were not spoiled for their true business by leaning on a rational system of ideas, who understood the poetic use of ideas. Tennyson tried to mix a little Huxley and a little Broad Church, without understanding either Broad Church or Huxley; the result was fatal, and what is worse, it was shallow. Miss Dickinson's ideas were deeply imbedded in her character, not taken from the latest tract. A conscious cultivation of ideas in poetry is always dangerous, and even Milton escaped ruin only by having an instinct for what in the deepest sense he understood. Even at that there is a remote quality in Milton's approach to his material, in his treatment of it; in the nineteenth century, in an imperfect literary situation where literature was confused with documentation, he might have been a pseudo-philosopher-poet. It is difficult to conceive Emily Dickinson and John Donne succumbing to rumination about "problems"; they would not have written at all.

Neither the feeling nor the style of Miss Dickinson belongs to the seventeenth century; yet between her and Donne there are remarkable ties. Their religious ideas, their abstractions, are momently toppling from the rational plane to the level of perception. The ideas, in fact, are no longer the impersonal religious symbols created anew in the heat of emotion, that we find in poets like Herbert and Vaughan. They have become, for Donne, the terms of personality; they are mingled with the miscellany of sensation. In Miss Dickinson, as in Donne, we may detect a singularly morbid concern, not for religious truth, but for personal revelation. The modern word is self-exploitation. It is egoism grown irresponsible in religion and decadent in morals. In religion it is blasphemy; in society it means usually that culture is not self-contained and sufficient, that the spiritual community is breaking up. This is, along with some other features that do not concern us here, the perfect literary situation.

II

Personal revelation of the kind that Donne and Miss Dickinson strove for, in the effort to understand their relation to the world, is a feature of all great poetry; it is probably the hidden motive for writing. It is the effort of the individual to live apart from a cultural tradition that no longer sustains him. But this culture, which I now wish to discuss a little, is indispensable: there is a great deal of shallow nonsense in modern criticism which holds that poetry—and this is a half-truth that is worse than false—is essentially revolutionary. It is only indirectly revolutionary: the intellectual and religious background of an age no longer contains the whole spirit, and the poet proceeds to examine that background in terms of immediate experience. But the background is necessary; otherwise all the arts (not only poetry) would have to rise in a vacuum. Poetry does not dispense with tradition; it probes the deficiencies of a tradition. But it must have a tradition to probe. It is too bad that Arnold did not explain his doctrine, that poetry is a criticism of life, from the viewpoint of its background: we should have been spared an era of academic misconception, in which criticism of life meant a diluted pragmatism, the criterion of which was respectability. The poet in the true sense "criticizes" his tradition, either as such, or indirectly by comparing it with something that is about to replace it; he does what the root-meaning of the verb implies—he *discerns* its real elements and thus establishes its value, by putting it to the test of experience.

What is the nature of a poet's culture? Or, to put the question properly, what is the meaning of culture for poetry? All the great poets become the material of what we popularly call culture; we study them to acquire it. It is clear that Addison was more cultivated than Shakespeare; nevertheless Shakespeare is a finer source of culture than Addison. What is the meaning of this? Plainly it is that learning has never had anything to do with culture except instrumentally: the poet must be exactly literate enough to write down fully and precisely what he has to say, but no more. The source of a poet's true culture lies back of the paraphernalia of culture, and not all the historical activity of an enlightened age can create it.

A culture cannot be consciously created. It is an available source of ideas that are imbedded in a complete and homogeneous society. The poet finds himself balanced upon the moment when such a world is about to fall, when it threatens to run out into looser and less self-sufficient impulses. This world order is assimilated, in Miss Dickinson, as medievalism was in Shakespeare, to the poetic vision; it is brought down from abstraction to personal sensibility.

In this connection it may be said that the prior conditions for great poetry, given a great talent, may be reduced to two: the thoroughness of the poet's discipline in an objective system of truth, and his lack of consciousness of such a discipline. For this discipline is a number of fundamental ideas the origin of which the poet does not know; they give form and stability to his fresh perceptions of the world; and he cannot shake them off. This is his culture, and, like Tennyson's God, it is nearer than hands and feet. With reasonable certainty we unearth the elements of Shakespeare's culture, and yet it is equally certain—so innocent was he of his own resources—that he would not know what our discussion is about. He appeared at the collapse of the medieval system as a rigid pattern of life, but that pattern remained in Shakespeare what Shelley called a "fixed point of reference" for his sensibility. Miss Dickinson, as we have seen, was born into the equilibrium of an old and a new order. Puritanism could not be to her what it had been to the generation of Cotton Mather—a body of absolute truths; it was an unconscious discipline timed to the pulse of her life.

The perfect literary situation: it produces, because it is rare, a special and perhaps the most distinguished kind of poet. I am not trying to invent a new critical category. Such poets are never very much alike on the surface; they show us all the varieties of poetic feeling; and, like other poets, they resist all classification but that of temporary convenience. But, I believe, Miss Dickinson and John Donne would have this in common: their sense of the natural world is not blunted by a too-rigid system of ideas; yet the ideas, the abstractions, their education or their intellectual heritage, are not so weak as to let their immersion in nature, or their purely personal quality, get out of control. The two poles of the mind are not separately visible; we infer them from the lucid tension that may be most readily illustrated by polar activity. There is no thought as such at all; nor is there feeling; there is that unique focus of experience which is at once neither and both.

Like Miss Dickinson, Shakespeare is without opinions; his peculiar merit is also deeply involved in his failure to think about anything; his meaning is not in the content of his expression; it is in the tension of the dramatic relations of his characters. This kind of poetry is at the opposite of intellectualism. (Miss Dickinson is obscure and difficult, but that is not intellectualism.) To T. W. Higginson, the editor of *The Atlantic Monthly*, who tried to advise her, she wrote that she had no education. In any sense that Higginson could understand, it was quite true. His kind of education was the conscious cultivation of abstractions. She did not reason about the world she saw; she merely saw it. The "ideas" implicit in the world within her rose up, concentrated in her immediate perception.

That kind of world at present has for us something of the fascination of a buried city. There is none like it. When such worlds exist, when such cultures flourish, they support not only the poet but all members of society. For, from these, the poet differs only in his gift for exhibiting the structure, the internal lineaments, of his culture by threatening to tear them apart: a process that concentrates the symbolic emotions of society while it seems to attack them. The poet may hate his age; he may be an outcast like Villon; but this world is always there as the background to what he has to say. It is the lens through which he brings nature to focus and control—the clarifying medium that concentrates his personal feeling. It is ready-made; he cannot make it; with it, his poetry has a spontaneity and a certainty of direction that, without it, it would lack. No poet could have invented the ideas of "The Chariot"; only a great poet could have found their imaginative equivalents. Miss Dickinson was a deep mind writing from a deep culture, and when she came to poetry, she came infallibly.

Infallibly, at her best; for no poet has ever been perfect, nor is Emily Dickinson. Her precision of statement is due to the directness with which the abstract framework of her thought acts upon its unorganized material. The two elements of her style, considered as point of view, are immortality, or the idea of permanence, and the physical process of death or decay. Her diction has two corresponding features: words of Latin or Greek origin and, sharply opposed to these, the concrete Saxon element. It is this verbal conflict that gives her verse its high tension; it is not a device deliberately seized upon, but a feeling for language that senses out the two fundamental components of English and their metaphysical relation: the Latin for ideas and the Saxon for perceptions—the peculiar virtue of English as a poetic language.

Like most poets Miss Dickinson often writes out of habit; the style that emerged from some deep exploration of an idea is carried on as verbal habit when she has nothing to say. She indulges herself:

There's something quieter than sleep
Within this inner room!
It wears a sprig upon its breast,
And will not tell its name.

Some touch it and some kiss it,
Some chafe its idle hand;
It has a simple gravity
I do not understand!

While simple hearted neighbors
Chat of the "early dead,"
We, prone to periphrasis,
Remark that birds have fled!

It is only a pert remark; at best a superior kind of punning—one of the worst specimens of her occasional interest in herself. But she never had the slightest interest in the public. Were four poems or five published in her lifetime? She never felt the temptation to round off a poem for public exhibition. Higginson's kindly offer to make her verse "correct" was an invitation to throw her work into the public ring—the ring of Lowell and Longfellow. He could not see that he was tampering with one of the rarest literary integrities of all time. Here was a poet who had no use for the supports of authorship—flattery and fame; she never needed money.

She had all the elements of a culture that has broken up, a culture that on the religious side takes its place in the museum of spiritual antiquities. Puritanism, as a unified version of the world, is dead; only a remnant of it in trade may be said to survive. In the history of puritanism she comes between Hawthorne and Emerson. She has Hawthorne's matter, which a too irresponsible personality tends to dilute into a form like Emerson's; she is often betrayed by words. But she is not the poet of personal sentiment; she has more to say than she can put down in any one poem. Like Hardy and Whitman, she must be read entire; like Shakespeare, she never gives up her meaning in a single line.

She is therefore a perfect subject for the kind of criticism which is chiefly concerned with general ideas. She exhibits one of the permanent relations between personality and objective truth, and she deserves the special attention of our time, which lacks that kind of truth.

She has Hawthorne's intellectual toughness, a hard, definite sense of the physical world. The highest flights to God, the most extravagant metaphors of the strange and the remote, come back to a point of casuistry, to a moral dilemma of the experienced world. There is, in spite of the homiletic vein of utterance, no abstract speculation, nor is there a message to society; she speaks wholly to the individual experience. She offers to the unimaginative no riot of vicarious sensation; she has no useful maxims for men of action. Up to this point her resemblance to Emerson is slight: poetry is a sufficient form of utterance, and her devotion to it is pure. But in Emily Dickinson the puritan world is no longer self-contained; it is no longer complete; her sensibility exceeds its dimensions. She has trimmed down its supernatural proportions; it has become a morality; instead of the tragedy of the spirit there is a commentary upon it. Her poetry is a magnificent personal confession, blasphemous and, in its self-revelation, its honesty, almost obscene. It comes out of an intellectual life towards which it feels no moral responsibility. Cotton Mather would have burnt her for a witch.

Emily Dickinson and the Limits of Judgment   Yvor Winters*

Antiquest felt at noon
When August, burning low,
Calls forth this spectral canticle,
Repose to typify.

When the poems of Emily Dickinson first began to appear, in the years shortly following her death, she enjoyed a period of notoriety and of semi-popularity that endured for perhaps ten years; after about ten years of semi-obscurity, her reputation was revived with the publication of *The Single Hound*, and has lasted unabated to the present day, though with occasional signs that it may soon commence to diminish. A good many critics have resented her reputation, and it has not been hard for them to justify their resentment; probably no poet of comparable reputation has been guilty of so much unpardonable writing. On the other hand, one cannot shake off the uncomfortable feeling that her popularity has been mainly due to her vices; her worst poems are certainly her most commonly praised, and as a general matter, great lyric poetry is not widely read or admired.

The problem of judging her better poems is much of the time a subtle one. Her meter, at its worst—that is, most of the time—is a kind of stiff sing-song; her diction, at its worst, is a kind of poetic nursery jargon; and there is a remarkable continuity of manner, of a kind nearly indescribable, between her worst and her best poems. The following poem will illustrate the defects in perfection:

*From Yvor Winters, *In Defense of Reason* (Denver: Swallow Press, 1938). pp. 283–99. Reprinted by permission of Ohio University Press/Swallow Press.

I like to see it lap the miles,
And lick the valleys up,
And stop to feed itself at tanks;
And then, prodigious, step

Around a pile of mountains,
And, supercilious, peer
In shanties by the sides of roads;
And then a quarry pare

To fit its sides, and crawl between,
Complaining all the while
In horrid, hooting stanza;
Then chase itself down hill

And neigh like Boanerges;
Then, punctual as a star,
Stop—docile and omnipotent—
At its own stable door.

The poem is abominable; and the quality of silly playfulness which renders it abominable is diffused more or less perceptibly throughout most of her work, and this diffusion is facilitated by the limited range of her metrical schemes.

The difficulty is this: that even in her most nearly perfect poems, even in those poems in which the defects do not intrude momentarily in a crudely obvious form, one is likely to feel a fine trace of her countrified eccentricity; there is nearly always a margin of ambiguity in our final estimate of even her most extraordinary work, and though the margin may appear to diminish or disappear in a given reading of a favorite poem, one feels no certainty that it will not reappear more obviously with the next reading. Her best poems, quite unlike the best poems of Ben Jonson, of George Herbert, or of Thomas Hardy, can never be isolated certainly and defensibly from her defects; yet she is a poetic genius of the highest order, and this ambiguity in one's feeling about her is profoundly disturbing. The following poem is a fairly obvious illustration; we shall later see less obvious:

I started early, took my dog,
And visited the sea;
The mermaids in the basement
Came out to look at me,

And frigates in the upper floor
Extended hempen hands,
Presuming me to be a mouse
Aground, upon the sands,

But no man moved me till the tide
Went past my simple shoe,
And past my apron and my belt,
And past my bodice too,

And made as he would eat me up
As wholly as a dew
Upon a dandelion's sleeve—
And then I started too.

And he—he followed close behind;
I felt his silver heel
Upon my ankle,—then my shoes
Would overflow with pearl.

Until we met the solid town,
No man he seemed to know;
And bowing with a mighty look
At me, the sea withdrew.

The mannerisms are nearly as marked as in the first poem, but whereas the first poem was purely descriptive, this poem is allegorical and contains beneath the more or less mannered surface an ominously serious theme, so that the manner appears in a new light and is somewhat altered in effect. The sea is here the traditional symbol of death; that is, of all the forces and qualities in nature and in human nature which tend toward the dissolution of human character and consciousness. The playful protagonist, the simple village maiden, though she speaks again in the first person, is dramatized, as if seen from without, and her playfulness is somewhat restrained and formalized. Does this formalization, this dramatization, combined with a major symbolism, suffice effectually to transmute in this poem the quality discerned in the first poem, or does that quality linger as a fine defect? The poem is a poem of power; it may even be a great poem; but this is not to answer the question. I have never been able to answer the question.

Her poetic subject matter might be subdivided roughly as follows: natural description; the definition of moral experience, including the definition of difficulties of comprehension; and mystical experience, or the definition of the experience of "immortality," to use a favorite word, or of beatitude. The second subdivision includes a great deal, and her best work falls within it; I shall consider it last. Her descriptive poems contain here and there brilliant strokes, but she had the hard and uncompromising approach to experience of the early New England Calvinists; lacking all subtlety, she displays the heavy hand of one unaccustomed to fragile objects; her efforts at lightness are distressing. Occasionally, instead of endeavoring to treat the small subject in terms appropriate to it, she endeavors to treat it in terms appropriate to her own temperament, and we have what appears a deliberate excursion into obscurity, the subject being inadequate to the rhetoric, as in the last stanza of the poem beginning, "At half-past three a single bird":

> At half-past seven, element
> Nor implement was seen,
> And place was where the presence was,
> Circumference between.

The stanza probably means, roughly, that bird and song alike have disappeared, but the word "circumference," a resonant and impressive one, is pure nonsense.

This unpredictable boldness in plunging into obscurity, a boldness in part, perhaps, inherited from the earlier New Englanders whose sense of divine guidance was so highly developed, whose humility of spirit was commonly so small; a boldness dramatized by Melville in the character of Ahab; this congenital boldness may have led her to attempt the rendering of purely theoretic experience, the experience of life after death. There are numerous poems which attempt to express the experience of posthumous beatitude, as if she were already familiar with it; the poetic terms of the expression are terms, either abstract or concrete, of human life, but suddenly fixed, or approaching fixation, as if at the cessation of time in eternity, as if to the dead the living world appeared as immobile as the dead person appears to the living, and the fixation frequently involves an element of horror:

> Great streets of silence led away
> To neighborhoods of pause;
> Here was no notice, no dissent,
> No universe, no laws.
>
> By clocks 'twas morning, and for night
> The bells at distance called;
> But epoch had no basis here,
> For period exhaled.

The device here employed is to select a number of terms representing familiar abstractions or perceptions, some of a commonplace nature, some relatively grandiose or metaphysical, and one by one to negate these terms; a number of statements, from a grammatical point of view, have been made, yet actually no concrete image emerges, and the idea of the poem—the idea of the absolute dissidence of the eternal from the temporal—is stated indirectly, and, in spite of the brevity of the poem and the gnomic manner, with extraordinary redundancy. We come painfully close in this poem to the irresponsible playfulness of the poem about the railway train; we have gone beyond the irresponsible obscurity of the poem about the bird.

This is technically a mystical poem: that is, it endeavors to render an experience—the rapt contemplation, eternal and immovable, which Aquinas describes as the condition of beatitude—which is by definition foreign to all human experience, yet to render it in terms of a modified human experience. Yet there is no particular reason to believe that Emily Dickinson was a mystic, or thought she was a mystic. The poems of this variety, and there are many of them, appear rather to be efforts to dramatize an idea of salvation, intensely felt, but as an idea, not as something experienced, and as an idea essentially inexpressible. She deliberately utilizes imagery irrelevant to the state with which she is concerned, because she cannot do otherwise; yet the attitude toward the material, the attitude of rapt contemplation, is the attitude which she presumably expects to achieve toward something that she has never experienced. The poems are invariably forced and somewhat theoretical; they are briskly clever, and lack the obscure but impassioned conviction of the mystical poems of Very; they lack the tragic finality, the haunting sense of human isolation in a foreign universe, to be found in her greatest poems, of which the explicit theme is a denial of this mystical trance, is a statement of the limits of judgment.

There are a few curious and remarkable poems representing a mixed theme, of which the following is perhaps the finest example:

Because I could not stop for Death,
He kindly stopped for me;
The carriage held but just ourselves
And Immortality.

We slowly drove, he knew no haste,
And I had put away
My labor, and my leisure too,
For his civility.

We passed the school where children played
At wrestling in a ring;
We passed the fields of gazing grain,
We passed the setting sun.

We paused before a house that seemed
A swelling of the ground;
The roof was scarcely visible,
The cornice but a mound.

Since then 'tis centuries; but each
Feels shorter than the day
I first surmised the horses' heads
Were toward eternity.

In the fourth line we find the familiar device of using a major abstraction in a somewhat loose and indefinable manner; in the last stanza there is the semi-playful pretence of familiarity with the posthumous experience of eternity, so that the poem ends unconvincingly though gracefully, with a formulary gesture very roughly comparable to that of the concluding couplet of many an Elizabethan sonnet of love; for the rest the poem is a remarkably beautiful poem on the subject of the daily realization of the imminence of death—it is a poem of departure from life, an intensely conscious leave-taking. In so far as it concentrates on the life that is being left behind, it is wholly successful; in so far as it attempts to experience the death to come, it is fraudulent, however exquisitely, and in this it falls below her finest achievement. Allen Tate, who appears to be unconcerned with this fraudulent element, praises the poem in the highest terms; he appears almost to praise it for its defects: "The sharp *gazing* before *grain* instils into nature a kind of cold vitality of which the qualitative richness has infinite depth. The content of death in the poem eludes forever any explicit definition . . . she has presented a typical Christian theme in all its final irresolution, without making any final statement about it." The poem ends in irresolution in the sense that it ends in a statement that is not offered seriously; to praise the poem for this is unsound criticism, however. It is possible to solve any problem of insoluble experience by retreating a step and defining the boundary at which comprehension ceases, and by then making the necessary moral adjustments to that boundary; this in itself is an experience both final and serious, and it is the experience on which our author's finest work is based.

Let me illustrate by citation. The following poem defines the subject which the mystical poems endeavor to conceal: the soul is taken to the brink of the incomprehensible, and is left there, for retreat is impossible, and advance is impossible without a transmutation of the soul's very nature. The third and fourth lines display the playful redundancy of her weaker poems, but the intrusion of the quality here is the result of habit, and is a minor defect; there is nothing in the conception of the poem demanding a compromise. There is great power in the phrasing of the remainder of the poem, especially in the middle stanza:

> Our journey had advanced;
> Our feet were almost come
> To that odd fork in Being's road,
> Eternity by term.
>
> Our pace took sudden awe,
> Our feet reluctant led.
> Before were cities, but between
> The forest of the dead.
>
> Retreat was out of hope,—
> Behind, a sealëd route,
> Eternity's white flag before,
> And God at every gate.

She is constantly defining the absolute cleavage between the living and the dead. In the following poem the definition is made more powerfully, and in other terms:

> 'Twas warm at first, like us,
> Until there crept thereon
> A chill, like frost upon a glass,
> Till all the scene be gone.
>
> The forehead copied stone,
> The fingers grew too cold
> To ache, and like a skater's brook
> The busy eyes congealed.
>
> It straightened—that was all—
> It crowded cold to cold—
> It multiplied indifference
> As Pride were all it could.
>
> And even when with cords
> 'Twas lowered like a freight,
> It made no signal, nor demurred,
> But dropped like adamant.

The stiffness of phrasing, as in the barbarously constructed fourth and twelfth lines, is allied to her habitual carelessness, yet in this poem there is at least no triviality, and the imagery of the third stanza in particular has tremendous power.

The poem beginning, "The last night that she lived," treats the same theme in more personal terms; the observer watches the death of a friend, that is follows the friend to the brink of the comprehensible, sees her pass the brink, and faces the loss. The poem contains a badly mixed figure and at least two major grammatical blunders, in addition to a little awkward inversion of an indefensible variety, yet there is in the poem an immediate seizing of terrible fact, which makes it, at least fragmentarily, very great poetry:

> And we, we placed the hair,
> And drew the head erect;
> And then an awful leisure was,
> Our faith to regulate.

Her inability to take Christian mysticism seriously did not, however, drive her to the opposite extreme of the pantheistic mysticism which was seducing her contemporaries. The following lines, though not remarkable poetry, are a clear statement of a position consistently held:

> But nature is a stranger yet;
> The ones that cite her most

> Have never passed her haunted house,
> Nor simplified her ghost.
>
> To pity those that know her not
> Is helped by the regret
> That those who know her, know her less
> The nearer her they get.

Nature as a symbol, as Allen Tate has pointed out in the essay to which I have already referred, remains immitigably the symbol of all the elements which corrupt, dissolve, and destroy human character and consciousness; to approach nature is to depart from the fullness of human life, and to join nature is to leave human life. Nature may thus be a symbol of death, representing much the same idea as the corpse in the poem beginning " 'Twas warm at first, like us," but involving a more complex range of association.

In the following poem, we are shown the essential cleavage between man, as represented by the author-reader, and nature, as represented by the insects in the late summer grass; the subject is the plight of man, the willing and freely moving entity, in a universe in which he is by virtue of his essential qualities a foreigner. The intense nostalgia of the poem is the nostalgia of man for the mode of being which he perceives imperfectly and in which he cannot share. The change described in the last two lines is the change in the appearance of nature and in the feeling of the observer which results from a recognition of the cleavage:

> Farther in summer than the birds,
> Pathetic from the grass,
> A minor nation celebrates
> Its unobtrusive mass.
>
> No ordinance is seen,
> So gradual the grace,
> A pensive custom it becomes,
> Enlarging loneliness.
>
> Antiquest felt at noon
> When August, burning low,
> Calls forth this spectral canticle,
> Repose to typify.
>
> Remit as yet no grace,
> No furrow on the glow,
> Yet a druidic difference
> Enhances nature now.

The first two lines of the last stanza are written in the author's personal grammatical short-hand; they are no doubt defective in this respect, but the defect is minor. They mean: There is as yet no diminution of beauty, no mark of change on the brightness. The twelfth line employs a meaningless inversion. On the other hand, the false rhymes are employed with unusually fine modulation; the first rhyme is perfect, the second and third represent successive stages of departure, and the last a return to what is roughly the stage of the second. These effects are complicated by the rhyming, both perfect and imperfect, from stanza to stanza. The intense strangeness of this poem could not have been achieved with standard rhyming. The poem, though not quite one of her most nearly perfect, is probably one of her five or six greatest, and is one of the most deeply moving and most unforgettable poems in my own experience; I have the feeling of having lived in its immediate presence for many years.

The three poems which combine her greatest power with her finest execution are strangely on much the same theme, both as regards the idea embodied and as regards the allegorical embodiment. They deal with the inexplicable fact of change, of the absolute cleavage between successive states of being, and it is not unnatural that in two of the poems this theme should be related to the theme of death. In each poem, seasonal change is employed as the concrete symbol of the moral change. This is not the same thing as the so-called pathetic fallacy of the romantics, the imposition of a personal emotion upon a physical object incapable either of feeling such an emotion or of motivating it in a human being. It is rather a legitimate and traditional form of allegory, in which the relationships between the items described resemble exactly the relationships between certain moral ideas or experiences; the identity of relationship evoking simultaneously and identifying with each other the feelings attendant upon both series as they appear separately. Here are the three poems, in the order of the seasons employed, and in the order of increasing complexity both of theme and of technique:

1

A light exists in spring
Not present in the year
At any other period.
When March is scarcely here

A color stands abroad
On solitary hills
That science cannot overtake,
But human nature feels.

It waits upon the lawn;
It shows the furthest tree
Upon the furthest slope we know;
It almost speaks to me.

Then, as horizons step,
Or noons report away,
Without the formula of sound,
It passes, and we stay:

A quality of loss
Affecting our content,
As trade had suddenly encroached
Upon a sacrament.

2

As imperceptibly as grief
The Summer lapsed away,—
Too imperceptible, at last,
To seem like perfidy.

A quietness distilled,
As twilight long begun,
Or Nature, spending with herself
Sequestered afternoon.

The dusk drew earlier in,
The morning foreign shone,—
A courteous, yet harrowing grace,
As guest who would be gone.

And thus, without a wing,
Or service of a keel,
Our summer made her light escape
Into the beautiful.

3

There's a certain slant of light,
On winter afternoons,
That oppresses, like the weight
Of cathedral tunes.

Heavenly hurt it gives us;
We can find no scar,
But internal difference
Where the meanings are.

None may teach it anything,
'Tis the seal, despair,—
An imperial affliction
Sent us of the air.

When it comes, the landscape listens,
Shadows hold their breath;

When it goes, 'tis like the distance
On the look of death.

In the seventh, eighth, and twelfth lines of the first poem, and, it is barely possible, in the seventh and eighth of the third, there is a very slight echo of the brisk facility of her poorer work; the last line of the second poem, verges ever so slightly on an easy prettiness of diction, though scarcely of substance. These defects are shadowy, however; had the poems been written by another writer, it is possible that we should not observe them. On the other hand, the directness, dignity, and power with which these major subjects are met, the quality of the phrasing, at once clairvoyant and absolute, raise the poems to the highest level of English lyric poetry.

The meter of these poems is worth careful scrutiny. The basis of all three is the so-called Poulter's Measure, first employed, if I remember aright, by Surrey, and after the time of Sidney in disrepute. It is the measure, however, not only of the great elegy on Sidney commonly attributed to Fulke Greville, but of some of the best poetry between Surrey and Sidney, including the fine poem by Vaux on contentment and the great poem by Gascoigne in praise of a gentlewoman of dark complexion. The English poets commonly though not invariably wrote the poem in two long lines instead of four short ones, and the lines so conceived were the basis of their rhetoric. In the first of the three poems just quoted, the measure is employed without alteration, but the short line is the basis of the rhetoric; an arrangement which permits of more varied adjustment of sentence to line than if the long line were the basis. In the second poem, the first stanza is composed not in the basic measure, but in lines of eight, six, eight, and six syllables; the shift into the normal six, six, eight, and six in the second stanza, as in the second stanza of the poem beginning, "Farther in summer," results in a subtle and beautiful muting both of meter and of tone. This shift she employs elsewhere, but especially in poems of four stanzas, to which it appears to have a natural relationship; it is a brilliant technical invention.

In the third poem she varies her simple base with the ingenuity and mastery of a virtuoso. In the first stanza, the two long lines are reduced to seven syllables each, by the dropping of the initial unaccented syllable; the second short line is reduced to five syllables in the same manner. In the second stanza, the first line, which ought now to be of six syllables, has but five metrical syllables, unless we violate normal usage and count the second and infinitely light syllable of *Heaven*, with an extrametrical syllable at the end, the syllable dropped being again the initial one; the second line, which out to have six syllables, has likewise lost its initial syllable, but the extrametrical *us* of the preceding line, being unaccented, is in rhythmical effect the first syllable of the second line, so that this syllable serves a double and ambiguous function—it maintains the syllable-count of the first line, in spite of an altered rhythm, and it maintains the rhythm of the second line in spite of the altered syllable-count.

The third and fourth lines of the stanza are shortened to seven and five. In the third stanza the first and second lines are constructed like the third and fourth of the second stanza; the third and fourth lines like the first and second of the second stanza, except that in the third line the initial unaccented syllable is retained; that is, the third stanza repeats the construction of the second, but in reverse order. The final stanza is a triumphant resolution of the three preceding: the first and third lines, like the second and fourth, are metrically identical; the first and third contain seven syllables each, with an additional extrametrical syllable at the end which takes the place of the missing syllable at the beginning of each subsequent short line, at the same time that the extrametrical syllable functions in the line in which it is written as part of a two-syllable rhyme. The elaborate structure of this poem results in the balanced hesitations and rapid resolutions which one hears in reading it. This is metrical artistry at about as high a level as one is likely to find it.

Emily Dickinson was a product of the New England tradition of moral Calvinism; her dissatisfaction with her tradition led to her questioning most of its theology and discarding much of it, and led to her reinterpreting some of it, one would gather, in the direction of a more nearly Catholic Christianity. Her acceptance of Christian moral concepts was unimpaired, and the moral tone of her character remained immitigably Calvinistic in its hard and direct simplicity. As a result of this Calvinistic temper, she lacked the lightness and grace which might have enabled her to master minor themes; she sometimes stepped without hesitation into obscurantism, both verbal and metaphysical. But also as a result of it, her best poetry represents a moral adjustment to certain major problems which are carefully defined; it is curious in the light of this fact, and in the light of the discussion which they have received, that her love poems never equal her highest achievement—her best work is on themes more generalized and inclusive.

Emily Dickinson differed from every other major New England writer of the nineteenth century, and from every major American writer of the century save Melville, of those affected by New England, in this: that her New England heritage, though it made her life a moral drama, did not leave her life in moral confusion. It impoverished her in one respect, however: of all great poets, she is the most lacking in taste; there are innumerable beautiful lines and passages wasted in the desert of her crudities; her defects, more than those of any other great poet that I have read, are constantly at the brink, or pushing beyond the brink, of her best poems. This stylistic character is the natural product of the New England which produced the barren little meeting houses; of the New England founded by the harsh and intrepid pioneers, who in order to attain salvation trampled brutally through a world which they were too proud and too impatient to understand. In this respect, she differs from Melville, whose taste was rich and cultivated. But except by Melville, she is surpassed by no writer that this country has produced; she is one of the greatest lyric poets of all time.

A Poetry of Ideas
Richard Chase*

The pervasiveness of the idea of status is clear, though its significance is not, from almost any random reading of Emily Dickinson's verse. The fact that death is the fate of all living creatures may be conveyed in a number of ways without speaking of the "estate" death confers. But Emily Dickinson, in treating this theme, characteristically calls death "the common right / Of toads and men," the "privilege" of all. The poem beginning "Did the harebell loose her girdle" asks, in terms of a rather confused nature allegory, whether female creatures (the category seems extensive) lose caste by yielding to their lovers, and also whether the lovers lose caste (for "Eden" read "the innocent sexuality of women," and for "earl" read "lover"):

> Did the paradise, persuaded,
> Yield her moat of pearl
> Would the Eden be an Eden,
> Or the earl an earl?

There is no specific idea of sin in this poem. The specification is of status, though the exact kind of status in question is, as frequently happens, not very clear.

In "The child's faith is new" the poet, wishing to speak of the self-delusion of children, does so by saying that the child imagines himself to be a mightier sovereign than Caesar. Disillusion comes when the child perceives that men are men and not kings. If we take "My worthiness is all my doubt" to be a love poem (though as in several of the "love" poems it is disconcertingly difficult to separate the image of God from the image of the lover), we see that such terms as "worthiness," "merit," "qualities," "lowlier," "chiefest," and "elect" are preferred to the more usual vocabularies of the love lyric. Her love poems show a persistent impulse to establish lover and loved in a kind of legalized hierarchy, instead of picturing the ecstatic fusing of souls or weeping at the swift passage of time.

In nature she finds many and diverse analogies of the kinds of status she discerns among human beings and between human beings and God. There are the sovereign Alps and the meek daisies bowing at their feet. There are the queenly moon and the docile sea. There are the diamond

*From Richard Chase, *Emily Dickinson* (New York: William Sloane, 1951), pp. 139–47. Copyright 1951 by William Sloane Associates, Inc. Reprinted by permission of William Morrow and Co.

and the coal, the alabaster, topaz, or ruby and the lowly stone; there are the regal butterfly and the vulgar buttercup.

Some of Emily Dickinson's best poems involve an idea of status. For example:

> Presentiment is that long shadow on the lawn
> Indicative that suns go down;
> The notice to the startled grass
> That darkness is about to pass.

This poem, like Marvell's "To His Coy Mistress," defines the inevitability of solar motion in terms of the fated coming of death. Yet this idea, presented in the first two lines, finds a new specificity in the second couplet, where "darkness" is imagined as a king whose heralds have already announced to a startled populace the approach of the royal entourage.

The beautiful poem beginning "There's a certain slant of light," to say no more about it here, conveys an impression that the "imperial affliction" of "despair" which enigmatically comes to us from heaven on winter afternoons endows the recipient with a kind of *noblesse oblige*—the fortitude and compassion of those who are royal but troubled and wounded.

Such a poem as "I died for beauty" does not directly pose a metaphysical problem of the relation of truth to beauty, as does Keats in the "Ode to a Grecian Urn." The emphasis is on status. It is not only in the realm of metaphysics that truth and beauty are congruent. They are equal, as two queens or dukes are equal, according to an imaginary order of rank, analogues of which may be seen throughout the universe.

Status, as we noted in the last chapter, is conferred by an influx of divine or at least mysterious energy. The poem called "The sun just touched the morning" may be taken as expressing, at a rather low level of intensity, the essence of Emily Dickinson's trope of "estates." The "morning," newly instinct with the ray of the sun, is blissfully "raised." She feels "supremer" and innocently ventures forth on her gay holiday in pursuit of her "wheeling king." Yet the "haughty" sun in its appointed course not only bequeaths the joy of queenly rank but also leaves "a new necessity." This new necessity is the renunciation of her crown, which "the morning" now loses as she flutters and staggers back to her lowly estate. The central trope of Emily Dickinson's poems could be said to be similar to the myth of Cinderella, if in the fairy tale the marriage of the heroine with the prince meant marriage with death and "living happily ever after" referred to eternity.

In her fictional use of status, as in her psychology, Emily Dickinson is akin to Melville, Hawthorne, and James rather than to Whitman, Emerson, and Thoreau. Whitman does not make much of the idea of status. For Emerson and Thoreau the soul of every man is rather too expandable and retractable ever to allow him to dispose himself into orders of rank.

But Melville, though politically democratic, worked out an extensive myth of the human lot in the new world which he derived from his own secularized idea of the fall of man, and this gave him an imaginative order of spiritual, moral, and intellectual rank which occurs throughout his work. In Hawthorne the idea of status is an almost purely moral order of relation among men according to their involvement with other men or their estrangement from them. And James, the novelist of manners and morals, deals intricately with the question of status within American and European society and within the international scene, evolving finally a far-reaching mythical order of redemption in the late novels, in which the intrepid investigator might find interesting parallels to ideas of redemption entertained by our poet.

Nearly everything in Emily Dickinson's personal, cultural, and historical background brought home to her the question of status. Although certainly not a feminist, in the public, crusading, nineteenth-century meaning of the word, she shared with other intellectual women of her time an interest in "the position of women." The romantic English society novels by women authors which she avidly read in her early years were intensely conscious of rank. Mrs. Child and Margaret Fuller—not to mention that ardent crusader for women's rights, T. W. Higginson—were strikingly on the American scene, posing to the thoughtful the problem of woman's position in a society which had abandoned the social structure of aristocracy and along with it most of the certainties as to women's rights and duties. Mrs. Browning and George Eliot, whom Emily Dickinson read and admired, were concerned with the status of feminine intellectuals as well as with that of working women. The Brontës dealt with the problem even more radically than Mrs. Browning or George Eliot, understanding the lot of women not only from the social point of view of feminism but from the point of view of their deepest biological and spiritual characteristics as these were threatened by the overbearing force of men like Rochester and Heathcliff or the inscrutable power of the universe which seemed to find special instrumentalities both for enslaving or destroying women and for providing them with the basis for their ascendancy in society, intellect, and spirit. Inevitably, Emily Dickinson's poems on Charlotte Brontë and Mrs. Browning confer royalty upon these writers. Once a plain bird, Charlotte Brontë enters heaven as a nightingale. To read Mrs. Browning's poems is to witness a general promotion among the ranks of nature: the bees become butterflies, the "low inferior grass" is newly resplendent. And Mrs. Browning's poetry impels one to place a diadem on a head already too high to crown.

Coming closer to home, we may note that although Emily Dickinson did not have to struggle for social position, she would certainly have been made aware that she already had it by the tradition of the provincial pre-eminence of the Dickinson family and also, doubtless, by her father's somber affirmations of respectability. There was indeed a tradition of spinsterhood and even poetry-writing among New England women. But though her father seems never to have pressed Emily unduly either to marry or to remain a spinster, she must nevertheless sometimes have regarded spinsterhood as a status to be explained and established. With the exception of her sister nearly all of her young women friends were married.

I would suggest, however, that these considerations are of minor importance compared with the mere fact of the existence of such a father and such a daughter within the isolated family circle. Edward Dickinson does not appear to have been an ogre of any kind; he was certainly no Patrick Brontë nor even an Edward Barrett. Yet to a "little girl" he must have seemed formidable enough, with his solemnity and his terseness, with the rigidity and anxious remoteness of his being, with his long silences and his grave legislative disposal of family matters. And Emily Dickinson, so she says, remained a "little girl" all her life; as we have seen, she often expressed her desire, particularly in the letters of about her twentieth year, to be really and exclusively a little girl. In the family circle, in short, there was status, real and symbolic. Her father was "imperial," she was "low." Yet Emily had a good deal of her father's temperament, his integrity and independence, his willingness to be outspoken, something of his austerity and of his impatience with incompetence, weakness, and confusion. Both the similarity and the dissimilarity of father and daughter compelled her to the consideration of her "estate."

If Emily Dickinson's imagined hierarchy contains only two classes, the nobility and the commoners, we may well look to the family relationship for one influence upon this dispensation. If the lowly achieve status through ravishment by unspeakable power, we may again remember, without specific psychoanalytic intent, the relation of father and daughter. If the poems in which Emily Dickinson is most inarticulate and confused tend to divide themselves most strikingly into a series of inexplicable abstractions on the one hand and an inert substratum of concrete words on the other, we may again be justified in recalling the relationship of father and daughter. A major technical flaw in Emily Dickinson's poetry is the lack of perspicuity in her abstract words. We shall have occasion to note several ways of accounting for this failure. But the account would not be complete without recalling the possibility that the first sense of abstraction a child attains is derived from its father, a mere "presence" as compared with the palpable reality of the mother. And we should want to recall too the abstraction of myth and idea with which the daughter endows her father in response to the feelings of guilt which rise between them. The father, beheld as an aggressor, is more easily admitted to the mind of the daughter as a speechless or ineffable abstraction than in his human reality. After early childhood Emily doubtless discovered that in the passive and ineffectual Emily Norcross Dickinson she had, as she said in later years, "no mother." The defection of her mother made her relationship with her "pure and terrible" father even more exclusive than it might otherwise have been.

One might add that her father's profession undoubtedly helped to confirm the idea of status in her mind. As Tocqueville pointed out, with its practice and theory of status, the legal profession was one of the few real analogues of aristocracy in nineteenth-century America.

And certainly of great importance is the heritage of New England Calvinism, the most legalistic of religions. There is considerable warrant in the Covenant Theology for ideas of legally defined position, since this theology was an attempt to clarify the relation of man to a capricious God by coming to an agreement with Him on where, under different conditions, He stood and where man stood. Calvinism, of course, implies a severely simple two-class order, first in its doctrine of salvation and, second, in its stress on the immediate relationship of man with God. The doctrine of justification through faith urged perpetual attention to one's status in relation to God. And as she uses it in her poetry Emily Dickinson's idea of status may be regarded as the doctrine of justification translated into a private language of romance.

The fall of man and man's sinfulness, as we have seen, play almost no part in Emily Dickinson's poetry. She does not, as Melville does, characteristically picture an Eden in which in the past the individual has lived and from which he has fallen. Nor does she, like Hawthorne, describe the ravages of sin upon the human personality. She has so much the sense of loss and desolation that she regards them as almost exclusively the quality of life. When she speaks of Eden as apart from "home," she usually means heaven, the heaven which lies in the future. She has not fallen. She *is* fallen. Her idea of sin is almost entirely confined to "conscience" and to the abdication or guardianship of the moralizing part of the mind. But even the few poems which treat of these matters show that our poet was more interested in psychology, or possibly the fated and limited quality of human action, than she was in moral judgments. She was a realist and a seer. No moralist can delve such abysses in the universe.

We have yet to specify exactly what kinds of "estate" Emily Dickinson adumbrates, and I am not sure that this can finally be done with perfect clarity. In very general language, the queenly or upper status meant to her the following things: 1) the condition of being blissfully "domestic," of enjoying a redemptive sense of fulfillment or vitality of spiritual health, a condition which may be achieved through immediate visitations of grace; 2) the achievement of mature womanhood or the involvement of oneself in the sacramental occasions of a woman's life through love and "marriage"; 3) accession to the absolute ground of immortality through death; 4) the achievement of seerhood and the station of prophetic poet, and ultimately of immortality, through beauty and truth. The lower status is simply the opposite of the upper. When one is not regal or an "Empress of Calvary," one has either missed the great transmuting experiences or, having had them and achieved regality, one has had to renounce them. Renunciation is the condition of earthly life, since the only absolute status is immortality.

Art and the Inner Life   Robert E. Spiller*

For Emily Dickinson (1830–1886), retreat was into the absolute. The recluse of Amherst, Massachusetts, became one of the great poets of all time, and perhaps the greatest of all women poets, without stirring from her garden in the quiet New England town. Her universe was that of the soul; her special task was to make that universe articulate. This she did in gem-like verse that resembled nothing written before or since.

Was her poetry the expression of life lived or of life repressed? Does she tell of experience or wish? So successful was she in guarding her secrets that it is almost impossible now to reconstruct the life out of which her poetry was made, even if ever it was in any way specific. She writes of God, man, and nature with a knowledge that does not seem possible in one so sheltered. Never was there a peron to whom so little happened who suffered and rejoiced with such intensity. She knew love and death as few have known them and survived, and yet who it was she loved and lost, her friends and biographers are unable or unwilling to agree upon.

There is a temptation to start with the stereotype of the New England nun, of which another writer of the day, Mary Wilkins Freeman, made a famous story. There was something about the way women lived in the late nineteenth century that encouraged repression. Glimpses of Sophia Hawthorne, Olivia Clemens, and many another idealized and sheltered wife tend to reveal an image of neuroticism that had provided its own system of values. Pale, dressed in white, devoted to their husbands and children, or consecrated to their God, they were waited upon, protected, repressed. The sex that was not permitted expression in literature was not even openly acknowledged in life.

The unmarried woman often died at an early age of the restrictions put upon her by society. Dress and habits allowed no free exercise that could promote health. Driven in upon herself, she lived intensely in the mirror of her own unrealized passions, and burned out her energies in silence. For her, Emily Dickinson provided a voice. Nature was her close and loving, although sometimes exacting, friend. Her religion had no church because she could converse directly with her God on personal terms. Whether she loved this man or that, or none at all except in her

*From Robert E. Spiller, *The Cycle of American Literature* (New York: Macmillan Publishing Co., 1955) pp. 164–69. Copyright 1955, 1956 by Macmillan Publishing Co., Inc. Reprinted with permission of Macmillan Publishing Co., Inc.

imagination, makes little difference to her poetry, for she knew love with a depth and violence that could come only from repression. Death, too, was always present, but whether it was someone dear to her who had just died or the sudden conviction of death itself is unimportant. Because most other avenues of expression were closed, her brief stanzas come to hold the distillation of all that it means to be human. They are her letters to the world, which she wrote but failed herself to mail.

No one who knew her well seemed to think of Emily Dickinson as morbid or withdrawn. Happy and outgoing, she loved and was loved by her family and her circle of intimate friends. Edward Dickinson, her father, was a man of considerable means and strong personality, a lawyer and treasurer of Amherst College; Emily Norcross, her mother, the exact opposite, was gentle and dependent, devoted to the care of her family until after her husband's death in 1874, when she became an invalid. Her younger daughter Lavinia, or "Vinnie," like Emily, never married, but did not share the beauty of Emily's spirit. Austin, the eldest, in the pattern of his father became a lawyer and leading citizen of Amherst, which he never left. He married Emily's early friend Susan Gilbert, a woman of aggressive wit and worldly charm, and lived next door to his parents' home on Main Street, where "Sister Sue" became for many years the confidante of the poet.

To her close-knit family Emily devoted herself completely after one year at Mount Holyoke Seminary. There had been nothing unusual about her childhood in its activities and friends, but her retirement from the world does seem to have had a deliberate intention to prompt it. She had attended district school and Amherst Academy, where she was known as a wit, and she loved her garden. To her friends she was outgoing and affectionate. She seldom left Amherst, although she had been to Boston on occasion, and once, at the age of twenty-three, to Philadelphia and Washington. Only in her unwillingness to "renounce the world" for a heavenly master did Emily seem different from her fellows; her independence made her hesitant to accept the joy of a nineteenth century Christian conversion. She felt herself too worldly! When she found that she could not share the unquestioning faith of her fellow students, she did not return to the seminary. Her own retirement from society came soon after, but it was to preserve rather than to renounce the self—there was more Yankee than Calvinist in her move. Perhaps she had been reading Emerson's recent essay on "Self-Reliance." Certainly the faith to which she retired had the skepticism of the Transcendentalist rather than the submission to God's will of the Calvinist.

Perhaps a failure in love, as gossip has it, was the immediate cause. There was a young lawyer in her father's office whom she called her "tutor" and who, before his early death, encouraged her in poetry and in religion, and there was the Philadelphia clergyman whom Emily saw only on a few occasions before he moved to the Pacific coast but who retained "an intimacy of many years" in the "box in which his letters grew." Both or either of these could have provided a focus for unrealized passions in the sheltered imagination. In any case the experience was there, and it was sufficient to produce, within a very few years, a sheaf of poems such as no woman had ever before composed.

It is too easy to assume that feminine modesty and the shyness born of her withdrawal had caused the delay in publication of most of these poems until after her death. The symbol of the pale Indian pipes, which her neighbor Mrs. Todd drew for the cover of the first volume of her poems, was never approved by its author; and the poems which Emily Dickinson wrote were not the outpourings of a hurt and inward-turning spirit. Art offers two ways to those who turn to it from life: a blinded wandering in the deep recesses of a sickened personality, or the depersonalized and hard forms of disciplined and complete expression. Emily Dickinson chose the latter. Hers was the poetry of craftsmanship rather than that of confession. Apparently she failed to publish because she could not find a way to reach the world on her own terms, and she would not accept compromise. From the first, she was writing as though to be read, but she was satisfied merely to enclose her poems in letters to her friends rather than in the covers of a book if in that way they could be accepted without alteration. Sister Sue, Mabel Todd, Samuel Bowles, Helen Hunt Jackson, and Josiah Holland were among those to whom she showed them for advice.

Once she came near to finding an editor who could help her, but even he tried to alter her supposed carelessness of craftsmanship. Thomas Wentworth Higginson, clergyman and editor, to whom she sent her poems, was acute enough to recognize their worth, but even he tried to smooth out the violent rhythms and the more obscure meanings when he later helped to prepare them for print.

The poet herself was courteous when such advice was given her, but she quietly ignored it. She knew better than any of her "tutors" what she wished to say and she was exacting in her ways of saying it. The general reading public that asked for meter that is smooth, rhythm that is easy, and words that are limited to only one obvious meaning interested her not at all. She was willing to wait.

Like John Donne and the English metaphysical poets whom she so resembled, Dickinson's understanding of the meaning of words was subtle and complex, her ear for music could assimilate discord as well as concord, and her images were drawn from life and from books with a sure but infinitely various authority. Only the most complex art could be made to include the depths and variety of those things for which she demanded expression. The resources of American poetry which the metaphysics of Emerson had already stretched with images as violent as those of Herbert and Donne, and that Poe had enriched with a darker and more complex music, were further opened and deepened by these deceptively simple stanzas. Emily Dickinson sought to reconcile the finite to the infinite without relinquishing the integrity of the human soul or the validity of physical nature. In the idiom of New England theology that she had renounced, she caught and forced into expression the skepticism and doubts of the age of science which was to come. Not printed until the 1890's, and hardly understood until the 1920's, poems which were written shortly after the Civil War reached with the firm note of authority a public that had experienced a World War. Her retreat had been into a realm which does not change, and her letters were to a world which had, like her, reached a point of irreducible paradox. Fully disciplined art alone could stand firm against threatened chaos.

Emily Dickinson Complete   Arlin Turner*

The publication of Emily Dickinson's poems over the past three-quarters of a century makes a story no less unique than it has been exasperating to readers and students who have had to wait from one batch to another. The poet did not seek publication in her lifetime and saw only a few of her poems in print; most of her poems remained unpublished decades after her death; they have been the victims of garbled editing. It has been as if the poet herself, her relatives and friends, and concomitant circumstances all conspired to restrict and confuse the canon of her work. Her readers have been tantalized by having her poems dribbled out by two teams of editors who worked with separate materials and were not on friendly terms and who left doubt as to the textual accuracy of many of the poems published. Only now, sixty-nine years after Emily Dickinson's death, is there a complete and dependable printing of her poems. Thomas H. Johnson has published a definitive edition of poems and verse fragments, which run to a total of 1775.

When Emily Dickinson died in 1886, only seven of her poems had been printed, three of them in the Springfield, Massachusetts, *Republican* and the others in barely more suitable media. The fact that these were published without her approval, apparently, and underwent editorial "improvement" no doubt contributed to her decision against publishing. Whatever the causes were, she had decided before she entered her most productive period, from 1858 to 1865, to avoid publication.

After Emily's death her sister Lavinia discovered, to her great surprise she avowed, a locked chest, now one of the most famous chests in all literary history, which contained hundreds of poems. The fact that Lavinia was surprised tells a good deal about Emily in relation to those

*From the *South Atlantic Quarterly*, 55 (October 1956), 501–04. Reprinted by permission of the author and Duke University Press, copyright 1956.

around her. Everyone knew of her poems, and many of her correspondents had received stanzas or whole poems in letters. The poems
were a part of her and were as much taken for granted as the seclusion
which had grown more thorough with the years or the white clothing she
adopted when she came to think of herself as totally dedicated. But not
even Lavinia, who like Emily lived a lifetime, unmarried, in the Dickinson home, suspected that nearly a thousand poems had been carefully
copied off, gathered into neat packets, and laid away. Emily was queer;
no one had any doubt about it, and the poems were part of the queerness.
To be sure, there were some who took the poems more seriously—Thomas
Wentworth Higginson, whom Emily asked of her verse in 1862, "Does it
breathe?" and especially her friend Helen Hunt Jackson, who strove to
win Emily over to the idea of publication. Yet Emily passed through her
years of richest productivity and through the remaining decade of her life
without impressing even her closest associates as a poet of any consequence.

It may be possible to read something of the mind which produced the
poems in Emily's leaving the manuscripts to be discovered after her death.
What she intended or supposed would be done with them can only be conjectured. But can there be any doubt that if she had wanted them
destroyed she would have done it herself and that she expected Lavinia to
find the poems and begin arranging for their publication?

The steps which followed have been recounted in full: how a friend
of the Dickinsons, Mabel Loomis Todd, undertook to transcribe the
poems and, with the unenthusiastic help of Higginson, to edit them for
the publisher. Thus three series of poems and two volumes of letters were
issued. Then followed the estrangement between Mrs. Todd and Lavinia,
climaxed in the court suit which left no possibility of further collaboration
in printing Emily's works. After a lapse of almost twenty years began to
appear the series of volumes published by the poet's niece, Martha Dickinson Bianchi, and still later the volumes prepared by Millicent Todd
Bingham, daughter of Mrs. Todd. In all, sixteen volumes were published,
collections of poems or other volumes containing poems—enough surely
to get all the poems into print and also, one might suppose, to establish
dependable texts. But not so in either case. These volumes did form the
basis, however, for such a rise in Emily Dickinson's reputation as a poet
that to establish and print the text of her complete poems became the most
urgent need in American literary study. Such an undertaking became
possible when the Dickinson manuscripts and copyrights came into the
possession of Harvard University.

Mr. Johnson has employed the full battery of scholarly techniques to
accomplish his purpose. He has searched all discoverable manuscripts and
earlier printings to establish the canon of the poems. With Emily Dickinson this task was particularly complex, because she interpolated lines or
stanzas or complete poems in letters she sent to more than thirty cor-

respondents. To settle questions of text, Mr. Johnson has collated all versions of each poem. Here again special difficulties exist: A poem or parts of it may have been sent in two or more letters, with variations appropriate to the recipients and the contexts. Many of the poems, moreover, were left unfinished. Some exist in only a rough draft; others are in a fair copy but indicate alternate words or phrases or entire lines on which the poet remained undecided.

It was in making decisions in these unsolved debates of the poet's that the earlier editors met their greatest difficulties; perhaps in consequence they took liberties in making further emendations of their own. Mr. Johnson could lighten the weight of such decisions as he had to make, for in his plan, after selecting the preferred version ("the earliest fair copy") when more than one exist, he then reproduces any other versions if the differences warrant and notes every variant and every suggested change appearing in any manuscript or printed version.

Beyond establishing a text of the complete poems, Mr. Johnson's second major purpose has been to date the poems as closely as possible. For some the dates come readily from letters into which they were copied or with which they were enclosed—some undated letters can be dated by references within them. For poems which exist in undated holograph copies, the testimony of handwriting and paper experts has been called in. The facsimile copies included in the first volume of this new edition, together with the supplementary analysis of the handwriting year by year, suggest that the handwriting test is particularly trustworthy with Emily Dickinson. And when it is coupled with study of the paper and such other evidence as that furnished by the poet's own collecting of the poems into packets, or small manuscript volumes—when all the evidence is considered, the reader is satisfied with the editor's chronology, which he does not contend is more than approximate.

Publication of *The Poems of Emily Dickinson* is an important event in American literary history: it is a major step in clearing up one of the greatest enigmas that has ever existed in connection with an American author. It provides the sort of accurate, complete variorum text which exists for no other American poet except perhaps Sidney Lanier. It adds forty-one poems and fragments to those published earlier from the pen of Emily Dickinson. No doubt other variant copies will be found of some of the poems in letters not yet discovered or elsewhere; some of the lost holograph originals for copies that have been preserved may turn up; and it may be that new poems will appear from one source or another. But such new discoveries we know will be slight. Until recently we could not be sure that the best or even the largest part of the Dickinson poems were not yet to come; now we know where we stand. And evaluations which in the past have had to be at least in a degree tentative and provisional can now gain assurance.

Fortunately, too, our knowledge of Emily and the other Dickinsons and her relations with those around her has been augmented many fold, chiefly through the books published by Millicent Todd Bingham in the last ten years. With all the poems now and with a greatly clarified picture of the poet herself in her surroundings, we are in effect ready to attack for the first time with any real hope of success the puzzle of Emily Dickinson. The undertaking promises fascination for its own sake, but a considerable incitement derives from the consideration that Emily Dickinson is at the same time one of the greatest of our poets and one of the most enigmatic persons in literary history.

[Review of *The Letters of Emily Dickinson* (1958)]   Mario Maurin*

These letters were meant to to be sipped at leisure with puzzlement and delight, not to be swallowed whole and strung one to the other; they were meant to be received, not reviewed. To read over a thousand of them at a stretch, however varied invention and circumstance may make them, is both taxing and unfair. Our lungs are not designed for prolonged stays in such a rarefied atmosphere; nor is our wit able to respond, letter after letter, year after year, volume after volume, to a sting which, after all, only made periodic assaults on correspondents. If Emily Dickinson's poems gain by being read in quantities, it is because her originality requires the confirmation of achievement, but has found safe anchorage in poetic form and shares it with us; whereas in her letters the extreme singularlity of the person shines sharply through—alone.

It may be a pity, as Professor Whicher suggested in his classic study, that these missives cannot be published in the actual form they assumed on the sheet of writing paper. It would be easier for us to see how close to the borderline of poetry—of her own poetry—Emily Dickinson stayed at all times, and what an imperceptible change in the intensity of the current it took to magnetize the letter into a poem. *This Was a Poet* pointed out two early passages where meter and rhyme were fairly straining to burst out from the fetters of prose. There were others, and the disguise they wore was soon to be discarded. But a more accurate reproduction would still be a long way from easing the reviewer's task. Though not deeper, our world is wider than Amherst, and where, for us too, there is seclusion, we have grown accustomed to find it, not behind white fluttery curtains, but in the street, in our work, in our efforts to cope with the jagged demands or the smooth drone of daily activity. We are threatened by more ominous gods than the one Reverend Colton could invoke. This is

*From *NEQ*, 32 (Mar., 1959), 99–102. Reprinted by permission of the author and the *New England Quarterly* © 1959.

not to begrudge Emily Dickinson what she was or what her family allowed her to become, but to admit that she commands a firmer hold on our admiration and our affection than on our understanding or our patience. We cannot help sympathizing somewhat with stolid Mr. Higginson who, after one of his visits to Amherst, wrote about his "partially cracked poetess." Granted that the "crack" was superb; but the woman does make one uneasy. There are early letters of hers where humor and hysteria seem strangely coterminous. And there is a note of thin childlike cruelty in her fancy that will ring more than once.

The task of preparing a complete edition of the letters cannot have been an easy one; and Mr. Johnson, seconded by Mrs. Ward, has lavished so much care on it that the reader's gratitude must remain an inadequate reward. In most cases, dates have had to be conjectured both from internal evidence and from the poet's handwriting. Names, titles, and quotations have been identified. And the notes and introductory statements to the various sections show time and again that a sensitive hand is discreetly at the helm. My only quarrel with the editorial procedure followed in the text—and quarrel is too pompous a word—is that where misspellings have been preserved without any identifying symbol, the suspicion of a misprint remains. For instance, did Emily Dickinson write: ". . . found Father is great agitation at my protracted stay" (p. 111)? Other mistakes, like "liesure" and "Febuary," are more plausible, while "magazinine" has such a wonderful flavor that one would like to think it intentional.

The collection, though it has gathered all available material, remains inevitably spotty. It is amply representative, nevertheless, and one cannot expect that further discoveries would radically add to our knowledge of the poet—except perhaps in the case of communications to and from Charles Wadsworth and Judge Lord, for whom her devotion verged on exaltation. Many letters have been destroyed, many are lost. There are years, like 1857, for which we have none; others, like 1855–1856, 1863, 1866–1869, for each of which we have less than ten. The numbers grow larger after 1875, the high points being 1883 and 1884, which total 164 letters. But many of these are one-sentence messages sent to sister-in-law Susan across the lawn, congratulations, presentation or thank-you notes for flowers, short expressions of mourning and consolation at the death of a friend. Admirably pithy and tantalizing as they often are, they are not as revealing as the longer letters which Emily Dickinson wrote in her youth. Whereas the decade 1847–1857 yields here, roughly speaking, 170 letters which occupy 280 pages, the final decade of the poet's life yields three times as many communications which, however, occupy about the same number of pages. The gushing breathlessness of the early years has been tamed into wiriness and crispness of cadence.

Had not her brother lived in the house next door, there would have been more letters to him, and their absence is to be deplored. The ones she wrote him while he taught or studied in Boston are among the most spontaneous of the whole collection. In many of the others, even to her dearest friends, something forced steals over the expression and gradually becomes the norm. She has been taking possession of her own person, has grown into her own mask, has become aware of *something* that expects her to sharpen her clauses and to find seventy different ways of saying thank you. She belongs to that fastidious troupe for whom the world, each time, hangs on a sentence. As a consequence, almost everything she writes is quotable for wisdom or quaintness, though the tone may range from majestic to maudlin. She brings to mind the French précieuses of the seventeenth century, before the great onslaught of clarity did away with tortuous concision and transparence became the soul of elegance. They, too, "cultivated their differences"; for them too, singularity of expression was the obvious corollary of a refined mind. They raised up about themselves a private world, where everything had private value. This transfiguration of the commonplace turned water into crystal, flowers into jewels, lovers into gods, fact into anecdote and meaning. One recognizes here a fundamental attitude of poetry which was familiar to Emily Dickinson. That there is also delightful humor in her letters, should not surprise. Is not a common spring of poetry and humor to be sought in animism, or even in anthropomorphism? An inclination to duplicate everywhere the formalities of human society achieves humor; whereas bestowing human qualities and values where none obtain may achieve poetry.

What indeed lie at the root of Emily Dickinson's greatness are the sense of life and the capacity for love to which she gives memorable utterance in many of her letters. "The Charms of the Heaven in the bush are superceded [*sic*] I fear, by the Heaven in the hand, occasionally," she writes to Samuel Bowles; "Life is the finest secret," to Mrs. Holland; and to Maria Whitney, "I fear we think too lightly of the gift of mortality, which, too gigantic to comprehend, certainly cannot be estimated." Life, in its mystery, its intricacies, its unity, has supplanted the Puritans' God as the prime mover of her world. She perceives and feels it as forcefully, in her own way, as her contemporary Gerald Manley Hopkins. She can and does anticipate the Catalan poet Maragall's question: "If the world is so lovely, Lord . . . what more canst Thou give us in another life?" In her, familiarity with the deep does not breed contempt for the minute. Unexpected quarters yield an oblique confirmation: the closest parallel that may be found to some of her "nature" poems comes from the most powerful poet of her age, Victor Hugo, in *Les Chansons des Rues et des Bois*, where the same alliance of driving force, pin-point imagery and wit sparkles dazzlingly. What Hugo squanders with his immense visionary breath, she hoards; but her sentences coiled in the grass also lash out with viperine energy. The world for her was a treasure not to be wasted, and she is never more moving than when she goes about taking meticulous inventory of its riches. Then we recognize her as an Alice born on the other side of the looking-glass, and we truly know her wonderland was earth.

Circumference   Charles R. Anderson[*]

"Circumference" is a word that she returns to again and again. It is a pervasive image in her religious thinking and in her theory of art, though the meanings it carries are not always consistent. An exploration of its ambiguities seems in order. Significantly, she rarely used the kindred word "circle" with its suggestion of a bounded inclosure. Her term was usually "circumference," occasionally its synonym "circuit," both compounded from Latin roots meaning to carry or go around. The emphasis is on the motion of encompassing, suggesting an extension outward to include something larger than can be found at a particular static point. It is close to the meaning now rare but copiously illustrated in the *Religio Medici* of Sir Thomas Browne, an author she specifically named as a favorite. In his effort to define it as a sense of boundlessness radiating out from a center, opposite to the normal sense of a limiting circle, he cited the formulation of Hermes: The sphere of which the center is everywhere, the circumference nowhere (*Sphæra cujus centrum ubique, circumferentia nullibi*). Though Browne frequently limited "circumference" to the immediately surrounding environment, she began with this rare use and expanded it into a symbol for all that is outside. Her center is the inquiring mind whose business is circumference, intent upon exploring the whole infinity of the universe that lies before her.[1]

At times "circumference" seems associated with the idea of cosmic expanse, as opposed to the limited life centered on earth. "A Coffin—is a small Domain," she says, yet it contains "A Citizen of Paradise"; and realization of this larger meaning of mortality can become the rudiment of a new apprehension, ampler than the sun's, "Circumference without Relief— / Or Estimate—or End."[2] Again, expansion outward from the narrow center of death, the coming full circle of the individual spirit, will occur at the Resurrection, when the fragmented earthly life is made whole at last and "Circumference be full." Even in life, according to another poem, she could sometimes have a vision of touching the Universe and see herself as a lone "Speck upon a Ball" going out to "Circumference," but the vision was a transient one and quickly receded. These certainly suggest the meaning of circumference as attainment of the divine reality.

Ultimate circumference may well be the extension of understanding

*From Charles R. Anderson, *Emily Dickinson's Poetry: Stairway of Surprise* (New York: Holt, Rinehart and Winston, 1960), pp. 55–59. Reprinted by permission of the author.

from mortal limits to absolute fulfillment in immortality. But the image is more complex for her, even involute, and there are circumferences short of the celestial one that are not beyond the poet's reach. There are endless expansions for the spirit, opening out from the smallest center of consciousness to the fullest comprehension. But this growth cannot be attained too easily; it is more likely to be achieved through the vision and discipline of art than in the experience of life. The ecstacy of perfect love, she says in one poem, is a "new Circumference" too exalted for mortals, conditioned as they are by the 'little Circuit' of ordinary life.[3] Starting from these two concentric images, she goes on to develop her theme that the human way must go through pain and suffering to a fuller understanding of what heaven can be. It is only by encompassing the full circle of human possibilities that one is made ready to expand towards the divine circle. How grand the expansion can be even within limits of the mortal calendar leads her to exclaim in another poem: "Time feels so vast" her finite self tends to become engrossed in "this Circumference" to the exclusion of God. The poem concludes that this life is only a preface to eternity, preparing her by stages of growth "For the Stupendous Vision / Of His Diameters."

To couch her theory of art in religious terms was natural for one formed by such an environment. In her thinking the Creator became a model for the poet. The circumference of divine reality perceived through awe was at least a useful metaphor for the heaven-on-earth of his art achieved through the imagination. This linkage is made explicit in a quatrain written near the end of her life. Unsuccessful as a poem, its meaning is obscure without the accompanying letter, sent to the sculptor Daniel Chester French. She was writing to congratulate him for winning his fame (his momentary achievement of Circumference) "reverently," and since success is dust she begged God to keep him "fundamental" so he could achieve it again. The verses themselves are addressed to "Circumference," who is properly the "Bride of Awe" and so can be possessed only by the truly "hallowed Knight."[4] Even then, possessed just momentarily in his art, she apparently means, since all is a metaphor for the artist's dedicated love of his Muse. Only so does he achieve occasionally the revelation of full meaning.

The most startling use of the term occurs in a late letter: "The Bible dealt with the Centre, not with the Circumference."[5] This pronouncement is not so much baffling as unexpectedly bold. Set beside her own boast, "My Business is Circumference," it seems little short of blasphemous. Her poems are to accomplish something the Bible does not? Is she saying it is just a human record, the history of a religious people and a rule book for conduct, whereas her poetry will encompass revelation? She certainly searched the Bible for meaning, but though she found it a primary source for her imagery—most significantly in its most poetic

books, the Psalms, the Revelation, and the Gospel of St. John—she did
not find in it the divine reality.

Through Emerson she was well aware of the Transcendentalists' doctrine that all books, including The Book, are secondary to the fountain of
truth within, and she could go so far with them as to affirm "By intuition
Mightiest Things / Assert themselves—and not by terms."[6] But her kinship with her predecessors is more tenuous than with her successors,
especially some of the esthetic philosophers today. At any rate, like many
modern poets she found art the substitute for her inherited religion, the
only instrument of revelation left to her. Does she come then at last to
contradict her poem "Of Bronze—and Blaze," which says it is spiritual
pride to aim at celestial beauty since the poet's mortal lot is to make splen-
dors out of menagerie? Perhaps all can be reconciled in a sort of dialec-
tical sequence. The immediate leap into God is impossible, the poet
cannot be like the aurora. He must go back to the earth, the human experience of pain and suffering, and work out from there towards the
divine reality. She, also, may have to *deal* with the center, as the Bible
does, though her ultimate *business* is to explore out to the circumference.

A final poem, successfully using this term by embodying it in a controlled metaphor, may help to clarify her meaning:

> The Poets light but Lamps—
> Themselves—go out—
> The Wicks they stimulate—
> If vital Light
>
> Inhere as do the Suns—
> Each Age a Lens
> Disseminating their
> Circumference—[7]

The disjunctive "but" in the first line emphasizes the homely implement
of the lamp by which poets light the earthly way in contrast with the
celestial light of the suns in the second stanza (and the aurora in "Of
Bronze—and Blaze"), which remains a simile. This light is not made by
touching the words with a magical taper, but is kindled by a generative
power within the artifact, as in the case of the lamps of heaven. Each of
the key words that open out this meaning is of Latin origin, the only six
in the poem. "Stimulate," *to animate* according to her Lexicon, leads into
the life-giving idea of "vital." This is the necessary condition to be fulfilled in order that the wicks may "inhere" in the poets' lamps, just as the
heavenly wicks do in the suns, making them shine with a kind of immortality of their own. This comparison with the sun, center of her planetary
universe, places the poetic lamps at the center of her private universe.

At this point a new element enters, germane to the principal image,
which links this poem with those she wrote on fame. The "Lens" is the

glass of posterity through which the light is not only seen but magnified. The central meaning of a poem, its light, remains constant; succeeding ages merely interpret and reinterpret, broadening its effect. This is happily rendered by "disseminating," carrying both the idea of scattering abroad and the seminal nature of the poems as seeds. Such a connotation makes no break in the figurative language, however, for common usage has long abstracted the meaning of this word from its agricultural origins, as in the phrase "disseminating truth." The literal meaning of "Circumference" as the boundary of a circle (like the disks of the lamps) has been expanded by her special meaning into a sphere like the sun, radiating its light outward to infinity. If poets can light such lamps they are content to "go out" themselves, for death then becomes a means of going outward to illuminate the darkness surrounding the generations of man. The mortal life has been transfigured into the enduring life of their poems.

Notes

1. *Religio Medici: The Works of Sir Thomas Browne* (London, 1852), II, 333 and note. (This set was in the Dickinson family library.) Margery McKay was the first to point out this parallel (unpublished thesis, "Amazing Sense," Swarthmore College, 1936; see also H. E. Childs, "Emily Dickinson and Sir Thomas Browne," *AL*, XXII (Jan. 1951), 455–65. Browne and Dickinson were kindred spirits in many ways: intensely interested in all the minute phenomena of nature and death, combining an analytical skepticism with a generally spiritual orientation, employing a style marked by economy of expression and startling imagery. He was also, like her, a recluse who did not intend to publish, calling his *Religio Medici*, "a private exercise directed to myself." The concept of "circumference" is central to his philosophy and gives unity to his vast system of circle imagery. The poetry of Emily Dickinson is likewise rich in wheels, arcs, axes, cycles, discs, spheres, and orbits. But there is an important difference. His use of "circumference" has a strictly religious purpose, and attempt to define God; her emphasis is esthetic. (See also Thomas H. Johnson, *Emily Dickinson: An Interpretive Biography*. Cambridge, Mass., 1955, Chapter VI.)

2. "A Coffin is a small Domain" Poem #943. The next quotations are from Poem #515 and 378.

3. Poem #313. The next quotation is from Poem #802.

4. Poem #1620.

5. Letter #950. (See Johnson, pp. 140, 151–53; and Letter #261 where she lists "the Revelations" among her six favorite books.)

6. Poem #420. In her distinction between the center and circumference, Dickinson seems closer to the esthetic-religious positions of modern writers like Langer, Bergson, and Whitehead than to the Transcendentalism of Emerson.

7. Poem #883. (Other poems on circumference are 451, 633, 641, 680, 889).

Emily Dickinson and Isaac Watts: Puritan Hymnodists

Martha Winburn England*

A lyric poet stores in the recesses of being some idea of form that must be satisfied. That idea is affected by rhythms apprehended by the senses, and more deeply affected by rhythms comprehended within the physical frame. As words and as music, the hymns of Watts became involved with Emily Dickinson's vocal cords, fingers, diaphragm, and lungs very early in life.

She wrote at a time when poetry and music were felt to be closely related. She did not know the poetry of her two American contemporaries, Lanier and Whitman, who most successfully exploited elaborate musical forms, opera, cantata, oratorio, chamber music, symphony. "Of Poe," she said, "I know too little to think."[1] She knew the writings of others, notably Longfellow, who worked from complex musical models, but she had little experience with those forms of music. When she heard Haydn's *Creation* sung in Boston, she merely mentioned "2 concerts" and went on to a detailed description of Mount Auburn Cemetery.[2] When she heard Jenny Lind, she said, "I'd rather have a Yankee."[3] She professed herself content with music made in her own garden, hearing in the natural phenomena the sounds of bugle, banjo, guitar, drums, castanets, bands, trumpet, tambourin, orchestra, ballet, and opera. Amherst was not wanting in the music she loved. Even the whistling in the street delighted her.

She spoke of the singing of Amherst students, the bands that came to town with Welsh's Circus, the Germania Orchestra, Dodsworth's Band; but all her experiments in lyric form were based on music she herself made. At the age of two and a half years she played in some fashion on the first piano she had her hands on.[4] In advanced years she improvised on the rosewood piano that was the pride of her girlhood. Until her last illness, people came to her home after choir practice to sing for her. She had private music lessons, lessons at Amherst Academy and at Mt. Holyoke Seminary. We know her exercise book, the dance tunes, minstrel songs, sentimental ballads she admired. Once she poked fun at her sister's singing of a mournful ditty, but record shows that she herself at sixteen had found the song very touching.[5] She tried in her poems to transmute into high art those characteristic love songs of her era in which death seems to be the ideal of life and love. For a while the songs of Robert Burns held her interest, and she tried out his Scots dialect, stanza forms, and plaintive falling cadences in minor mode (192, 193, 205). She had the poetry and the music she liked. There was no lack of money to buy it and no restriction on her choice.

*From *Bulletin of The New York Public Library*, 69 (Feb. 1965), 83–116. Reprinted by permission of the New York Public Library.

The formal influence in all her poetry is the hymn. When music is considered along with hymn texts, that influence is seen as pervasive. Her poetry was written as Watts's was written, as most hymns are written, *par-odia*, to an existing tune.

If a hymn be defined as a lyric intended for congregational singing, she wrote none. Her poems were not so intended, have never been so used, would not be appropriate to such use. Yet she wrote no epic, drama, fiction, essay, sonnet, or villanelle, but only something she called hymns or psalms. Hymn meters set her meters. The range of the reading voice is restricted to hymn range. Vocabulary is impregnated with hymn vocabulary and strictly circumscribed by New England gentility. Questions are posed and answered with reference to religious thought.

She wrote nineteenth-century hymns. They differ from eighteenth-century hymns (especially from those by Watts) by their greater metrical freedom, freer use of enjambment, use of more images with no scriptural source. The voice is that of a lone singer rather than the voice of the congregation assembled. Lay writers knew and cared little about dogma and systematic theology. The songs at their worst were modes of sentimental self-expression, not songs in praise of God. Dozens of noble exceptions rush to mind from nineteenth-century hymnody, the more readily because the noble exceptions remain in use—but the generalizations hold.

As she adopted at times the stance of Dickens without ever adopting his social conscience, so in like manner she adopted gestures and situations from nineteenth-century hymns. Many of the hymns have an aura of medieval Catholicism like that which surrounds some work of Scott, Keats, Coleridge. She also could set up a typical situation of a medieval mystic. "Oh, Shadow on the Grass" (1187) is a beautiful incantation suggesting the medieval song "I sing of a maiden." But the point to that poem is the same as the point to her other poems that hint of a mystic encounter: there was no encounter, no certainty that the shadow was anything other than a shadow.

If I were able to perceive any evidence of the peculiar regional "transcentalism" and "Unitarianism" that have been thrust upon her by some critics, I should be glad to point them out. There are only such elements of mysticism and transcendentalism as are common to all orthodox Hebrew and Christian thinking. She was no Unitarian. The separate phrases of the Apostles' Creed make a fairly comprehensive index of her religious preoccupations.

She was a Puritan with a Puritan's attitude toward the Establishment, which is by definition a desire to purify it and recall it to the right ways. In her life, Watts had preempted control of the Establishment, and she saw a great deal that seemed wrong with Watts.

From first to last in all her writings, she never consciously alluded to him in any tone but criticism, any spirit but one of refutation. Her refusal to be awed by hell was more systematic than Huck's parody of the Sunday School lesson. Her statements on instructing children in uglification and derision are more impassioned than Alice's parodies of Watts's moralizing. It was 1862 when Alice's more sympathetic logician took her boating and silenced Watts's Busy Bee and laid out his Sluggard for his final repose. Emily Dickinson had been trying since 1850 to perform these last rites. Pending the day when computer experts shall program the texts of Watts, Dickinson and the King James Version, and prove by IBM that she attacked Watts's version,[6] we must take her word for it. Her celebrated statement on the subject (1545) says nothing is wrong with the Bible. It is the manner of singing it that is wrong. This poem is the record of her most careful revision. She tried out thirteen adjectives before she made a choice: "Had but the Tale a warbling Teller," children would listen gladly. Knowing Watts, one can see the consistency in her contradictory moods. Her marriage of jest and passion does not seem an unequal yoking of believer and unbeliever, but a true oneness of substance. Through every avenue of life, she learned from the Father of English hymnody how she would never write. That is an important thing for an author to learn. In her writing, she did not depart from the genre he fathered.

Mr. Austin Warren says that in some poems she "creates a counterpoint or descant on Watts."[7] These musical forms must arrive at harmony with the cantus firmus. She does perform this sort of musical exercise, but beside Mr. Warren's musical analogies, I will place another.

Miss Phyllis Bartlett called Emily Dickinson "an unorthodox religious poet—like Hopkins."[8] Unorthodox not in theology (Father Hopkins was orthodox) but in the poetic process that was Miss Bartlett's special study. Orthodoxy of poetics must be defined with reference to time and place. Hopkins and Emily Dickinson began with simple metrical ideas, he with the rhythms of common speech, choruses, refrains, nursery rhymes, weather saws,[9] she with hymn meters. Both poets developed metrical tactics that were unorthodox for their time and place. Now, descant and counterpoint describe methods of handling a hymn that were orthodox in the Valley. An unorthodox method was also at work in her poetry.

The method is parody in the usual sense: the imitation of an art form that handles any element of art so as to criticize the original form with more or less serious intent. In our day, Mr. T. S. Eliot's influence has converted the method to orthodoxy by his use of parody to produce poetry of serious intent. He frustrates the expectations raised by some familiar verse form, and turns the reader from lyric mood to critical evaluation of statements commonly associated with the original form. Emily Dickinson handled various elements of words and music so as to comment on statements commonly associated with the hymn form. Watts's is a statement of unwavering faith. She said that "we believe and disbelieve a hundred times an Hour, which keeps believing nimble."[10] In her determination to

"Tell all the Truth but tell it slant" (1129), she used her most un-dear preceptor as a monolith from which to slant, referring to his uprightness to define her angle of variation, whatever it might be at the moment.

She started with simple methods, parodying hymns and prayers as she sat in church and in letters, writing sermon parodies for *Forest Leaves*, the school paper. Her brother joined the game. He sent her a "psalm" to be sung to Greenville, a hymn tune composed by Jean Jacques Rousseau, and her answering letter was "Variations on Greenville."[11] It would be a *coup* to be able to attribute to Austin the parody on Greenville, "Go tell Aunt Dinah the old gray goose is dead," but these youthful efforts do not survive. Such pranks did not contravene piety or decorum. Her sermons were considered innocuous. Austin Dickinson knew that his letters were read by the whole family.

The whole family interjected into common discourse the rhythmic phrases of Bible and hymn, quoted or in parodic form. Mr. Dickinson wrote to tell his son that work had begun on the Amherst & Belchertown Railway, and the family would here "set up our Ebenezer." He alluded to I Samuel 7:12, a hymn by Robinson, and the doctrine of the Covenant, but he added an exultant and capitalized HA! HA!![12] Emily planned to go to heaven via that railway, as certain of her destination "As if the checks were given," that is, as if the conductor had already taken up her ticket (1052). The relation of this poem to Watts has been recognized.[13] It is more a counterpoint on Watts than a parody. A Valentine she wrote was published in the Amherst College paper in 1850; it contains a parody of Watts's Psalm 72.[14] Her first published poem (3) was a Valentine printed that year in the *Springfield Republican*. The verse rhymes some of the cliches in Latin and English that were offered to the young as guides for conduct, among them two lines from Watts. Many later poems used the two lines. With increasing complexity they were made to deal with important themes.

The first is "How doth the busy bee." In two very early poems that antedate the Valentine there are bees, buzzing and courting flowers. From the Valentine of 1850 on, her bee was a defiant counter-emblem to Watts's emblem, and her sententiae dispute his. Bees are idle. One poem (994) speaks of an abstemious bee, but one is forced to the conclusion that she was being ironic about the bee's exercise of self-control. For bees at best are irresponsible creatures (138, 1343), indiscriminate in their pursuit of *la dolce vita* (1627), and unmindful of the Judgment Day (620). They are seducers, traitors, buccaneers, given over to apostacy and heresies (81, 128, 134, 206, 213, 214, 230, 661, 896, 1220, 1224, 1339, 1526, 1628). Watts's bee also was "a reckless Guide."[15] Rascals though they were, they wore the very gems of heaven (916) and, with regard to the dichotomy of ordained versus contingent grace, they lived in this life by "Fuzz ordained, not Fuzz contingent" (1405). The admirable verse epistle from his friend Fly to Bee (1035) may parody Watts's less inspired hymns, some of which sound as if they might conclude "Yours truly, I. Watts"—but perhaps not.

When her nephew started to school, she sent him a poem with instructions that it be given to his teacher (1522). The bee's religion is not "Industry and Morals," but "the divine Perdition / Of Idleness." She footnoted the poem with two quotations from Revelation, one (Rev. 21:8) cited to "Jonathan Edwards," though she might have better cited it to Watts, who rhymed it and put it close beside his Bee:

> ev'ry liar
> Shall have his portion in the lake
> That burns with brimstone and with fire. (Song 15)

The other (Rev. 22:7) she signed "Jesus": "And let him that is athirst come." She thought boys had a hard life. She did not want Gilbert subverted by Wattsian notions, and for all her jokes, she dealt with vital matters.

The other line in the Valentine is taken from "There is a land of pure delight."

> Could we but climb where Moses stood,
>   And view the landscape o'er,
> Not Jordan's stream nor death's cold flood
>   Should fright us from the shore. (b,66)

Moses' distant glimpse of the Promised Land from Mt. Nebo she associates with "the Hill of Science," from which eminence the poet views with sarcastic rapture the "transcendental prospect" spread by the learned before her eyes.

Like the Bee, this line meanders through her poetry. It becomes (112) the "Voice of the Sluggard Emily," who longed to sleep "Thro' Centuries of Noon," but was prevented by various personifications of industry.

Then (168) she began to turn Watts's leading character against Watts as she did with the Bee. Moses himself opposes the narrowminded "Savants" who categorize nature. In this poem there is a hint of the same theme on which the Bee was made to comment: justice. Moses was allowed to view the Promised Land only from afar. Was the edict that kept him from Canaan a just one? Watts did not question its justice, but who can trust a Savant? The hint in this poem becomes the theme of the next one.

> Old Man on Nebo! Late as this—
> My justice bleeds—for Thee!   (597)

Then, as she had accumulated the Sluggard into her poems about the Bee, she began to pick up others of Watts's *Divine and Moral Songs*. Song 15, quoted above, tells of the fate of Ananias, "struck dead / Catch'd with a lie upon his tongue." Another *Moral Song*, "Innocent Play," is a bland injunction against wading, an argument from analogy that Emily Dickinson found irrelevent, illogical, and annoying: "If we had been ducks, we might dabble in mud." She fretted a good deal about the justice of that edict. One poem (1201) lumps the fates of Moses, Ananias, and the young dabbler as three prime examples of miscarriage of justice.

In similar manner more serious questionings of divine justice accumulate arguments from other encounters of Moses with Jehovah (Ex. 3:2; 33:11–23; Num. 11; 14:14; Deut. 3:27; 5:4–5; 31:1). Some experience of her own is made analogous to the incidents. As the bush had burned without being consumed, as the prayer on Sinai for full sight of God's glory had been denied, as the view of Canaan had been brief, so had she burned with cold fire, had been denied, had lost some earthly paradise after one glimpse (576, 597, 694, 1247, 1733).

The progressions of *Watts Entire* do not falter: The justice of God and the mercy of God are one attribute of Holiness which cannot be in conflict with Itself, which controls and contains all that exists. She took up her themes in youthful exuberance, with some ironic qualifications even then, but on the whole confident that the ideas could be domesticated into common parlance. There came comic rebellions, passionate rebellions, moods when the brief vision seemed worth anything it cost, moods when she felt that love and poetry had been born "coeval" from the glimpse, moods when she suspected poetry came more from the deprivation than the vision. She and Watts agreed that the matter was worth thinking about all one's life, and agreed that for whatever went wrong or came out right God was responsible. That is a fairly large area of agreement, but it left room for the exercise of the critical implement of parody. Watts seemed to disregard experience. He moved all too inevitably by progressions that were all too simple to his four-fold chord where mercy and righteousness, truth and peace met and kissed.

The three hymnbooks used by Emily Dickinson during the years when she went to church are the chief source of information about her knowledge of church song.[16] Daily from earliest years she knew the words, music, and styles of singing. Watts predominates; but all periods of church song are represented, the old metrical psalms, the era of Watts and his disciples, the era dominated by the Wesleys, the early romantic writers. Family letters and records, including the valuable background material compiled by Mr. Jay Leyda, give some idea as to which songs were especially important. Additional information is found in books, periodicals, and music known to have been in the home. All this material should be read against the history of American hymnody, with special attention to the disputes that have always gone along with church song.

In quotation or in parody, I find allusions to the hymns of Burkitt, Watts, Doddridge, Stennett, John Burton, Newton, Cowper, Robinson, and possibly Kelly, Hart, and Simon Browne. Later writers who are prominent in family records are Mrs. Barbauld, H. K. White, Bishop Heber, and James Montgomery.

The egregious omission is the Wesley hymns. About thirty of the hymns are in the three hymnbooks, most of them anonymous. Jonathan Edwards' suspicion of the very word *Arminian* may have been still active in the Valley to exclude them. If so, some apt hymnologists did the excluding. The three meters that interest me most with reference to Dickinson poetry are attributed to sound Calvinist names. "Jesu, Lover of my soul" is ascribed to Cowper, "Blow ye the trumpet" to Toplady, and "Love divine" to Whitefield. Wesley hymns may have been sung, but there is no mention of them. No single phrase indicates that the Dickinsons ever sang one—and Wesley phrases adhere powerfully to the memory.

In a study of prosody, however, the absence of the Wesleys' hymns does not by any means exclude Wesley influence. Watts wrote almost altogether in three stanza forms. Charles Wesley used almost a hundred. Subsequent writers adopted Wesley meters, and long before 1850 the influence had pervaded hymnody.

Metrical influences of the English romantic poets also are present. It is, as a matter of fact, chancy business proving any specific metrical influence in the lyrics of any American poet of this period if the poet went to church. The English romantic poets, Shelley excepted, had their lyrics conscripted into the service. Sir Walter Scott's version of *Dies Irae* from *The Lay of the Last Minstrel* is in two of her three early hymnbooks, properly ascribed to him. But the meters of other poets are present when their actual words are not. For example, Byron's *Hebrew Melodies* were used in other hymnbooks, but not in these three. In two of the books, however, is the song "Daughter of Zion, awake from thy sadness," not Byron's, but using Byron's general mood and his dactyllic tetrameter.

She quit going to church, but she read hymns and practiced hymn tactics all her life. She knew the hymns of Whittier first from magazine publication, then later in book form. She mentioned the work of F. W. Faber. The light verse movements of Ray Palmer of the American romantic school seem to have made themselves felt in two poems at least (34, 1237).

In English hymnody, the next great era was brought in by the writers of the Oxford Movement. Emily Dickinson did not speak of these writers, except once to tell her sister-in-law how to spell *Puseyite*, but her sister Lavinia owned an 1847 edition of *The Christian Year* by Keble, which is the fountainhead of that hymnody. Keble often rhymed long with short lines, a thing seldom done in eighteenth-century hymns. Emerson also used the trick, and she knew Emerson well; but her experimenting in this mannerism appears in association with phrases that make it appear that she imitated Keble. H. F. Lyte's broken pentameters—as opposed to the solider pentameters of Old 50th and Walworth—seem to have served her as model (381, 382). One poem (964) by mood, content, stanza form, and use of dialogue, suggests an experiment based on J. M. Neale's hymn from the Greek, "Art thou weary?"

American hymnody reacted to the revival of Unitarian interest in church song, and names that were dear to her were signed to hymns that contributed to that revival: Thomas W. Higginson, J. G. Holland, Emerson, Hale, Lowell, Pierpont, Bryant, Longfellow, Parker. Names of other writers she admired are in hymnbooks in her home. "The night is come, like to the day" is from *Religio Medici*. Five hymns by Mrs. Browning are in Henry Ward Beecher's *Plymouth Collection* (1850). I know of no use of the Brontë hymns in American hymnbooks before the 1870s, but the poems were known to her in her girlhood and the influence is apparent. She spoke of no other public event with such delight as she felt in the visits of Edwards A. Park; few names are more honored in American hymnography.[17] But the important name is Watts.

Watts's early book *Horae Lyricae* shows him a resourceful and ambitious metrist. He set insoluble problems for himself and did not solve them completely; no poem is satisfactory throughout as poetry, though there are brilliant spots. But he learned skill in the weighing and disposition of syllables, and *Watts Entire* is a metrical triumph. The texture of his verse differs as widely from that of his predecessors in church song as does that of Emily Dickinson from, say, Mrs. Barbauld's, whom she admired. She and Watts were well matched as metrists, with delicate ears for nuance, sensitive awareness of musical conventions absorbed from childhood on, and audacity to revolutionize a metrical situation.

In all hymnody they are the two notorious offenders with false rhyme. They loved it. Watts's rhyme is not "slip-shod," but works by phonetic laws that are easily seen when his rhyme-words are examined. Emily Dickinson, beginning her career with a large vocabulary of rhyme-words learned by ear from hymns, including a large vocabulary of false rhyme learned from Watts, went as far beyond his liberties as he went beyond the conventions of English verse.[18] About 50% of his rhyme is false. He felt, however, a need for true rhyme at the close of a hymn. His half-rhymed stanzas often change to full rhyme in the last stanza, and about 77% of his final rhyme is true, even when one counts as false those rhymes allowed by convention (come-home, abroad-God, word-Lord, etc.) Years of usage had accustomed her to expect a hymn to close in true rhyme on a simple major chord (called in her hymnbooks "the flat key") or minor chord ("the sharp key"). The ear, anticipating the norm, will be lulled only by the expected sound. Where she departed from that convention, her sound patterns should be considered in assessing her poetic intention, for it is at this point the hymn convention is most vulnerable.

Notes

1. *The Letters of Emily Dickinson*, ed. Thomas H. Johnson and Theodora Ward, 3 vols. (1958), II 649.

2. Jay Leyda, *The Years and Hours of Emily Dickinson*, 2 vols. (1960), I 112, prints a review of the performance. See *Letters* I 36.

3. *Letters* I 121.

4. *Letters* I 33.

5. *Letters* I 34, 111.

6. Bible concordances have long existed; *A Concordance to the Poems of Emily Dickinson*, edited by S. P. Rosenbaum, has just been published by Cornell; *Watts Entire* may wait some time.

7. Austin Warren, p. 105 in *Emily Dickinson: A Collection of Critical Essays*, ed. R. B. Sewell (1963): see also John Crowe Ranson, p. 99–100. See Thomas H. Johnson, *Emily Dickinson: An Interpretive Biography* (1960), 70–77.

8. Phyllis Bartlett, *Poems in Process* (1951), 84–87.

9. Gerard Manley Hopkins, "Author's Preface," *Poems*, 3rd ed. (1948), 9.

10. *Letters* III 728.

11. *Letters* I 201, 234–236. George Frisbie Whicher, *This Was A Poet* (1938), 176.

12. Leyda I 233.

13. James Davidson, "Emily Dickinson and Isaac Watts," *Boston Public Library Quarterly* VI (1954), 141–149.

14. *Letters* I 92.

15. *Letters* II 604.

16. *The Psalms, Hymns, and Spiritual Songs of the Rev. Isaac Watts, D.*, *to which are added, Select Hymns, from other Authors: and Directions for Musical Expression*, ed. Samuel Worcester. Known as *Watts & Select*, it was first published in 1819.

Church Psalmody . . . Selected from Dr. Watts and Other Authors, ed. Lowell Mason and David Greene (1831). *Village Hymns . . . a Supplement to Dr. Watts's Psalms and Hymns*, ed. Asahel Nettleton (1824). Used also at Mt. Holyoke Seminary.

17. *Letters* I 271–272. Park's Sabbath Hymn Book was the most scholarly of the century; five copies from the Dickinson home are in Houghton Library. When Louis Benson wrote *The English Hymn*, his only important predecessor in the study of hymnology was *Hymns and Choirs* (1860), by Park and Phelps.

18. Watts divided the phonetic spectrum in two parts, apparently, and freely rhymed any dark vowel sound with any other, any light vowel sound with any other. He did not rhyme dark with light vowels, either in vowel rhyme of suspended rhyme, except in a few cases. One is the sibilant; any sibilant seemed to serve in itself as a rhyme without consideration of the preceding vowel sound; thus, he occasionally rhymed peace-pronounce, etc. The long *o* rhymed thus: boast-frost-trust; hope-prop-up; shone-son; stroke-flock; goat-foot, road-clod; groan-dawn. But long or short *o* did not rhyme with *a, e, i*. In vowel rhyme such matchings occur more frequently than in suspended rhyme, but the rule is the same. Any nasal consonant was made equal to any other. He rhymed *m* with *n*, *n* with *nd* and *ng*, and (rarely) *m* with *ng*. *F* and *v* are equivalent. Both he and Emily Dickinson sounded *l* and *r* so lightly that the sounds might be ignored in rhyming. He rhymed thought-not-note-vault-court. Emily Dickinson rhymed dark with light vowel sounds, and accepted many consonants as equivalent that were distinguished by Watts. Whicher (244–246) lists some of her principles of rhyming.

The Voice of the Poet   Brita Lindberg-Seyersted*

It is obvious that Emily Dickinson had an immense need to communicate with the world around her. She seems to have been a lively and exacting talker, and we have ample evidence of her activity as a writer of letters; in later life the *written* word became her chief vehicle for conveying love and affection, concern and consolation, reproach and irony. Her schoolgirl letters are chatty and exuberant; reading her letters gives the impression of listening to someone who simply cannot stop talking, someone rather infatuated with her own voice and verbal pranks. The earliest extant letter in her hand, written on April 18, 1842 to her brother away at school, is an almost uninterrupted stream of disparate bits of information about herself and the Dickinson household, punctuated, not with periods or commas, but only with the dashes she would later use in her poetry to indicate pauses for breath. Her role as the Dickinson family wit is enacted with great gusto in the somewhat later letters to her schoolfriend Abiah Root. With some self-consciousness she emphasizes that sharing such drollery marks the freemasonry of intimate friendship; in a long, rambling letter of February 23, 1845, she expresses the hope that "this letter wont be broken open. If it is folks will wonder who has got so much nonsense to tell, wont they?"[1]

Her friends and members of her family have testified to Emily's early displays of a spoken and written wittiness. In 1893, a schoolfriend, Emily Fowler Ford, reminisced how, in the literary group to which they both belonged, Emily Dickinson was one of the two most sparkling humorists, delighting her friends with droll mock-sermons.[2] Her niece, Martha Dickinson Bianchi, remembered long after Emily's death how she used to give life to the conversation with "some terse conclusion", "a verbal rocket". "Detail was anathema to her," said Mme Bianchi in describing how her Aunt Emily "loved to fence in words" and "loved a metaphor, a paradox, a riddle . . ."[3]

Contemporary testimony seems to agree that Emily Dickinson's voice was soft and low-pitched. (All references are from the last two decades of her life.) MacGregor Jenkins, a playmate of Martha Dickinson, observed: "Her [Miss Emily's] voice I can never forget—clear, low-toned, sweet."[4] Martha Dickinson recalls in *Emily Dickinson Face to Face* that "[Aunt Emily's] low-pitched voice was the instrument of an unconscious artist, almost husky at times of intensity, sweetly confidential, exciting in moments of extravaganza or 'outrage,' satiric, sympathetic, breathless in turn."[5] In a letter written to his wife on meeting Emily Dickinson for the first time, Thomas Wentworth Higginson records Emily's entrance line, handing her guest two lilies: "[she] said, 'These are my introduction' in a

*From Brita Lindberg-Seyersted, *The Voice of the Poet: Aspects of Style in the Poetry of Emily Dickinson* (Cambridge, Mass.: Harvard Univ. Press 1968). pp. 15–31. Reprinted by permission of the author.

soft frightened breathless childlike voice . . ."[6] Mabel Loomis Todd, Emily Dickinson's first editor, never *saw* her, but through frequent conversations carried on "between the brilliantly lighted drawing-room where I sat and the dusky hall just outside where she always remained, I grew very familiar with her voice, its vaguely surprised note dominant."[7] Emily Dickinson's voice may have contained a note of surprise; her manner of speaking certainly had the power to surprise and bewilder. Her way of talking and writing had grown more and more allusive; there was an impatience with the long-winded explanation, the superfluous word. "I don't speak things like the rest"[8] was her excuse for withdrawing and selecting "from an ample nation" a few privileged friends for interviews, truly a "Queen Recluse" (to borrow her much-admired Samuel Bowles's teasing phrase),[9] receiving her dutiful subjects. In her fifth letter to Colonel Higginson (August, 1862), evidently in reply to a complaint of his about poems enclosed in her preceding letters as being "Beyond [his] knowledge", she asks, only half credulously, "You would not jest with me, because I believe you—but Preceptor—you cannot mean it?" She is clearly disappointed in her newly acquired Preceptor's literary insights; already in this early letter, she brings in a note of good-natured mockery in her somewhat smug but precise statement about her linguistic peculiarities: "All men say 'What' to me, but I thought it a fashion—".[10]

In "All men" was included also Emily's family circle:

> My father seems to me often the oldest and the oddest sort of a foreigner. Sometimes I say something and he stares in a curious sort of bewilderment though I speak a thought quite as old as his daughter. And Vinnie, . . . it is so weird and so vastly mysterious, she sleeps by my side, her care is in some sort motherly . . . ; and the tie is quite vital; yet if we had come up for the first time from two wells where we had hitherto been bred her astonishment would not be greater at some things I say.[11]

She became more and more enchanted with the playful and serious uses of words—"How lovely are the wiles of Words!"[12]—learning "Gem-Tactics" as she metaphorically described her apprenticeship while practicing with base materials.[13] To her friend, Joseph Lyman, she recalled, "We used to think, Joseph, when I was an unsifted girl and you so scholarly that words were weak & cheap. Now I dont know of anything so mighty."[14] Everybody seemed to recognize her peculiar and original "Tactics". Her sister-in-law, recipient of more of Emily's poems than anyone else (276),[15] wrote perceptively in an unsigned obituary of "Miss Emily Dickinson of Amherst":

> Her talk and her writings were like no one's else. . . . A Damascus blade gleaming and glancing in the sun was her wit. Her swift poetic rapture was like the long glistening note of a bird one hears in the June woods at high noon, but can never see. . . . quick as the electric spark in her intuitions and analyses, she seized the kernel instantly, almost impatient of the fewest words, by which she must make her revelation.[16]

To Susan Dickinson, away on a visit or even just next door going about her busy life, Emily, almost up to the time of her death, sent messages in prose and verse. Colonel Higginson, with his *Atlantic Monthly* article, "Letter to a Young Contributor",[17] opened the door to a more than twenty-year-long correspondence with the Amherst "Scholar", wherein he acted as the bewildered but fascinated supplier of literary advice never adopted. Although the relationship was a disappointment to her in many respects, she always felt deep gratitude to him for *listening*, because, as she said, he had saved her life by doing so.[18] In the letter where she acknowledges her great debt to Higginson, two or three other sentences reveal her social situation: isolation versus need for communication. In response to Higginson's invitation to her to visit Boston—"You must come down to Boston sometimes? All ladies do."[19]—she politely but emphatically declines the offer with the excuse that "I do not cross my Father's ground to any House or town." In her urgent wish to thank Higginson, failing a personal interview, she relies on letters to convey both thoughts and feelings: "A Letter always feels to me like immortality because it is the mind alone without corporeal friend. Indebted in our talk to attitude and accent, there seems a spectral power in thought that walks alone— . . ."[20]

Thirteen years later, Emily Dickinson repeated the opening line of the letter just quoted from in an almost identical form, "A Letter always seemed to me like Immortality, for is it not the Mind alone, without corporeal friend?".[21] This allows us a glimpse into her workshop. To judge from such repetitions, and the ample evidence of a painstaking, artistic process from mere jottings on scraps of paper through varying worksheet stages to the finished products of fair copies, she seems often to have stored her preliminary literary efforts the way writers frequently do, and reworked them later; sometimes she may not have remembered that she had used a phrase or a line before.

In communicating with the outside world Emily Dickinson employed the medium of poetry as well as that of prose. "This is my letter to the World", she proudly announces in a poem which leaves us in no doubt that she views herself as the transmitter of a message, which as she says in the last stanza is addressed to her "Sweet—countrymen—."[22] At times, indeed, the verse is hard to distinguish from the prose, and vice versa. This has naturally created problems for the editors of Dickinson's letters and poems. For example, a letter-poem sent to friends shortly before their departure for Europe was hesitatively printed in the 1955 edition of the *Poems* to include a question which, as the 1958 edition of the *Letters* shows, is part of the slight prose framework for bracketing the three-line poem which is a less personal statement and consequently more deliberately literary. The "I" of the concluding wellwishing for a happy journey (which is a quotation from the Psalms) corresponds to a more general "We" in the poem, and the direct apostrophe of the opening line,

"Dear", links it with the last line in its immediacy. The character and tone of the stanza is quite different from the prose frame in this matter of personal concern. The following constitutes the whole message:

> Is it too late to touch you, Dear?
>
> We this moment knew—
> Love Marine and Love terrene—
> Love celestial too—
>
> I give his Angels charge—
>   Emily—[23]

Sometimes the poet had difficulty in finding the appropriate setting for her poetic messages. This can be seen in the drafts of a letter replying to one of Helen Hunt Jackson (February, 1885). The prose letter affords only the flimsiest pretext for bringing in two poems, "Take all away from me, but leave me Ecstasy" and "Of God we ask one favor".[24] The themes of the poems concern the ecstasy of the inner life and religious defiance before an impassible and exacting God. The prose contexts for these poems, which contain two of the central themes in her canon, are inappropriately trivial. Earlier in the same year, Emily Dickinson had tried to fit the first poem into a letter-message; in fact the poem is the kernel of the letter, which, typically, glides in and out of prose and verse. These same lines are included in a letter a third time during the year, now as prose.[25] It seems as if, to an ailing Emily Dickinson—she spent much of her days now propped up in bed—they reasserted the crucial importance of the inward life, of the wealth bestowed upon her by Ecstasy.

One of Emily Dickinson's most poignant and, at the same time, most aristically controlled letters—written to Sue after the death of Emily's beloved nephew Gilbert—contains a perfect blend of prose and poetry. The poetic element is there from the opening line, in the diction and the imagery; gradually, the rhythm becomes more metrical; four consecutive sentences written as prose do in fact make up a stanza with three beats to the line, initial capitals, unorthodox "rhymes" faintly suggested (knew–no; Dervish–his), with alliteration (knew–no–niggard; were–wild), consonances (Life–full) and (approximate) assonances (full—Boon).[26] The line following this "prose stanza" is also metrical and poetic. Prose then returns, only to give way to verse still written as prose. After another three prose sentences, the writer breaks out openly into a straightforward poetic stanza, which in its concentrated beauty is a crystalization of her view of the mystery of death and of her profound sense of loss. I quote this remarkable letter in full:

Dear Sue—
  The Vision of Immortal Life has been fulfilled—
  How simply at the last the Fathom comes! The Passenger and not the Sea, we find surprises us—

Gilbert rejoiced in Secrets—
His Life was panting with them—With what menace of Light he cried "Dont tell, Aunt Emily"! Now my ascended Playmate must instruct *me*. Show us, prattling Preceptor, *but the way to thee.*[27]
He knew no niggard moment—His Life was full of Boon—The Playthings of the Dervish were not so wild as his—
No crescent was this Creature—He traveled from the Full—
Such soar, but never set—
I see him in the Star, and meet his sweet velocity in everything that flies—*His Life was like the Bugle, which winds itself away, his Elegy an echo—his Requiem ecstacy—*
Dawn and Meridian in one.
Wherefore would he wait, wronged only of Night, which he left for us—
Without a speculation, our little Ajax spans the whole—

> Pass to thy Rendezvous of Light,
> Pangless except for us—
> Who slowly ford the Mystery
> Which thou hast leaped across!

Emily.[28]

The poems Emily Dickinson sent to her friends were either enclosures on separate sheets, or they were incorporated in the prose text. To Susan Dickinson, who actively shared her literary interests and whose approval the poet strove for,[29] she sent many of her poems as artistic products, without falling back on the excuse provided by the needs of everyday communication. It was natural that Higginson, her literary mentor, should receive the poems undisguised for evaluation and criticism. In later life, she usually incorporated her verses in letters to friends, in part or whole.

Because Emily Dickinson in her later letters often moved freely from prose to poetry, and sometimes actually put down a poem—elsewhere written as verse—as a prose passage, and because the style of the letters is similar to that of the poems, scholars do not always agree on what is and what is not verse in the Dickinson canon. On the manuscript pages of her letters, lines of poetry may spread across the whole page.[30] In reviews of the 1955 Harvard Edition of the *Poems*, variant readings of prose as opposed to poetry have been presented in a few instances.[31] Obviously the letters and the poems were created out of the same need for communication and self-expression; both categories were artistic products: she usually made drafts for both the letters and the poems, particularly in later years; some letters may never have been sent off, some were perhaps not intended for a recipient's eyes.[32] Certain types of poems, for instance the "Wife" poems[33] and other love poems, among them the frankly erotic "Wild Nights—Wild Nights!",[34] were rarely shared with anyone. It is worth noting, however, how confident and bold Emily Dickinson was at the outset of her correspondence with Higginson: in her second letter she included a poem—"There came a Day at Summer's full"

(No. 322)—where the communication of love and the inevitable renunciation are poignantly enacted.

The time, place, and sex of our poet certainly explain sufficiently her reluctance to share her most intimate thoughts and emotions with a listener-reader. But there seems to be more to her "discretion" than these conventions: words, and perhaps especially her own words, both fascinated and awed her to such an extent that she wanted no witness to the expression of her most naked ideas and feelings. Late in life, in apologizing to a friend for repeatedly refusing to see him, she once wrote: "I had hoped to see you, but have no grace to talk, and my own Words so chill and burn me, that the temperature of other Minds is too new an Awe—".[35]

When, in April 1862, Emily Dickinson offered her poems to the world,[36] as she saw it incarnated in the man of letters, Thomas Wentworth Higginson, she probably did so for two main reasons: she felt convinced that she had something to offer as a poet, and, presumably disappointed in her sister-in-law's advice, she realized that she desperately needed the guidance and opinion of a professional. Her growing confidence in her creative faculty and eventual fame as a poet is evidenced both in a letter and a poem probably composed in 1861. In a note to Susan Dickinson acknowledging her praise of a poem, Emily Dickinson writes, "Could I make you and Austin—proud—sometime—a great way off—'twould give me taller feet—".[37] The poetic counterpart is

> I shall keep singing!
> Birds will pass me
> On their way to Yellower Climes—
> Each—with a Robin's expectation—
> I—with my Redbreast—
> And my Rhymes—
>
> Late—when I take my place in summer—
> But—I shall bring a fuller tune—
> Vespers—are sweeter than Matins—Signor—
> Morning—only the seed of Noon—   (No. 250)

She pleaded her case to Higginson: "The Mind is so near itself—it cannot see, distinctly—and I have none to ask—".[38] It was about this time that she copied into one of her "packets" of poems the following stanzas, a statement of purpose and the prayer of a maturing artist:

> This is my letter to the World
> That never wrote to Me—
> The simple News that Nature told—
> With tender Majesty
> Her Message is committed
> To Hands I cannot see—
> For love of Her—Sweet—countrymen—
> Judge tenderly—of Me   (No. 441)[39]

Like so many others of her poems, this one is written in the first person singular. To attempt an identification of the "voice" of a poem with its author is a precarious thing. Emily Dickinson was explicit on this point of speaker as opposed to author when, in her fourth letter to the Colonel, she warned "When I state myself, as the Representative of the Verse—it does not mean—me—but a supposed person."[40] Hesitant, in spite of her boldness in approaching him, and afraid of exposure—"That you will not betray me—it is needless to ask—since Honor is it's [sic] own pawn—"[41]—it seems natural that she should need this protection of the assumed personality; especially since out of the thirteen (possibly twelve[42]) poems she had so far enclosed in her letters to him (in one instance incorporated in a letter), eight are written in the first person singular.[43] Often the "I" describes the processes of nature: a magnificent sunrise; the working of the wind, "that fleshless Chant"; a bird caught in the act of eating an angleworm raw.[44] However, she also included poems of a more personal, confessional character; in addition to "There came a Day at Summer's full", there is the equally personal tribute to an addressee whose "Riches—taught me—Poverty."[45] The speaker in another three poems is a "we", reducing the number of poems without a first person pronoun to only two of the thirteen, a ratio which is fairly representative of her poetry of the years around 1860.[46]

The autobiographical element in poetry and fiction may of course appear in various guises and as a factor of varying importance. One extreme, where nothing but the actual experiences form the substance of the literary product, may be represented by Marcel Proust's almost maniacal attempts to recapture his own past, with subtletly and precision;[47] the other is manifested in an impersonal distillation of reality in which the writer records experiences and events, *erlebt* or, more frequently, imagined, from a more or less detached vantage point. Flaubert, whose goals were comprehensiveness and universality, used the means of impartiality, impersonality, impassivity, and objectivity.[48] Nineteenth-century English poetry because of its lyric strain was often centered on the pronoun "I", and poems of an outright confessional or autobiographical nature occupy a significant part of Romantic as well as Victorian poetry.[49] Ballads and epic poetry written about Romanticism may represent an objective tradition. Although I shall not relate Emily Dickinson's verse to her biography as a more or less faithful record of the events of her life, I suggest that she expressed her thoughts, feelings and parts of her experience in her poems as she did in her letters, and with even greater frankness in the former. Many areas and topics were not touched upon in her correspondence, but the erotic passion of some of her love lyrics can be glimpsed even in her letters, as, for instance, in the so-called "Master" letters,[50] and some of the fragments of her notes to Judge Otis Lord.[51] Her poetry is very much "centrallyrik" to use a Swedish term, that is poetry of a highly personal, often confessional character.[52] Partly because of the similarity to the letters, we may infer that the poems are expressions of the poet herself, and even more fully and freely so than her letters. The two kinds of writing are products of the same emotional and artistic need for expression.

In Emily Dickinson's case then it would seem a fallacious rigorousness to exclude all thought of a connection between the "I" of the poems and Emily Dickinson herself.[53] Her warning to Higginson may be seen as part of the protective mask of the "Young Contributor" to whom he had addressed his article, the "Scholar" dutifully reciting to the great "Preceptor." At the same time, it is of course also a stressing of the greater degree of "detachment" that distinguishes the artistic creation from the straight reporting of fact. Robert Frost insisted on this distinction when he said that a poem is an *act*, not a report.[54] Emily Dickinson's letters are seldom mere reporting; often they present the sort of detachment that characterizes the literary product (also in their prose passages). Her "occasional verse" might be seen as being one step further away from the letters in the direction of the expression of a "supposed person"; their stronger connection to a situation in reality makes them less "detached" than the "pure" verse. Reading through her letters, especially the early ones, one cannot help observing in them a fair amount of posing, another method for achieving detachment and disguise. Emily's brother, on reading some of the Higginson letters after her death, remarked with a smile that his sister "definitely posed" in them.[55] But, it is only fair to add, she probably also "posed" to other correspondents *and* to her brother. Indeed in a way one might say that the poet always "poses", as does the writer of letters who is conscious of an artistic aim beside the practical one of mere communication.

Some of Emily Dickinson's messages in verse are clearly of an occasional type. We may distinguish different kinds of occasional poems in the Dickinson canon. One which can be described as occasional in the full sense of word, is directly addressed and sent to an actual person. This group of poems consists mostly of the verses which apostrophizes or mentions Susan Dickinson by the names "Sue" or "Dollie", the latter a pet-name for Susan.[56] A few of these are extant only in the form of a direct message—for instance poem No. 218, "Is it true, dear Sue?", evidently sent next door to her sister-in-law the moment Emily heard about the birth of Susan's first son. One variant within this group borders on a type of adaptation described below: the special version of a regular packet poem personalized for the occasion. Typical is No. 1400, from which she extracted two stanzas and substituted "Susan" for the original poem's "nature." The effect for the reader-addressee may have depended on her knowledge of the original.[57]

Emily Dickinson had a small set of standard poems to accompany the gift of flowers, leaves, etc. The following is such a poem:

> South Winds jostle them—
> Bumblebees come—
> Hover—hesitate—
> Drink, and are gone—

> Butterflies pause
> On their passage Cashmere—
> I—softly plucking,
> Present them here!   (No. 86)[58]

Sometimes she dispatched poems, whole or in part, as congratulatory or consolatory notes for special occasions. Several elegies belong with this group, for instance:

> Go thy great way!
> The Stars thou meetst
> Are even as Thyself—
> For what are Stars but Asterisks
> To point a human Life?   (No. 1638)[59]

There were also verses which could easily be adapted for the particular addressee, although not apostrophizing the name directly. One of these touches on friendship, "Brother of Ingots—Ah Peru— / Empty the Hearts that purchased you—" (No. 1366). One variant was sent to Sue ("Sister of Ophir"), another commemorated the death of a young Amherst professor ("Brother of Ophir"). Thomas Johnson, in his Dickinson biography, states that "In later years almost all poems were intended for enclosure in letters to friends."[60] Although it is true that these later poems were given their final form as part of a letter or as an enclosure, I think that the verb "were intended for" subordinates the creative act to the stimulus of the external occasion too much. A perusal of Emily Dickinson's later poems and letters would indicate that the *occasion* itself seldom or never prompted the initial composition of the poems; the first drafts of poems, unfinished or fragmentary, probably already existed in the poet's scrap basket; a special event, or the need to reply to a friend's note, then afforded the necessary impetus for a decision on the final form of the often fragmentary lines. Significantly she never sent rough or even semi-final drafts to her correspondents.[61] Often the poem does not actually fit the context of the letter; it seems rather different from the prosaic framework, and more fraught with meaning.

Most of the occasional verse, particularly the openly occasional type, in which the addressee is apostrophized or referred to, is of inferior artistic quality (perhaps because it is not sufficiently "detached", not enough "art"). This circumstance alone would make one hesitate to accept Thomas Johnson's suggestion that poem No. 1620, "Circumference thou Bride of Awe", was written for a special occasion. It was incorporated into a letter to the sculptor Daniel Chester French, on the unveiling (in 1884) of his statue of John Harvard in front of University Hall in Cambridge, Massachusetts, and Johnson believes it was written for this event.[62] The poem involves one of Emily Dickinson's most challenging keywords, "Circumference", and is of high poetic value. The short stanza reads in its worksheet form:

> Circumference thou Bride of Awe
> Possessing thou shalt be

> Possessed by every hallowed Knight
> That dares to covet thee

No other internal or external evidence as to the poem's occasional character is offered by Johnson than that it was incorporated in a letter to the sculptor. But most of the poems of the 1880s were thus sent off, and there seems no reason to select this one as written for an occasion, especially since, according to Johnson, this procedure would apply to almost all of the late poems. (Most of the "Circumference" poems had been written in the early 1860s, that is, the period when Emily Dickinson was most productive.)[63]

To summarize my observations on Emily Dickinson's occasional verse: there is a small, clearly defined group of explicitly occasional poems, mostly directed to Susan Dickinson; a less distinct group of personal messages without explicit mention of the addressee; a few standard poems to accompany the gift of flowers, etc.; a larger group containing poems which were used more than once as messages to friends, in identical or slightly altered form; and, perhaps a special group, much of the later verse, the composition of which, it seems important to emphasize, was not *caused* by an outward event, but was prompted by the immediate need for communication with friends. It cannot be maintained that a characteristic feature of Dickinson's verse is its occasional nature. Although in her later years it often took the final form of a delivered message, it was created by an *inner* need for expression and communication.

Notes

1. *The Letters of Emily Dickinson*, eds. Thomas H. Johnson and Theodora Ward, 3 vols., Cambridge, Mass., 1958, Vol. I, p. 11. This edition will be referred to as *Letters*.

2. *Letters of Emily Dickinson*, ed. M. L. Todd, New York, 1931, pp. 123–132. Cf. also Martha Dickinson Bianchi, *The Life and Letters of Emily Dickinson*, Boston, 1924, p. 32: "[Emily] sent her young friends off into fits of laughter over her impromptu stories . . ."

3. Martha Dickinson Bianchi, *Emily Dickinson Face to Face*, Boston, 1932, pp. 39 f.

4. Quoted in Jay Leyda, *The Years and Hours of Emily Dickinson*, 2 vols., New Haven, 1960, Vol. II, p. 240 from Jenkins' *Christian Union* article, Oct. 24, 1891.

5. Leyda, p. 17.

6. *Letters*, II, p. 473.

7. Quoted from Mable Loomis Todd's notes by Millicent Todd Bingham in *Ancestors' Brocades: The Literary Debut of Emily Dickinson*, New York, 1945, p. 12.

8. From "My Personal Acquaintance with Emily Dickinson" by the poet's cousin, Clara Newman Turner, c. 1900 (quoted by Leyda, II, p. 481). Cf. Leyda, I, p. xxi: "A major device of Emily Dickinson's writing, both in her poems and in her letters, was what might be called the 'omitted center' . . . the deliberate skirting of the obvious. . . ."

9. In a letter of [March?] 1863 to Austin Dickinson (Leyda, II, p. 76).

10. *Letters*, II, p. 415.

11. Transcript made by Joseph B. Lyman of a letter reportedly written by Emily Dickinson (quoted by Richard B. Sewall, "The Lyman Letters: New Light on Emily Dickinson and Her Family", *Massachusetts Review*, Autumn 1965, p. 766).

12. *Letters*, II, p. 612, June 1878.

13. Cf. *The Poems of Emily Dickinson, Including variant readings critically compared with all known manuscripts*, ed. Thomas H. Johnson, 3 vols., Cambridge, Mass., 1955, No. 320. This edition will be referred to as the Harvard Edition, abbreviated HE, or as *Poems*.

14. Quoted by Sewall, op. cit., p. 774, from Lyman's transcript.

15. *Poems*, III, p. 1197.

16. Quoted in Leyda, II, p. 473.

17. Vol. IX, No. LIV, April 1862, pp. 401–411.

18. *Letters*, II, p. 460.

19. *Letters*, p. 462, May 11, 1869.

20. *Letters*, p. 460.

21. *Letters*, III, p. 752.

22. *Poems*, No. 441 (early 1862).

23. *Letters*, III, p. 865. Notice the repetition of the final phrase in two other letters of 1885; one to Samuel Bowles, Jr.: "I give 'his Angels Charge—' " (*Letters*, III, p. 887), the other to Mrs. J. A. Sweetser: ",I give his angels charge!' " (ibid., p. 877).

24. *Poems*, Nos. 1640 and 1601. In the *Letters* (III, pp. 866–868), the date given for the later poem is March 1885, not 1884 as stated in the note on the poem in the 1955 *Poems*. Cf. David J. M. Higgins, "Emily Dickinson's Prose", *Emily Dickinson: A Collection of Critical Essays* (ed. Richard B. Sewall, Englewood Cliffs, N.J., 1963), where these drafts are discussed (pp. 160–166). Cf. also Theodora Ward, *The Capsule of the Mind: Chapters in the Life of Emily Dickinson*, Cambridge, Mass., 1961, p. 112.

25. Letter to Samuel Bowles, Jr. (*Letters*, III, p. 888). Poem No. 323, "As if I asked a common Alms", presents another example of verse lines being written as prose: of three MSS, two are arranged as verse, the last, written c. 1884, as prose (*Poems*, I, pp. 253 f.). It is interesting to note that of the eight-line poem's initial capitals, four (those introducing every other line) have been kept, thus indicating that for the writer the passage retained some of its poetic features.

26. For a discussion of unorthodox rhymes, see Brita Lindberg-Seyersted, *The Voice of the Poet* (Cambridge, Mass., 1968), Chap. III.

27. Italics mine in this and the following sentences.

28. *Letters*, III, p. 799, early Oct. 1883.

29. See commentary on, e.g., No. 216 in *Poems*, I, pp. 152–154.

30. E.g. poem No. 1648 incorporated in letter No. 1043. Cf. review of HE by John L. Spicer in the *Boston Public Library Quarterly*, VIII, July 1956, pp. 136–140, esp. pp. 137–138 which reproduces a facsimile of the letter.

31. See reviews by, e.g., Spicer (see above n. 1) and Jay Leyda, "The Poems of Emily Dickinson", *New England Quarterly*, XXIX, June 1956, pp. 239–245.

32. I am thinking of the so-called "Master" letters.

33. E.g. Nos. 199, 271, 461, and 1737. No. 1072, "Title Divine—is mine!", *was* sent, probably to Samuel Bowles. A later copy was sent to Sue.

34. No. 249. For other love poems presumably not sent, see, e.g., Nos. 246, 247, 339, 453, 456, and 480.

35. *Letters*, III, p. 758.

36. In the first letter, she enclosed four poems, the composition of which stretched over the years 1859–1862 (according to the HE chronology): "Safe in their Alabaster Chambers—" (No. 216), "I'll tell you how the Sun rose—" (No. 318), "The nearest Dream recedes—unrealized—" (No. 319), and "We play at Paste—" (No. 320).

37. *Letters*, II, p. 380. The young Emily Dickinson is quoted as having said: "I have a

horror of death; the dead are so soon forgotten. But when I die, they'll have to remember me" (see Leyda, II, p. 481).

38. *Letters*, II, p. 403.

39. Early 1862. For a description of the "packets" (Thomas Johnson's term), see *Poems*, I, p. xviii. Emily Dickinson's sister referred to them as "volumes" (ibid.). The poet herself never mentions them.

40. *Letters*, II, p. 412, July 1862.

41. *Letters*, p. 403, April 15, 1862. Emily Dickinson consistently wrote the pronoun in the possessive case "it's". In the following pages I shall reproduce without notice all her idiosyncrasies of spelling.

42. Leyda suggests the possible inclusion of a fourth poem, "A Bird came down the Walk—" (No. 328), in the April 25, 1862 letter to Higginson (Leyda, II, p. 56). His authority for this conjecture is Higginson's own statement to the fact in his *Atlantic Monthly* article of Oct. 1891. On the evidence of the folds of the MS. letters and poems, Thomas Johnson believes that Higginson's memory was at fault (see *Letters*, II, p. 405).

43. I.e. almost two thirds of the total number (61.5%). The corresponding percentage for all poems of 1860 is 60.9% (39 poems out of 64).

44. *Poems*, Nos. 318, 321, and 328.

45. *Poems*, No. 299. It has been suggested that Emily Dickinson wrote this poem in memory of her "earliest friend", Benjamin Newton (see *Poems*, I commentary p. 220).

46. For a statistical analysis of the output of three separate years, see Lindberg-Seyersted, p. 32.

47. A Proust biographer, George D. Painter, classifies *A la recherche du temps perdu* as a "creative biography" (*Marcel Proust: A Biography*, Volume I, London, 1959, p. xiii). Another scholar terms it as "*essai* of self-analysis" (Leo Bersani, *Marcel Proust: The Fictions of Life and of Art*, New York, 1965. p. 4).

48. Cf. B. F. Bart, "Flaubert's Concept of the Novel", *PMLA*, LXXX, March 1965, pp. 84–90.

49. Cf. Kristian Smidt, "Point of View in Victorian Poetry", *English Studies, A Journal of English Letters and Philology*, XXXVIII, Feb. 1957, pp. 1–12. Smidt says apropos of the "gigantic 'I'–consciousness" (of an Arnoldian, rather than Emersonian kind: self-dependence, not self-reliance) which arose in the Victorian period: This 'I'-consciousness must have been one of the main reasons for the extraordinary 19th-century spate of poetry in the first person, particularly of the confessions and the autobiographical pieces in which we find the poets grappling directly with the problem of their own age and of all time" (p. 9).

50. *Letters*, II, Nos. 187, 233, and 248. The editor suggests that the Rev. Charles Wadsworth may have inspired the earliest letter. Millicent Todd Bingham (*Emily Dickinson's Home: Letters of Edward Dickinson and His Family*, New York, 1955, p. 421) regards Samuel Bowles as another possible "Master". Theodora Ward, after surveying the possible candidates, leaves the question open, with a strong suggestion for some hitherto totally unknown man, "a man who came into her life for only a short time" (*The Capsule of the Mind*, p. 153). Jay Leyda also believes that the "Master" is not to be found among the men already known (*The Years and Hours of Emily Dickinson*, p. lxi). It would seem that there may be two addressees: one for No. 187, and another for Nos. 233 and 248, the tone of the former letter being quite different from that of the other two, written later.

51. E.g. *Letters*, II, Nos. 559–563; III, Nos. 645, 750, 780, 790, 842, and 843.

52. In *Svensk Uppslagsbok*, 2nd ed., Malmo, 1947, "centrallyrik" is thus defined: "lyrik av djup och väsentlig art, som utgör ett omedelbart (ej berättande el. reflekterande) uttryck för diktarens känsla och stämning." Goethe's 'Uber allen Gipfeln" is often given as an example of "centrallyrik". The *OED* defines *lyric* as "directly expressing the poet's own thoughts and

sentiments"; the OED definition corresponds to the Swedish "omedelbart . . . uttryck för diktarens känsla" but seems a wider definition. *Dictionary of World Literature*, ed. Joseph T. Shipley, New Revised Edition, Paterson, N.J., 1964, has a brief definition: "the general use of 'lyric': a (usually) short, personal poem." Cf. John Stuart Mill, "Thoughts on Poetry and Its Varieties", *Dissertations and Discussions, Political, Philosophical, and Historical*, Vol. I, London (1859) 1867: "Poetry is feeling, confessing itself to itself in moments of solitude . . ." (p. 71). "Lyric poetry . . . is . . . more eminently and peculiarly poetry than any other . . ." (p. 85). I shall use "lyric" to cover both kinds: "centrallyrik" as well as the wider concept of the personal poem which may also include reflection, not only feeling and mood.

53. In *The Capsule of the Mind*, Theodora Ward analyzes Emily Dickinson's inner life by means of the poems and the letters; the author acknowledges the "serious danger of drawing false inferences" (p. vii), but claims as a basis for her procedure the conviction that "the poet himself speaks through [the poem]" (p. viii). Her postulate seems reasonable, as does her exemplification of it in her six "Chapters in the Life of Emily Dickinson".

54. See Reuben A. Brower, *The Poetry of Robert Frost: Constellations of Intention*, New York, 1963, p. 3.

55. Quoted from Mabel Loomis Todd's journal by Millicent Todd Bingham in *Ancestors' Brocades*, p. 167. In "Dramatic Poses in the Poetry of Emily Dickinson" (unpubl. diss., Stanford Univ., 1962), Thomas R. Arp treats of poses adopted by Emily Dickinson in poems and letters.

56. Addressed to or mentioning "Sue" or "Susan" are Nos. 14 ("One Sister have I in our house"), 218 ("Is it true, dear Sue?"), 818 (variant, "I could not drink it, Sue"), 1400 (variant, "But Susan is a Stranger yet—"), 1401 ("To own a Susan of my own"); referring to "Dollie" are Nos. 51 ("I often passed the village"), 156 ("You love me—you are sure—"), and 158 ("Dying! Dying in the night!"). Nos. 818 and 1400 are variants of packet copies, evidently "personalized" for the occasion. Other poems of this type with other addressees than Susan Dickinson are 163, 222, and 1410. No. 227 is another clearly occasional poem, not naming the addressee, but including the poet's name.

57. See also No. 1619, "Not knowing when the Dawn will come", which in another version commemorating the death of Helen Hunt Jackson substitutes the authoress for Dawn: "Not knowing when Herself may come".

58. This poem was included, with a flower, in her second letter to Higginson (see Spicer, review *B. P. L. Quarterly*, p. 142). Other "flower" poems are Nos. 1094 and 1579.

59. Sent to Judge Lord's relative B. Kimball (see *Letters*, III, pp. 860 f.) and to another friend (ibid., p. 863). Other elegies are Nos. 164, 1489, and 1599. No. 1156 is a congratulatory note.

60. *Emily Dickinson: An Interpretive Biography*, Cambridge, Mass., 1955, p. 52.

61. See *Poems*, III, commentary p. 1081.

62. *Poems*, III, commentary p. 1112.

63. Other critics differ on the role and number of occasional poems; see, e.g., Richard B. Sewall, ed., *Emily Dickinson: A Collection of Critical Essays*, p. 3: "We are thus constantly reminded of the occasional nature of many of the poems." Albert J. Gelpi, *Emily Dickinson: The Mind of the Poet*, Cambridge, Mass., 1965, p. 126, n.*: "[The poem 'Circumference thou Bride of Awe'] is one of the very few poems of Emily's written for an occasion."

Proud Ephemeral

Hyatt H. Waggoner*

To Emerson's way of thinking, the profile of a sphere implies a center. The essay "Circles," of which the poem "Circles," prefixed to it, is a partial condensation, begins with the eye, "the first circle," moves outward to the horizon, which is a segment of the spherical earth, and then back to the center to define it in the third sentence of the essay: "St. Augustine described the nature of God as a circle whose centre was everywhere, and its circumference nowhere." That one may realize the presence of God everywhere, anywhere, in all experience, is the unstated Emersonian conviction underlying the poem. *This* is what would make a new birth possible, if nature's proud ephemerals only knew it. It seemed to Emerson that man's situation was at once precarious and immensely hopeful.

Emily Dickinson made it her business as a poet to scan the profile of the sphere, but the harder she scanned it, the less she thought she knew what it signified. Perhaps the profile of the sphere, when fully understood, would turn out to be a "purposeless circumference," an emblem not of birth but of death. Perhaps at the center there was only an emptiness and a silence. Perhaps man could not bear what was signified. More remote from the mystical tradition than Emerson, she devoted herself to attempting to define what Emerson had said was intrinsically undefinable. If Emerson's faith, which rested ultimately on a *way* of "seeing," was only partially and theoretically available to her, at least she knew what it *felt* like to be, as she put it, "a speck upon a ball," a proud ephemeral clinging precariously to nowhere. Preferring the more imagistic word "evanescent" to Emerson's "ephemeral" as a description of the dying self, she spent a lifetime exploring the ambiguities latent in Emerson's paradoxical combination of "ephemeral" with "proud."

Her personal situation and her psychic necessities joined forces with her religious and philosophic heritage to make the experience of living in constant awareness of the coming of death, and the imaginative realization of dying as the climactic experience of living, become the subjects that increasingly preoccupied her and that give her verse its special quality. Like Pain and Bradstreet and Taylor before her, she seldom lost sight of the grave. They would have agreed perfectly with the definition she offered her Norcross cousins in a letter of 1863: "Life is death we're lengthy at, death the hinge to life." Death and Immortality became the chief speakers in a poetic debate she carried on with herself on the subject of the evanescence, or the possible permanence, of life and love.

But of course is it not necessary to go back to the Puritan poets of the seventeenth century, of whom she so often and so sharply reminds us, to

*From Hyatt Waggoner, *American Poets From the Puritans to the Present* (Boston: Houghton Mifflin, 1968) pp. 181–222. © 1968 by Hyatt Waggoner. Reprinted by permission of Houghton Mifflin Co.

find an analogue for her sensibility. The Puritan mind was still intact in Amherst, and not unknown even in Concord, however contemptuously Emerson might ignore its presence and the truths it witnessed to. Emerson's own Aunt Mary Moody Emerson had ridden through Concord on a donkey dressed in her shroud. She had made the shroud herself and had worn it daily as an outer garment, to remind herself, and perhaps others, of mortality. Her idiosyncrasy seemed to Emerson, who was fond of her and felt indebted, a charming example of a self-reliant willingness to follow "whim." If Dickinson had known Aunt Mary, surely she would have understood better than Emerson why one might thus choose to try to get in the habit of the tomb. She herself in the end chose to wear only white, a color that contained as many ambiguities for her as it had for Melville in his explication of "The Whiteness of the Whale."

But Emerson was perceptive about his Aunt Mary in one respect: she did not really share the attitudes of the new age he was helping to initiate; she was old-fashioned and in the end rather out of touch. But there was nothing old-fashioned about Dickinson. However she might share a style of life, created as a symbolic gesture, with Emerson's aunt, her mind was thoroughly contemporary. Comparisons with the Puritans, or even with Emerson's eccentric relative, will prove thoroughly misleading if they suggest that she ought to be thought of as typical of an earlier age rather than her own. Her seclusion was not from books or ideas. Intellectually, she was a woman of her time with an extremely intelligent and well-stocked mind. Alice James's *Diary* provides a closer analogue to her literary situation than Anne Bradstreet's *Tenth Muse*.

The sister of Henry James and William James was eighteen years younger than Emily Dickinson, but she died only six years later. In 1889, already an invalid for years and knowing she had not long to live, she turned from keeping a commonplace book to keeping a personal diary. Her motive for the change she put down as her first entry: "I think that if I get into the habit of writing a bit about what happens, or rather doesn't happen, I may lose a little of the sense of loneliness and desolation which abides with me." In the entries that follow, "Life is reduced," in the words of Leon Edel in the Introduction, "largely to the simple existential fact—as it was for her. . . . The claim of life against the claim of death—this is the assertion of every page . . ." Reading it after her death, brother Henry thought it constituted "a new claim for the family renown."

That she had hoped for this result is nowhere explicit but may be guessed not only from the care with which she dictated revisions in her final entries, after she was too weak to write, but from the definition of genius she quoted inaccurately from brother William's *Psychology*, a definition she could not fail to see as encouraging to the literary ambition of a dying woman keeping a diary: "William says in his *Psychology*: 'Genius, in truth, is little more than the faculty of perceiving in an unhabitual way.' This seems to the sisterly mind, or heart rather, more felicitous than the long-accustomed 'infinite capacity for taking pains' . . ."

Looking at life from the perspective of death, reducing all issues finally to "the claim of life against the claim of death"—such a way of perceiving was no longer common in the last half of the nineteenth century, as it had been among the Puritans. It tended to be characteristic now only of invalids or the very elderly. It was not, as William James was soon to put it, "healthy-minded." (But as James also said, a little later, "Even prisons and sick-rooms have their special revelations.") Whether healthy-minded (whatever that means) or not, in Dickinson's poems, as in Alice James's *Diary*, it produced an awareness that broke through the habits, proprieties, and utilities that normally protect us from too sharp a realization of experience. Knowing herself a proud ephemeral, as Emerson had put it, the poet scanned both the "profile of the sphere," the circumference of reality, and its minutest irregularities, searching for a revelation of meaning that would make a "new genesis" possible. She saw all things freshly, as though for the first, and the last, time. The "genius" of Dickinson's poetry, that which gives it both its uniqueness and its value, rests finally on an unhabitual way of perceiving, an angle of vision that found both formal and thematic expression.

A Plank In Reason   John Cody*

One will inevitably misunderstand and trivialize much of Emily Dickinson's life and poetry if one fails to grasp the full intensity of her suffering and the magnitude of her collapse. For this reason let me state at the onset my thesis that the crisis Emily Dickinson suffered following the marriage of her brother was a psychosis.[1] The proof of this consists in the poet's description of psychological states that occur only in psychosis and in explicit statements in prose and verse which can scarcely be interpreted in any other way.

One such statement, already quoted, occurs in a letter to her cousins. Here Emily Dickinson speaks of having a "snarl in the brain which don't unravel yet,"[2] the phrase being embedded in a paragraph remarkable for its tense and nightmarish quality. What can this "snarl in the brain" be but a delusion which the poet herself recognizes as such? A complex of powerfully obsessive thoughts obtaining a strangle hold on one's mental life might conceivably constitute a "snarl in the brain." This and a state of

*From John Cody, *After Great Pain: The Inner Life of Emily Dickinson* (Cambridge, Mass.: Belknap Press of Harvard Univ. Press, 1971), pp. 291–315. Reprinted by permission of the author and the Belknap Press of Harvard University Press. © 1971 by the President and Fellows of Harvard College.

psychotic confusion seem to be the only two conditions which would justify such a description. The rest of the paragraph, however, rules out the neurotic obsessive state. The intense fear, the poet's shutting herself up in her room, her need to keep all the gas jets burning to light up the imaginary danger—these are not the concomitants of neurotic obsessive-compulsive states. Can there be serious doubt that here Emily Dickinson is disclosing the fact that she has undergone a psychotic episode? Certainly the poems support this conclusion.

In poem no. 280 (about 1861), "I felt a Funeral, in my Brain," the poet describes an experience of gradually increasing depression which finally becomes overwhelming to such a degree that it seemed to her "That Sense was breaking through." Finally there comes the line "And then a Plank in Reason, broke, / And I dropped down." She is here saying that she suffered a prostrating depressive illness which culminated in a loss of rationality.

It has been argued that the "I" in Emily Dickinson's poems does not refer to herself but, as she said, to a "supposed person." But the poem depicts not an event, which can easily be invented, but an experience. We must ask ourselves whether anyone, even a poet, can portray a feeling state that he has not himself undergone. And if one grant that this is possible, what could possibly motivate a person to attempt to express what he never felt? It may be replied that Emily Dickinson knew what ordinary depressions were and may even have had some acquaintance with severe neurotic ones and that, drawing on such experiences, she could imaginatively have extrapolated and projected the psychotic intensification of depression that is expressed in the poem. However, the intense depersonalization expressed in the phrase "I thought— / My Mind was going numb" and the sense of estrangement conveyed by the image of the universe resonating with the poet's projected despair like a mighty tolling bell convey an intensity of disintegration and a confounding of inner experiences with outer reality which reflect a profound insight into the specific pain of the psychotic state. Where could this insight have come from if not from Emily Dickinson's own inner life? The simplest and most natural explanation is that in this poem Emily Dickinson is talking about herself, that she is describing a real experience which actually happened to her, and that, in the line "And then a Plank in Reason, broke," she is revealing that she had been the victim of a psychological crisis that was not an ego-sparing and relatively benign neurosis, but a reason-disrupting, prostrating psychosis.

Poem no. 937 (about 1864) gives further support to this conclusion in the perfection of its description of a psychotic thought disorder. The poem reads:

> I felt a Cleaving in my Mind—
> As if my Brain had split—

I tried to match it—Seam by Seam—
But could not make them fit.

The thought behind, I strove to join
Unto the thought before—
But Sequence ravelled out of Sound
Like Balls—upon a Floor

Here, directly and without equivocation, the poet discloses her awareness that her thinking has become disordered. Her mind feels "split"; she has an urgent need to reestablish the broken continuity of her intellectual processes. She vainly invokes conscious effort to correct and order the play of mental operations that ordinarily proceed spontaneously and effortlessly. Thought now follows thought without the usual connecting links, seemingly arbitrarily and incoherently. She strives to join one idea to another, but all sense of logical sequence is gone and she is unable to restore it by an act of will. The final two lines are obscure and one cannot be certain what image the poet had in mind. The obscurity may even be deliberate and meant as a graphic demonstration of the am biguity and confusion produced by the deranged mental functioning.

A popular interpretation is that the "Balls" upon the "Floor" create an image of confusion—with balls of yarn dropped and rolling in all directions and becoming hopelessly entangled, rather like a "snarl in the brain." But balls of yarn do not unravel; they unwind, and they make no sound, which in the poem is said to be unraveled of sequence. "Sequence ravelled out of Sound" therefore may possibly mean that the regular patterns of thought construction and their vocal expression became disrupted, lost their normal rhythm, and trailed off into silence like the sound a ball makes when dropped on a floor: the ball strikes the floor, bounces in ever-diminishing oscillations until the sounds of impact crowd together, lose their intensity, and dwindle into silence. Whether or not either reading is correct, the intent of the poem is clear; it confesses that the poet reached a point at which she was no longer in command of her thought processes.

The foregoing references—the snarl in the brain, the broken plank in reason, and the cleavage in the mind—appear to be sufficient justification in themselves for concluding that the crisis in Emily Dickinson's life was a psychosis. With this conclusion as guide I will examine, solely as psychological documents, other poems, my aim being a deepened understanding of the poet's inner life.

In the preceding chapter, beginning with the simplest nonspecific depressions and anxieties, I traced in her letters the emotional repercussions of Emily Dickinson's life situation and inferred the progression of these reactions to ever more highly elaborated, idiosyncratic, and crippling symptoms. It is not surprising that the poems, intrinsically more self-revelatory than the letters, provide further evidence of the same psychological trends. Although many of the poems reflect commonplace emotional states, others clearly communicate anguished and broken reactions to markedly adverse situations. These portray the ego in collapse, crushed between irreconcilable opposing forces: on one side, prodigious inner needs, on the other, unyielding environmental facts. These poems have almost no existing prose counterparts. They uniquely reveal a height of turmoil and psychic disintegration only obscurely adumbrated in the remainder of our biographical sources.

In my analysis no effort will be made to review the poems in the chronological order of their composition. Instead, they will be arranged in a sequence that corresponds to the gradually developing clinical picture of an actual psychotic illness. What justifies this approach is the fact that it is the only way to render the process understandable. Also, for my purposes, the chronology of composition is more or less irrelevant: A large percent of Emily Dickinson's poems could not have been written at the time the poet was living through the circumstances they depict. Obviously, a person depressed to the point of immobility, or one whose thought processes are unable to follow a rational sequence, cannot write a coherent poem. Emily Dickinson's poems are, almost without exception, perfectly coherent. Therefore, the poems evoked by her illness must largely have been written in retrospect. Moreover, there is no reason to believe that in composing the poems delineating her breakdown the poet necessarily followed the same order in which the symptoms actually presented themselves. A further reason for disregarding chronology is that the creation of most of the poems under consideration occurred within a two- or three-year period—not a long interval in a psychiatric illness.

What I shall attempt is a reconstruction of the phases of Emily Dickinson's illness from the point of view of its phenomenology. The underlying dynamics leading to the illness have been covered in preceding chapters. Here I am concerned only with the form the illness took and the sequence of clinical appearances it presented—that is, the way the poet herself felt her illness, comprehended it, and recorded it.

Psychosis, or the breaking down of the sense of reality, consists in the encroachment upon consciousness of desires, memories, fears, and former states of the personality that are ordinarily unconscious—the eruption of unconscious life into the field of consciousness and the conclusion and disorganization that ensues.

Let me start with the early harbingers of illness as well as with certain premonitions and predispositions of the poet that existed before her emotional and psychic disturbance became manifest. A precarious psychological state at this time, though subjectively intense, would not have been such as to command the attention of others. It appears unlikely, for example, that Emily Dickinson's parents, in the early stages of her illness, would have been aware of its potential seriousness. For the same reason, many of the poems reviewed and interpreted in the next few pages may not impress one as unduly ominous.

As I have noted, Emily Dickinson's earliest distress consisted of simple depression. Her letters and poems indicate that her illness began with feelings of sadness that gradually increased in intensity. Some cherished dream had to be relinquished and was replaced by a feeling of despair. She mourned the loss of her hopes with accumulating vehemence and desolation. Probably it was in the later phases of this period of deepening melancholy that the earliest prodromal manifestations of her breakdown occurred.

The early stages of her depression were deceptively mild. In poem no. 111 (about 1859) the poet contemplates the joy and friendliness of nature and asks herself why she has feelings of sadness: "Wherefore mine eye thy silver mists . . . ?" In no. 353 (about 1862) she describes the deliberate forcing of a smile, the careful preparation of a happy facade for the purpose of deceiving others and hiding the misery inside. The same kind of smiling depression is presented in no. 514 (about 1862), in which she speaks of a woman's smile as being painful to see because one knew that it was erected to disavow and conceal a mortal wound.

Depressive reactions foreboding a psychotic outcome are almost invariably accompanied by feelings of remorse and guilt and a sense of unworthiness sometimes so all-encompassing that suicide may seem to be the only appropriate recourse. In poem 744 (about 1863) the poet tells of being haunted by guilt at the memory of "Departed Acts," and she calls her condition the "Adequate of Hell." The poem goes on to speak of the soul's past as being illuminated with a match, as if it were something unwholesome and sinister, hidden in a cellar. The same theme appears in poem 753 (about 1863), in which the poet speaks of quailing before the accusations and disdain of her soul, which she finds more painful to endure than "a finger of Enamelled Fire." Again in no. 1598 (about 1884) "Conscience" is represented as seeking her pillow at night, questioning " 'Did you' or 'Did you not' " and threatening damnation and hell, "the Phosphorous of God.

Either in her depression or in the subsequent phase of impending reality severance with its attendant panic, Emily Dickinson seems to have contemplated suicide. Such a measure is, of course, familiar to everyone as a consequence of depression. It is less well known that self-destruction may commonly be resorted to as a final desperate effort to escape the terror that accompanies a threatened personality disintegration in psychosis. The Dickinson poems that deal with the suicide theme are exclusively depressive in nature. If such a means of deliverance occurred to her at the height of her break with reality, she did not record the fact.

A kind of romantic languor invests certain of the early suicide poems. In no. 50 (about 1858) she writes as one who, having decided to die, contemplates the things she will miss and wonders what will be the reaction of her environment, including her family, to her death.

In no. 51 (about 1858) she describes a cemetery. She says that when she passed by it as a girl she did not know the year of her death. The implication is that she now knows when this event will take place. The poem concludes with a message to a female loved one to the effect that the poet will wait for her in the grave and will welcome her when the beloved herself dies.

In another poem, no. 146 (about 1859), the poet wonders if anyone would care if "On such a night" a "little figure" (presumably herself) should slip from its chair and lie "Too sound asleep." She then paints a picture of the busyness of life and reflects that all activities and aspirations have a common goal—the "little knoll" in the graveyard. None of these poems have great power and they seem to represent a sentimental toying with the idea of self-destruction at times of mild depression.

Perhaps, as no. 1692 (undated) suggests, the poet once actually attempted suicide. Here she speaks of the difficulty of asserting one's "right to perish" because the "Universe" will do all it can to thwart the effort.

A common theme of nineteenth-century romanticism is the fantasy of the reunion of sundered lovers beyond the grave. In no. 277 (about 1861) Emily Dickinson considers the implications of not awaiting a natural death. What if she should kill herself, she asks ("burst the fleshly Gate"), to be with her beloved? The reward, according to the poem, consists in being beyond the reach of the pains and frustrations of earth, whose clamor would then be meaningless to her.

More somber and suggestive of an earnestness lacking in the poems are some of the prose comments on the theme of suicide. In an 1877 letter Emily alludes to Austin's unhappiness in his marriage, speaks of his insomnia, and concludes shrewdly, "Sorrow is unsafe when it is real sorrow."[3] What worries her seems to be her belief, drawn from her experience of years before, that grief is a menace because it makes the thought of suicide enticing. Similarly, following a long silence on Higginson's part after his wife's death, Emily grew worried and wrote, "I cannot resist to write again, to ask if you are safe? Danger is not at first, for then we are unconscious, but in the after—slower—Days."[4] And to her cousin Louise Norcross she expresses consolation for some sorrow and implies that once she too had felt an impulse to die, "when rallying requires more effort than to dissolve life, and death looks choiceless."[5] And in the following undated fragment, the designated experience in which "Life stands straight," though not clearly grief, must be that or some similar reaction of profound shock or dismay, for its menace is similar. "Tis a dangerous moment for any one," she writes, "when the meaning goes out of things and Life stands straight—and punctual—and yet no contents come."[6]

Fortunately for American letters, Emily Dickinson braved out her despair and did not destroy herself to escape the frightful anxieties of psychological disorganization. To conceive and carry out a plan for self-destruction presupposes a certain degree of organization and available energy. The poems testify that when the poet's crisis came she was too prostrated by it to be able to implement such an escape, even if that is what she had desired. The early stages of her depression were apparently not unbearable. But the depressive symptoms gradually became mixed with more malignant psychic processes.

The earliest subjective experiences of an impending psychotic episode may be transient and minor breaks with reality that occur suddenly and persist only for a few seconds or minutes. These minor estrangements and depersonalizations are almost invariably concomitants of severe depressive states and in themselves do not necessarily presage a psychosis. Yet every psychotic episode probably gives advance notice of its imminent arrival through increasingly severe and protracted experiences of estrangement and depersonalization, such as I have noted in Emily Dickinson's letters. The poet has also given numerous vivid descriptions of them in her poems. For one lacking her expressive genius the essence of these experiences is extremely difficult to convey in words.

Paul Ferdern, a close friend and pupil of Freud, was one of the first psychoanalysts to concern himself with these phenomena. Regarding the experience of depersonalization, he wrote, "we all know the earnest, and always somewhat uncanny, complaints with which severe cases of depersonalization describe their condition or rather their changing condition. The outer world appears substantially unaltered, but yet different; not so spontaneously, so actually, near or far; not clear, warm, friendly and familiar; not really and truly existing and alive; more as if in a dream and yet different from a dream. At heart the patient feels as if he were dead; and he feels like this because he does not feel. His feeling, wishing, thinking and memory processes have become different, uncertain, intolerably changed. And yet the patient knows everything correctly, his faculties of perception, of intellect, and of logic have not suffered at all . . . time, place and causality are recognized and properly applied in finding one's bearings, but they are not possessed spontaneously and self evidently."[7] When Emily Dickinson wrote: "I heard, as if I had no Ear," and "I saw, as if my Eye were on Another," and "I dwelt, as if Myself were out" (poem no. 1039, about 1865), she was probably recollecting an experience similar to the ones described by Federn.

The merging of Emily Dickinson's depressive symptoms into episodes of severe estrangement is clearly traceable. Although she seems at times to have thought that her despair dropped upon her with catastrophic suddenness, the letters and the poems reveal an insidious onset. The depressed moods she has recorded swelled gradually from mild loneliness and melancholy to crushing agony and frustration. The onset of a relentless state of estrangement seems to have been a feature of the depths of this depression.

The psychoanalyst Marguerite Sechehaye described the symptom of estrangement in her interpretive supplement to the *Autobiography of a Schizophrenic Girl*. The body of the book was written by Madame Sechehaye's patient Renée following her recovery after years of intensive full-time care in the therapist's home. Madame Sechehaye writes, "Renée's introspection reveals that the earliest disturbing subjective symptom bears uniquely on the perception of reality. Suddenly objects become enormous, cut off, detached, without relation to one another; space appears limitless . . . Normally the world of objects is perceived on a relative scale, each thing in its allotted space, coordinated by angles of vision. Each object is perceived in its relation to another, and in relation to the ground on which it stands. Further, a utilitarian function is attributed to seen objects: a chair is used to sit on. [In states of estrangement] objects no longer appear in inter-individual relationships. The spaces separating and arranging them on different planes are eliminated. This is why each object appears as a whole in itself, cut away, detached, larger than life, and why space seems limitless, without depth or control, without the successive planes lending a third dimension . . . In proportion as Renée loses subjective self-awareness, she increasingly localizes her feelings in things. The boundaries separating the inner world of thinking from the outer world of reality shade off, then fade out. Objects are alive, they become threatening, they sneer, they torment her."[8]

Renée describes one of her own experiences of estrangement thus: "One day, while I was in the principal's office, suddenly the room became enormous . . . Everything was exact, smooth, artificial, extremely tense; the chairs and tables seemed models placed here and there. Pupils and teachers were puppets revolving without cause, without objective. It was as though reality, attenuated, had slipped away from all these things and these people. Profound dread overwhelmed me, and as though lost, I looked around desperately for help. I heard people talking but I did not grasp the meaning of the words. The voices were metallic, without warmth or color."[9] When Emily Dickinson writes, "I clutched at sounds— / I groped at shapes— / I touched the tops of Films— / I felt the Wilderness roll back / Along my Golden lines" (no. 430, about 1862), she appears to be describing an experience very much like Renée's. The poem projects a desperate need to hold onto reality, which has become tenuous and impoverished. The sounds and shapes of the active, real world are slipping through her fingers; her senses no longer put her in contact with the living world, now hazy and without substance. The familiar environment, transformed and estranged, becomes an uninhabited wasteland. In four lines the poet has given us a powerful recreation of an experience of intense estrangement.

Emily Dickinson's repeatedly used symbols, the sea and the volcano, were eminently appropriate for expressing the encroaching menace of her mental illness. The inner transformations that lead to the breakdown of rational thought and reality contact generate two fears: (1) that one will lose control over one's erotic and destructive impulses: and (2) that one's unique and separate mental existence will undergo disintegration in a psychic death. The first of these is related to the "volcano poems," the second, to those concerned with the sea.

It has been stated previously that a psychosis is a process in which instinctual and repressed elements of the psyche, ordinarily unconscious, burst into consciousness, destroying the integrity of the personality. Environmental stresses combined with constitutional predispositions precipitate this breakthrough. It results in the ego's yielding its autonomy before the pressures of previously subjugated destructive and sexual impulses to such an extent that the ego no longer controls them, at which point they erupt into waking life like burning lava. In the most benign of the "volcano poems" (no. 1748, undated) the poet remarks, in images of a slumbering volcano, on the inscrutable reticence of nature, which keeps its plan for destructiveness a secret. Then she speculates upon the possible reasons why human nature cannot do the same. In poem no 1705 (undated) she wryly remarks that she need not travel to view a volcano—that one may be contemplated at home. It has been said that in this poem she alludes to her father's red hair and fiery personality, but other "volcano poems" suggest a degree of potential destructiveness that she would have been unlikely to ascribe consciously to her father. For example, no. 175 (about 1860) states that great inner pain and destructiveness ("Fire, and smoke, and gun") may be long concealed, and the features of one's face may not for some time betray the violence that smolders within. The final stanzas of this poem reveal uncertainty regarding the security of this control. She asks: What if the forces of creativity and the nurturing of life ("Vineyard") are overthrown? Can there afterwards be a resurrection of sanity and peace?

The inner potential for bursting controls, symbolized by Vesuvius, is recognized in poem no. 601 (about 1862) as characteristic of a passionate few. "Natures this side Naples" remain unaware of the latent upheaval that others conceal within themselves.

Another poem, no. 1677 (undated), expresses the same general idea:

> On my volcano grows the Grass—
> A meditative spot—
> An acre for a Bird to choose
> Would be the General thought—
>
> How red the Fire rocks below—
> How insecure the sod
> Did I disclose
> Would populate with awe my solitude

Emily Dickinson believed that if her family knew how little her calm exterior revealed the true state of turmoil within her and how brittle her control really was, they would have consigned her to a solitude complete except for "awe."

In addition to the "volcano poems," many others testify that Emily Dickinson found her psychic equilibrium extremely difficult to maintain. No. 530 (early 1862) may be interpreted as expressing the idea that the instinctual drives and pressures of the unconscious are impossible to contain: the fire "You cannot put . . . out," the flood "You cannot fold" and "put in a Drawer" in that poem can be regarded as symbols of erotic and destructive impulses. In no. 576 (about 1862) the poet reflects on the comforts that religion might have offered her had she retained her childhood faith. She then proceeds to describe her intense feelings of insecurity and imbalance:

> And often since, in Danger,
> I count the force 'twould be
> To have a God so strong as that
> To hold my life for me
>
> Till I could take the Balance
> That tips so frequent, now,
> It takes me all the while to poise—
> And then—it does'nt stay—

The poet's disturbance, manifested by gradually increasing depression, fears that latent forbidden impulses were in danger of imminent eruption, and the feeling of precarious psychological equilibrium, ultimately took on aspects of a more serious disorder. As has been mentioned, one of the ego characteristics of the potential or borderline psychotic is that he, unlike the normal or neurotic person, has an awareness of the unconscious forces that underlie his illness. That is to say, the forces are no longer unconscious. Indeed, his consciousness is flooded with material that his previous relatively stable state had repressed, and such a situation is the hallmark of a psychotic illness.

The "sea poems," in contrast with the "volcano poems," are not related to fears that one's potential violence might evade control and endanger others. Here the anxiety is related to an inner threat to one's self—to one's psychic integrity. In the normal personality in the waking state there exists a feeling of continuity of bodily and mental reactions and relations that we think of as our inner selves. One's thinking processes—memories, sensory impressions—and one's characteristic reactions and relationships with others—in short, all the conscious and preconscious operations of our psychological lives—are enveloped and integrated within this feeling of personal continuity. The rest of the world is separate and distinct from ourselves. There exists a feeling of a frontier at which the heterogeneous external world stops and our personal, integrated inner world begins. Psychoanalytical terminology speaks of an "ego boundary" separating us from all that is not ourselves. It is important to note that this feeling of the circumscribed extension of our inner life into time and space and its impenetrability and separateness is an *ego* feeling; it does not invest the unconscious operations of the id—the primitive drives and all the memories and experiences that have been repressed from awareness or have never been conscious. The inner core of the feeling of one's unique existence and physical and mental discreteness therefore excludes one whole area of psychic life—the unconscious.

The ego feeling is so much taken for granted by the healthy personality that one's attention is rarely directed to it. It permeates all that transpires in one's waking mind with the unreflecting certitude that these are *my* thoughts, *my* waking consciousness. A sense of separateness from the external world of these inner operations is felt with great security. It is taken for granted that what is outside is real and not a part of one's self. The major premise of our rational lives is based on this elementary distinction between self and non-self—on the intactness and maintenance of this certain feeling of having a securely bounded ego. As Paul Federn says, "The basis of sanity is correct and automatic recognition of this breach between subjective mental individual experiences in the world and the knowledge of the status of the world that actually exists. Sanity means dealing with the world and with one's self with the faculty of distinguishing clearly between them."[10] When Emily Dickinson says, "A Plank in Reason, broke," and she felt herself dropping into a chasm of "Finished knowing," she appears to be describing the sensation of one experiencing a sudden loss of ego boundaries—the "plank" that supports one's conscious and rational psychological life gives way and plunges one into an awful abyss in which the external world and the inner unconscious, both equally "not me", have become difficult to distinguish from one another.

To be submerged, drowned in a vast sea, lost, alone, helpless—this is the subject of many Dickinson poems. The sea, a most important and frequent symbol, is used to represent many different experiences, for example: the loss of one's self in death (no. 30, about 1858); the separation from security and safety and the sense of being isolated from others (no. 48, about 1858, and no. 905, about 1864); the feeling of being lost in a vast, uncharted, unknown expanse (no. 52, about 1858); the exultation of escape from the mundane and limiting—the afflatus of creativity (no. 76, about 1859); the loss of one's individual identity through absorption or fusion with another person (no. 162, about 1860); a complete abandonment of one's self through erotic passions (no. 249, about 1861); or the buffeting of violent emotions (no. 368, about 1862). These divergent experiences, all appropriately symbolized in various ways by images of the sea, are depicted as pleasurable when the self is imagined as merging with a larger, security-providing, beneficent reality, and as unpleasurable when the larger reality in which the self is immersed carries the connotations of loneliness, isolation, or turbulent chaos. The common denominator in all these "sea poems," however, regardless of the pleasurability of the feeling, is the poet's experience of a diffusion of herself—of the blurring of her own boundaries until she becomes lost in the infinite or expands into infinity herself.

One may recognize in these poems the weakening of ego boundaries that has been discussed earlier as a prerequisite of psychosis. Just as Emily Dickinson's "volcano poems" depict the pressure of emotional forces within the personality—the threat of eruptive violence versus the effort to control and repress these forces—so the "sea poems" depict other predispositions for the same process of psychotic breakdown. In these latter poems the danger with which the poet is concerned is not that presented to others through her latent destructiveness, but that which is felt as a threatened dispersal of the integrity of her own personality.

It should be pointed out that not every experience of a loosening of ego boundaries is indicative of serious mental disorder. Normal persons may have the sensation when thrilled by any of the arts—especially, perhaps, music. The experience may be found in the contemplation of nature—a starry night, for example, or a startling panoramic view. "Breathtaking" is a word often applied to pleasurable experiences in which the ego undergoes a sudden expansion. A partial loss of ego boundary occurs also at the moment of orgasm. Perhaps this is one reason that some persons, aware of a psychotic propensity within themselves, will avoid sexual intercourse; being frightened of their increasing inability to distinguish the processes within their own minds from what is happening in the outer world, they become fearful of anything that weakens their already enfeebled sense of psychic separateness.

Emily Dickinson both courted and feared this experience of ego expansion and weakening of psychological boundaries. She recognized true poetry because it evoked this reaction: "If I feel physically as if the top of my head were taken off, I know *that* is poetry."[11] Yet her "sea poems" are often full of dread. It would appear that she was well aware that unless one kept one's guard up the unconscious was likely to trespass. Poem no. 520 (about 1862) is an interesting demonstration of this insight:

> I started Early—Took my Dog—
> And visited the Sea—
> The Mermaids in the Basement
> Came out to look at me—
>
> And Frigates—in the Upper Floor
> Extended Hempen Hands—
> Presuming Me to be a Mouse—
> Aground—upon the Sands—

But no Man moved Me—till the Tide
Went past my simple Shoe—
And past my Apron—and my Belt
And past my Boddice—too—

And made as He would eat me up—
As wholly as a Dew
Upon a Dandelion's Sleeve—
And then—I started—too—

And He—He followed—close behind—
I felt His Silver Heel
Upon my Ancle—then my Shoes
Would overflow with Pearl—

Until We met the Solid Town—
No One He seemed to know—
And bowing—with a Mighty look—
At me—The Sea withdrew—

The poet here says that she started out casually and "visited the Sea"—in other words, she focused her attention on her deepest and most inward psychic processes. "The Mermaids in the Basement" then came out to look at her—that is, psychic curiosities and fantasy creatures appeared—and the poem indicates that she was not alarmed by this sudden appearance. "Frigates in the Upper Floor," presuming her to be stranded and in trouble, offer her rope so she can come aboard. The "Frigates" may be interpreted as representing the ego defenses that are alarmed by this dallying with the unconscious. They offer her a solid deck of reality before she is engulfed. The poem relates how the poet ignores the warnings and in her innocence is almost submerged before she realizes what is happening. She becomes aware of the possibility of imminent drowning—inundation by the unconscious and the instinctual drives, especially, in this poem, the erotic ones: "the tide . . . made as He would eat me up." The ego defenses are at last heeded and the poet beats a panicky retreat from the unconscious. She returns to reality, "the Solid Town" so unlike the fluid fantasies of the id.[12]

With the sea representing the vast unconscious (in terms of "infinity," "immensity," "tremendousness," and so on) and drowning in it representing the loss of one's psychic integrity in psychosis, the image of the boat becomes an appropriate means of delineating the ego which rides separate and distinct upon the surface of the id.

A strange little poem (no. 107, about 1859), possibly expressive of this ego-id relationship, speaks of a little boat seduced to its destruction by a seemingly gallant sea. The poem gives no clue to what catastrophe the poet had in mind—perhaps consciously she was merely referring here to a dashed hope. In no. 30 (about 1858) it is clear that the little boat represents a life; it sinks beneath the waves of death, but from an angel's vantage point its destination is heaven. In no. 48 (about 1858), the poet is "at sea," troubled and questioning and telling her soul that "Land" may still exist.

None of these and similar poems taken individually can be given a definitive interpretation. However, in the context of the poet's entire oeuvre plus all available biographical information, they reflect her preoccupation with that fragile craft—her conscious rational mental life—riding on a vast, formless, elemental power—the unconscious instinctual drives. Even when the theme takes the form of the soul's confrontation with eternity, it seems likely that the terms of the problem—survival or dissolution, life or death, haven or desolation—reflect not only the poet's philosophical speculations but also, on another level, her uneasy awareness of the precariousness of her sanity.

It may appear paradoxical that the same symbol—the sea—can refer equally to two seemingly opposite psychic states. On the one hand, it denotes the miseries of trackless isolation, on the other (as in poems, 249, 212, and 162), to the union with the beloved. However, there is no real contradiction. One's sense of individual identity is lost when unconscious material (which is devoid of ego feeling) is projected to the external world. This causes the world to appear strange and alien and produces a feeling of uncertainty as to what is within and what without. A sense of separate existence can be lost equally when the tenuousness of the Ego boundaries allows a fusion of one's identity with that of another person.

Clinical experience offers frequent examples of this phenomenon. In such *folie à deux*, the victims, most frequently a mother and daughter, experience themselves as one person. They so confound their past and present lives that neither knows for certain whether any single event has befallen herself or the other. So intimate is this fusion that when hospitalization brings about a separation each may feel that she herself has died, and it is a therapeutic necessity to arrange frequent meetings to reassure each other of the other's (and therefore her own) continuing existence.

Of course this extreme situation is the end point of certain compelling needs that in other persons merely tend in the direction of the psychological union with another. The full-blown psychotic process of fusion can occur only when both individuals have an irresistible impulse to merge, an impulse which seems to reflect a need for a security and strength that neither can find alone. When Emily Dickinson writes (no. 284)

> The Drop, that wrestles in the Sea—
> Forgets her own locality—
> As I—toward Thee—

she reveals a susceptibility to the kind of total immersion of identity described above. Though the word "wrestles" suggests an opposing impulse to retain separateness, the sum effect is an impression of the poet's readiness for intense identification and her awareness of ego boundaries that were at times unduly fluid.

Such fluidity or flexibility of ego boundaries, though psychologically perilous, may from the viewpoint of an artist be of inestimable value. Creative artists, without necessarily being psychotic, characteristically have an intuitive grasp of unconscious dynamisms without being overpowered by the unconscious forces—the raw instincts, conflicts, and forbidden impulses. The creative artist with his ego still rational, intact, and in contact with reality can tolerate a certain amount of inspection of this dangerous and ordinarily prohibited territory. It is as though his ego were more tolerant, more flexible, less easily alarmed than those of the ordinary person or the neurotic, whose egos maintain a constant rigid guard against the id. The artist, in contrast, appears to be able to turn to the dark places of his own mind for material for his art and bend the inner enemy to his own purposes.

Emily Dickinson's poetry affords us an outstanding example of the artistic use of psychodynamic insight, much of which was undoubtedly a combined product of extraordinary poetic gifts and intrepid self-confrontation. Some of it, one suspects, was also the result of her experience of, and reflections upon, the flooding of her personality by unconscious processes during a psychotic illness. The "sea poems," in conveying a sense of immersion in a vast and foreign element, probably to some degree derived from this aspect of her experience.

Poem no. 1225 (about 1872), though not one of her "sea poems," suggests that the poet was aware of processes within herself that even an artist has no business knowing.

> It's Hour with itself
> The Spirit never shows.
> What Terror would enthrall the Street
> Could Countenance disclose
>
> The Subterranean Freight
> The Cellars of the Soul—
> Thank God the loudest Place he made
> Is licensed to be still.

The poem says that the deepest self-knowledge must be hidden from the view of others. It is obvious from the context that the kind of self-knowledge referred to is not the self-awareness that a realistic person builds up through self-observation and ordinary introspection. It is not a continuous process but instead a kind of insight that occurs only at intervals: the spirit's "Hour with itself." The poem says that the knowledge is felt as a burden ("Freight") and associated with dark, hidden, buried, and perhaps unwholesome things (symbolized by the words "Subterranean" and "Cellars of the Soul"). The poet reacts to what she encounters at these times as to something overwhelmingly impelling and commanding of attention; she calls it the "loudest Place" that God has made. The poem concludes with the observation that should this knowledge be made known to others they would be appalled. What would most likely thus "enthrall" and terrify "the Street"? Most probably those propensities of the dark and troublesome side of human nature associated with sexuality, madness, and murder as they are manifested as agents of the unconscious. The poet herself, one suspects, was enthralled by them and terrified as well.

Another poem (no. 1203, late 1871) reveals Emily Dickinson's awareness that one's past experiences are never dead and buried once and for all. Instead the influence of the experiences remains alive within us and is capable of exerting an effect on the present. Sometimes, according to this poem, a recurrence of memory induces pleasure, sometimes disgrace. The final stanza, "Unarmed if any meet her [the Past] / I charge him fly / Her Faded Ammunition / Might yet reply," might be paraphrased in psychodynamic terms thus: Should the past be revived as one's defenses—that is, repressions—become inoperable ("Unarmed"), one would be confronted with a dangerous situation best avoided ("I charge him fly"); for the past and influences of the past are invested with the potentiality for violence, capable of destroying the present. The poem offers a clear exposition of the hazardous state of one whose consciousness is faced with a return of the repressed, a situation that obtains most painfully during the early stages of a psychotic illness.

Emily Dickinson's awareness that a glimpse into the hidden depths of personality should be avoided because it exposes one to the danger of being overwhelmed is also expressed in poem no. 1182 (1871), similar to that above. It compares "Remembrance" (by which we may understand all the stored residues, conscious and unconscious, of one's past experience) with a house that has a "Rear," a "Front," a "Garret" containing "Refuse" and a "Mouse," and "the deepest Cellar." Paraphrased, the poem reads: Some memories can be reviewed openly and publicly ("Front" of the house), others are more private—perhaps reserved for one's family or one's self ("Rear" of the house). Other memories are inconsequential and trivial and like refuse accumulate in stored nooks in the mind ("a Garret"), where they may be allied with discreditable memories akin to vermin and unclean things ("a Mouse"). The "Garret" and "Mouse" are Emily Dickinson's symbols for what in psychoanalytic terms would correspond to the suppressed and the denied. These are contents of the mind that are preconscious, that is, they are accessible to consciousness should one choose to focus attention on them. However, because of their unpleasant nature the personality tends to avoid dwelling on them and in a sense denies their existence.

Then there is a deep and hidden abyss of the mind whose contents are to be guarded against lest they overwhelm one ". . . the deepest Cellar / That ever Mason laid— / Look to it by its Fathoms / Ourselves be not pursued." This stanza refers to the unconscious and the most deeply buried and fearful things of the past, which must remain unconscious if the repressed is not to return and overtake one in psychosis.

Emily Dickinson has written several other poems in which aspects of the personality are likened to a house with many compartments, but none more strikingly reveals her awareness of the stirring of disavowed memories and threatening unconscious propensities than the one beginning "One need not be a Chamber—to be Haunted" (no. 670, 1862). Here she tells us that the psyche has "Corridors" that are "Haunted" with a ghost that is more to be feared than any real "Assassin"—that is, the unconscious may threaten to overflow into consciousness in psychosis, bringing with it a feeling of terror and imminent dissolution.

Evidence of Emily Dickinson's unusual awareness of psychic processes that ordinarily go unnoticed by the mass of mankind can be found on almost every page of her writings. One might justifiably assert that such observations constitute a major portion of her subject matter. Moreover, her formulations of her other major themes—death, love, and nature—in addition to the philosophical and externally descriptive characteristics they possess, are almost invariably colored and livened by psychological insight. This penetrating subjectivity lends depth and fascination to her work regardless of the ostensible subject matter. It would appear, however, that these qualities were dearly bought at the expense of emotional balance and inner security. The ego flexibility and tolerance of the artist that enriched and deepened her poetic gifts appears also, in Emily Dickinson, to have been an ego weakness carrying with it a perilous vulnerability to psychic disorganization.

A weakened ego in thrall to unconscious processes, depression, estrangement, and depersonalization, anxiety that violent impulses could no longer be contained, and feelings of being adrift in a void—these predispositions and premonitory symptoms inexorably ushered in the psychotic climax. In poem no. 1123 (about 1868) she writes:

A great Hope fell
You heard no noise
The Ruin was within
Oh cunning wreck that told no tale
And let no Witness in

A cherished dream has evidently collapsed and now lies in silent ruins within the poet's mind, unsuspected by her environment. The next stanza tells of her difficulty in understanding her loss:

> The mind was built for mighty Freight
> For dread occasion planned
> How often foundering at Sea
> Ostensibly, on Land

Here again the mind is likened to a ship which feels itself in imminent danger of being swallowed up by a sea of emotions evoked by the crash of her hopes.

Despair now becomes complete and overwhelming and the poet's ego undergoes increasing disorganization. In poem no. 378 (about 1862) she describes the condition of utter psychological collapse:

> I saw no Way—The Heavens were stitched—
> I felt the Columns close—
> The Earth reversed her Hemispheres—
> I touched the Universe—
>
> And back it slid—and I alone—
> A Speck upon a Ball—
> Went out upon Circumference—
> Beyond the Dip of Bell—

At this point the "Plank in Reason" broke. The poem tells us that happiness and religious reassurance (heaven) were denied her and that there seemed no way out of the dilemma that faced her. Even the familiar consolations and pursuits of ordinary life ("Earth") became distorted and psychologically unavailable. The whole universe appeared to evade her perception and opened out into an enormous void. She felt alone, stranded, the only discrete speck of consciousness upon a planet ("Ball") that swam in nothingness. Then her consciousness itself eddied out into the void and was lost to itself and submerged too deeply in infinity and boundlessness to be summoned by any signal from reality ("Beyond the Dip of Bell").

Probably when Emily Dickinson wrote her cryptic letter to T. W. Higginson saying she "had a terror—since September—I could tell to none,"[13] she was alluding to a recurrence or foreboding of an illness such as this. Anyone who has once witnessed this terrible sundering of the personality's connection with reality will never forget it. When the severance is relatively sudden, as appears to be the case with Emily Dickinson, and not a gradual slipping away, the experience is probably the most terrifying one that can befall a human being. Contrary to general belief, the person undergoing a psychotic break with reality frequently realizes that he is the victim of a catastrophic alteration—not only of the world but of himself as well. He knows that everything seems changed, that his home and family and friends look different and seem to behave strangely; and, especially early in the illness, he may know that it is he himself and not the world that is no longer familiar. As the process of disorganization continues, the world appears more and more alien. Initially, only the person's curiosity may be aroused by intermittent false observations of minor and mysterious alterations in familiar things. A book, for example, may appear on the mantle when the person is certain that he just put it on the end table, or the cat may have a strange and *knowing* look on its face that is somehow disturbing. Soon, however, curiosity gives way to anxiety, which increases as the feeling of strangeness begins to pervade everything in the environment. The person may then fly to someone loved and trusted for protection and beg like a child to be soothed and comforted. In the ambience of a strong and warm personality the uncanny fears may disappear and the world may resume its former comfortable aspect. However, if the refuge he is trying to find becomes impossible because the loved one has also shared in the general alteration, his anxiety gives way to terror. The loved and trusted person may well act accepting and sympathetic, but the sufferer now senses his behavior only as acting. The feeling that the friend or relative is now somehow sinister is reinforced by the very "perfection" with which the friend goes through the expected and familiar gestures, now experienced as studied or simulated. Later all the family and friends begin to seem like imposters or robots and only the shell of the real world seems to remain. As with Renée, Madame Sechehaye's patient, everything that is perceived may come to seem suspended in a great vacuum. The feeling of immense space may alternate with the feeling that all one observes is two-dimensional, like a motion picture that is plotless, meaningless, and flat.

The fear that is evoked at the onset of a psychotic breakdown is not due solely to the apprehension that one is suddenly in a new and unfathomable world. Such feelings are augmented by uncertainty, adumbrated in Emily Dickinson's "volcano poems," about one's ability to control bodily reactions and physical movements. The fear arises that one may do everything that one most dreads doing. The repressive powers of the ego are breaking down. Aggressive, destructive, and erotic impulses, formerly forbidden to consciousness by the conscience and sense of propriety, now command the center of awareness. Because such proscribed and denied impulses have, during health, remained unconscious, they have never been invested with the ego feeling that allows one to recognize one's inner thoughts and other mental operations as one's own. For this reason, they are perceived as an encroachment from outside, and the afflicted person feels in the control of an external and invisible power. A woman, for example, may feel that she is about to kill her beloved children despite all her efforts to prevent the terrible deed. In her desperation to safeguard them she may hide or discard all knives and scissors in the house. Or she may rush from the house or beg her family to tie her up or lock her in a room out of reach of her children.

The dread of impending loss of control may become unbearable. To ward off the dreaded act a person may throw himself violently into some substitute activity—anything, however unreasonable it may appear, to escape the demands of a destructive demon that seems to have taken hold of him. A man, for example, may attempt to exhaust himself breaking up furniture or smashing windows. Or he may get into his car and drive at top speed without having any destination in mind. Frequently, as a last resort, the victim may injure himself, sever his radial arteries or shoot himself, rather than be forced (as he experiences it) to injure his loved ones. Such persons fear their own murderous potentialities so greatly that they seek a jail cell or enter a seclusion room in a mental hospital with the greatest avidity. It is impressive to witness the relief such patients exhibit when they realize that external controls will be substituted for the inner ones they believe they have lost or are in danger of losing. (Fortunately those patients who actually lose control are few, and of those few a still smaller percentage are actually dangerous to others).

Not uncommonly, victims of incipient ego breakdown are, despite their panic, rational and perfectly oriented to the environment. Hallucinations and systematized delusions are secondary effects of the primary breakdown and may appear only later as the illness progresses, or they may never appear—the broken ego boundaries may seal over, as it were, and the psychotic reaction subside. The answer to the question whether Emily Dickinson's breakdown included these dramatic derivatives of the primary loss of reality or whether she made a rapid recovery without progressing to them will be considered in later pages.

To summarize my hypothesis so far: Emily Dickinson's writings, taken in the aggregate, point to a break with reality that was the culminating point of a prodromal depressive reaction. With the abandoning of certain cherished hopes the depression deepened in severity until the poet was prostrated. Then, mingled with these feelings of hopeless misery, episodes of estrangement and depersonalization intervened, along with fears of losing impulse control. All these symptoms probably increased in duration and intensity until the breaking point was reached and the poet succumbed to a psychotic illness.

Notes

1. It is useful to think of the various "neuroses" and "psychoses," including the many "schizophrenia" subgroups, not as fixed states, but as representing points on a continuum from a hypothetical completely "normal" extreme to a hypothetical completely disorganized extreme. An individual's position, which may continually shift along the scale, is determined by the degree to which his thought, feeling and behavior are disorganized by stressful life situations. "Neurosis," nearer the "normal" end, implies hampering and rigid ego defenses, a strong capacity for repression, and the maintenance of contact with what is ordinarily called reality. "Psychosis" involves a diminished capacity for repression, an uneasy and potentially disorganizing openness to unconscious processes, and weak, unstable, or extreme defenses which, to varying degrees, call for a sacrifice in reality contact. Though points as they approach the disorganized end of the scale are traditionally and loosely called "illnesses," the

present state of psychiatric knowledge does not justify regarding either neurosis or psychosis as a disease entity.

2. *Letters*, II, 424, no. 281 (Emily to Louise and Frances Norcross, late May 1863).

3. *Letters*, II, 581, no. 501 (Emily to Mrs. Jonathan L. Jenkins, late May 1877).

4. *Letters*, II, 594, no. 522 (Emily to T. W. Higginson, early autumn 1877).

5. *Letters*, II, 500, no. 380 (Emily to Louise Norcross, late 1872).

6. *Letters*, III, 919 (prose fragment 49).

7. Paul Federn, *Ego Psychology and the Psychoses* (New York, Basic Books, 1952), pp. 40, 41.

8. Marguerite Sechehaye, *Autobiography of a Schizophrenic Girl* (New York, Grune and Stratton, 1951), pp. 110–115.

9. Sechehaye, p. 7.

10. Federn, *Ego Psychology*, p. 229.

11. *Letters*, II, 474, no. 342a (T. W. Higginson to his wife, August 16, 1870).

12. Clark Griffith, in *The Long Shadow: Emily Dickinson's Tragic Poetry* (Princeton, Princeton University Press, 1964), pp. 18–24, offers an excellent analysis of the poem's erotic implications. My identification of the personality components with which the poem deals is perfectly compatible with his interpretation.

13. *Letters*, II, 404, no. 261 (Emily to T. W. Higginson, April 25, 1862).

Emily Dickinson's "Double" Tim: Masculine Identification

Rebecca Patterson*

The several biographers and editors of Emily Dickinson have usually been content to ignore the poet's masculine claims, although these claims bulk large. Again and again, the poet describes herself as a boy—a boy possessed, moreover, by an unappeasable desire to return to the mother, symbolized in such objects as houses and rooms, food, nectar, and the like; but neither this symbolism nor the boy-identity has attracted much critical notice. Theodora Ward's *The Capsule of the Mind*, with its gingerly excursion into the poet's masculine alter ego, forms a partial but interesting exception. The approach is Jungian, and Mrs. Ward specifically mentions Jung as her authority for the assertion that such mental power as a woman possesses belongs to her masculine side, whereas the feminine element in a man is "soul." She finds this idea borne out in the more "philosophical" poems (many of them in the form of "definitions" and employing the "phraseology of the text books") written in the years 1863–1865, after the poet had suffered a tragic love affair and had extracted from the now vanished lover "the masculine element that set her mind free."[1]

This masculine power of text book and definition appears to be also

*From Rebecca Patterson, "Emily Dickinson's 'Double' Tim: Masculine Identification," *American Imago*, 28 (Winter 1971), 330–62. Reprinted by permission of the Wayne State University Press, © 1971.

the more distinctively lyrical power of the years 1860–1862. Speaking of the poet's double, the boy Tim, in an 1860 poem beginning "We don't cry—Tim and I" (196),[2] Mrs. Ward observes that Emily's "shy masculine counterpart . . . 'reads a little Hymm'—an act that is prophetic of his true function" as the part of her mind that is able to create.[3] Although Mrs. Ward never quite clarifies this point, it would seem that the males of both sexes have a monopoly of the creative power. Men writers rarely stress their femininity, seldom yearn after their lost little girlhood, and do not appear to recollect their pinafores or to imagine themselves playing with dolls again. The converse can be demonstrated of Emily Dickinson and the woman writers she particularly admired, all of whom, in some sense. yearned after their lost boyhood.

Like other biographers, Mrs. Ward betrays a troubled concern with the childish tone of many poems. Of one beginning "God permits industrious Angels— / Afternoons—to play—" (231), Mrs. Ward says the image of the boy playing with the angel could not have originated in the mind of a thirty-year-old woman, "but was certainly carried over from the impressions of childhood."[4] She does not seem to have observed what is going on in the poem. This school boy has been summoned from a game of "marbles" to play the game of love with an enchanting angel and stranger, two names Emily Dickinson repeatedly gave the lost beloved, and with an obvious allusion to the Biblical injunction: "Be not forgetful to entertain strangers: for thereby some have entertained angels unawares."[5] In a poem which appears to fall in early 1859, she identifies with the Gymnast Jacob wrestling with the Angel, who is emphatically hailed as "Stranger!" (59). Also relevant are these lines in poem 895: "Never to pass the Angel / With a glance and a Bow." But, of course, her work is full of poems lamenting her failure to hold the beloved stranger.

Mrs. Ward is equally positive that young Tim was an imaginary companion invented by a child of five or six. She notes the curious childlike language, the poet's surprising regression, "at a time when her creative flood was reaching its height, . . . to the mood of a lonely child, burdened with a secret fear," and the odd fact that instead of projecting herself into an imaginary companion of the same sex, the little Emily invented for her alter ego a boy named Tim.[6] Mrs. Ward might well have recalled the candid language with which the Dickinsons' friend Samuel Bowles congratulated another friend on the birth of a son: "I am glad it is a boy. Boys are institutions. They have a future, a positive future. Girls are swallowed up,—they are an appendage,—a necessary appendage, it may be,—probably they are—but still they are appendages."[7] Possibly a sensitive, very intelligent and gifted little girl growing up in such a climate would try to avoid destruction—being "swallowed up"—by escaping into an imaginary boy-self. The evidence, however, suggests that the boy-self was both creation and creator of her belated productivity, though not in Mrs. Ward's sense, and that this particular Tim was born about February 1859.

During the early months of 1859, the poet's sister-in-law, Susan Gilbert Dickinson, entertained an old school friend, the handsome and charming Kate Scott Turner, and Emily spent many of her evenings with them. Apparently one such visit was prolonged until nearly midnight, and the poet was fetched home by her bossy father. In a note sent to her sister-in-law the following morning, she wryly describes herself as an "unfortunate insect" and her father as a "Reptile." Pasted above the joking message is a woodcut clipped from the *New England Primer* showing a youth (Emily) pursued by an upright, wolf-like creature with a forked tail, the "Reptile" of her misleading caption (L214). Although she cut away the letterpress, she doubtless reminded Sue and Kate, or they remembered, that the woodcut illustrated the letter "T" and these verses: "Young Timothy / Learnt sin to fly." There is no evidence that the little Emily ever "played with" an imaginary little Tim, but it is quite clear that the twenty-eight-year-old woman playfully identified herself with the Puritan youth Timothy fleeing from "sin."[8]

The poet's boyishness was a recognized part of the family joke-lore, as shown by her own comments about being told to behave better "when I was a Boy" (L571) or about little Ned inheriting "his Uncle Emily's ardor for the lie" (L315) or by the signature "Brother Emily" in a letter to her Norcross cousins (L367); and this boyishness was apparently not unknown to outsiders. On reading the poem "A narrow Fellow in the Grass" (986), Sam Bowles delightedly asked where "that girl" got her knowledge of farming and Sue Dickinson laughingly replied, "Oh, you forget that was Emily *'when a boy'!*"[9] Sue's joking answer was intended to remind Bowles of earlier incidents, for he too was aware of Emily's masculine identity.

In late June 1877, in an unusually reminiscent mood (her old friend Kate had once more been visiting in the house next door), the poet signed a letter to Bowles, "Your 'Rascal,' " adding, "I washed the Adjective" (L515). She was alluding to a passage in *The Old Curiosity Shop* in which Dickens explains that Mr. Brass was in the habit of treating his sister Sally like another man, a feeling "so perfectly reciprocal, that not only did Mr. Brass often call Miss Brass a rascal or even put an adjective before the rascal, but Miss Brass looked upon it as quite a matter of course." And Dick Swiveller, Mr. Brass's clerk, is so accustomed to the manliness of Sally Brass that he "would sometimes reward her with a hearty slap on the back, and protest that she was a devilish good fellow, a jolly dog, and so forth." Later in the story, Miss Brass is reported to be disguised as a sailor, or as a soldier in the Foot Guards.[10]

Now, an 1861 letter in which Emily Dickinson calls Bowles the "Swiveller" and signs herself the "Marchioness" suggests that labeling each other in this fashion was a game with them (L241). The temptation to call Emily a mannish "Sally Brass" or "Rascal" (Dickens says "provoking rascal" and hints at a stronger adjective) would be most likely to arise upon any hint of feminist sympathies, and about 5 August 1860, the poet was clearly on the aggressive and open to the charge of being Sally Brassish. In Amherst to report the August Commencement, Bowles was taking a little time off to refresh himself at the house of his friend Austin Dickinson, when a discussion arose that waxed almost as warm as the weather. Months later, he would write with some pride to his close friend Maria Whitney that she and two or three unnamed women had given him a new understanding of the disabilities of their sex.[11] It can be no more than a guess that the unnamed women were Emily and her sister-in-law and perhaps Kate Turner, but it is a certainty that the conversation that August day turned on the position of women, and that Bowles was annoyed. In her letter of apology Emily hopes that Bowles will forgive and respect his "little Bob o' Lincoln" (L223). Characteristically she is a boyish bird.

There are no boy poems in handwriting earlier than 1860, and two of the three examples of that year may be dismissed as casual: "School Boys" hunt pine cones in the bough overhead (161); "Death . . . Never was a Boy," that is, a boy like herself (153). The Tim poem of late 1860 is the first clear assertion of her new masculine identity. A poem written perhaps a year later describes the temptation of some strawberries growing just beyond a fence. She could climb the fence—and berries are "nice"; but if she spoiled her apron, God would scold. On second thought, she guesses He would try to climb too, "If He were a Boy"—like Emily (251). Another 1861 poem, "Did we disobey Him?," confesses her inability to forget. If the lover were such a dunce, Emily would continue to "Love the dull lad—best—" Can the other person not love the dull lad Emily? (267). In a poem, probably written in late 1861, "The nearest Dream recedes—unrealized" (319), "School Boy" Emily is "Homesick for steadfast Honey," but admits that no bee "brews that rare variety."

Of these 1860 and 1861 poems, except for the "Tim" poem, it may be said that the poet does not unequivocally identify herself as a boy. The comparison with God is not completed; the "dull lad" shifts and evades; the school boy is as elusive as his bee. Beginning with 1862, however, she quite clearly and deliberately adopts the boy identity for specific poems. In "There's been a Death, in the Opposite House" (389), she, or rather he, remembers—"when a Boy"—watching a house of death, seeing a mattress flung out, wondering "if it died—on that," finding in the minister's stiff walk a suggestion that this man now owns the mourners—"And little Boys—besides—" Perhaps the boy-identity struck her as peculiarly suited to graveyard themes. In a letter of 25 April 1862 to T. W. Higginson, she speaks of a terror she has suffered "since September" and adds, "and so I sing, as the Boy does by the Burying Ground—because I am afraid—"

(L261). An 1864 poem, "Who occupies this House?" (892), describes the graveyard as a "curious Town" with houses old and new. The poet would not care to build among such silent inhabitants but rather where birds assemble and "Boys" like herself are "possible." Another 1864 poem, "How the Waters closed above Him" (923), might suggest an attempt to poetize some local tragedy. It describes feelingly the solitary anguish of the drowning youth, the pathos of his "unclaimed Hat and Jacket," the ironic beauty of the pond spreading her water lilies "Bold above the Boy." This boy is Emily herself perishing beneath her symbolic lilies.

Several boy poems written about 1862 deal with the pain of lost love. The first of these describes the attractive power of the distant, feminine moon over a masculine—and curiously juvenile—sea: With her "Amber Hands," she "leads Him—docile as a Boy—" In the final stanza, this inconstant moon is transmogrified into a beloved "Signor" and the poet identifies with the "Boy" sea (429). In a second 1862 poem, she appears to represent herself as a masculine "Black Berry" which wears "a Thorn in his side" (like Christ, with whom she often identifies), but stoically conceals the pain and goes on offering his berries to the passerby. There is no mistaking the tender self-pity of the final line, "Brave Black Berry" (554). In like manner, she murmurs "Brave Bobolink" over a boyish bird (a self-symbol, as in her August 1860 letter to Bowles) whose longed-for nesting tree has been cut down (755). In another 1862 poem, she is once more locked within the lonely prison of herself, dreaming of the pools in which she plashed when "Memory was a Boy" (652). An early 1863 poem, which makes a detailed contrast between loveless North and erotic South, says that "playing Glaciers—when a Boy" taught her to long for the fire of love (689). She sent a copy of this poem to Samuel Bowles, reminding him once more of Emily "when a boy" (L283).[12]

After 1865, the love theme being effectually dead, and with it most of her symbolism, she used the boy-identity to voice her opinions on religious or moral subjects. According to a Christmas poem which illustrates her rather curious pal-ship with Jesus, the road to Bethlehem has been considerably improved "Since He and I were Boys" (1487). An 1879 poem, to which she gave one of her rare titles, "Diagnosis of the Bible, by a Boy" (1545), expresses a strong and increasing hostility toward the religious instruction she had received in childhood. "Boys that believe," she says, "are very lonesome" or even "bastinadoed," and the "Boys" that do not "are lost." A poem of late 1871, written in an equally unregenerate mood, tells of pulling off her stockings and wading just to be disobedient. The "Boy that lived for 'Ought to' " might go to Heaven at death, and then again he might not. After all, God had treated Moses unfairly (1201). That this disobedient wading was a live and permanent memory is demonstrated by an undated prose fragment written after her mother's death in late 1882: "Two things I have lost with Childhood—the rapture of losing my shoe in the Mud and going Home barefoot, wading for Cardinal flowers and the mothers reproof" (PF117). Apparently the child Emily was as much a tomboy as her mother permitted her to be.

Besides the boy poems already described, there is poem 968 with its "Excellenter Youth" and poem 717 about the "Beggar Lad" who cries, "Sweet Lady—Charity," to a bowing, smiling, *feminine* world taking its cruel "Cambric Way." Finally, there are some fifteen or sixteen poems in which she confers on herself various masculine titles of nobility. Since she may call herself indifferently girl, bride, or earl within the same poem, the titles earl, duke, prince, or king have a reduced sexual significance, as have also boy, lad, and youth, but they do manifest a preference for the important male role. The belted earl is a more striking figure than his appendage, the countess.

In a rather curious poem "He" puts the "Belt" around her life, and she hears the "Buckle snap." Since she—or perhaps "He"—folds up her "Lifetime" as a "Duke" would fold the title deed to a kingdom, the poem appears to have a religious flavor, but it is the religion of erotic love so constant throughout her poetry. The oddity consists in depicting herself as a medieval nobleman undergoing investiture or "belting" at the hands of his sovereign (273). In another poem, the now indifferent beloved will regret not speaking to "that dull Girl" when the latter becomes an "Earl"; but what with "Crests," with "Eagles" on her "Buckles" and in her "Belt," with "Ermine" as her familiar wear, the newmade "Earl" will be indifferent too (704). In a poem beginning "The Malay—took the Pearl— / Not—I—the Earl," the Malay has got away with the "Jewel" (and the lover is often figured as a gem) which "Earl" Emily desperately wanted (452). Of a wild rose, she says she would rather "wear her grace" than be "Duke of Exeter" or have an "Earl's distinguished face," although in some of her marriage poems it is precisely like an "Earl" that she wants to hold her "Brow" (138, 473). Rejoicing in some unspecified happiness, she calls herself "Prince of Mines," but in a poem about childhood loneliness she pictures herself as a "Prince cast out" of his "Dominion" (466, 959). After the virtual disappearance of the love theme in 1865, the few royal-name poems concern themselves with death and are of a more general nature.

Masculine titles are only part of the evidence pointing to a boyish side. It has been noticed that she links the forbidden sport of wading to her little-boy self, plays a boyish game of marbles, wrestles with an "Angel"—no doubt the one who interrupts the marble game—and wrings a blessing from this "Stranger." She is the "Loaded Gun" that roams in "Sovereign Woods" with her curiously passive "Master," and hunts the "Doe." When she speaks for her "Master," that is, fires herself, she smiles like a "Vesuvian face" letting its "pleasure through," and a "cordial light" glows on the "Valley." No enemy on whom she lays a "Yellow Eye" or an "emphatic Thumb" ever stirs a second time. But at night she prefers to stand ascetically on guard rather than lay herself on the "Eider-Duck's Deep Pillow" (754).[13]

The imagery so far examined has been conspicuously and persistently juvenile. She is a boy, a lad, a childish prince; even her earls tend to be childlike or girlish. In her letters as well as in her poems, a tendency to revert to childhood under particular pressures can be detected again and again; for example, when Susan Gilbert became engaged to Austin Dickinson and hence "lost" to Emily, or when Kate Turner apparently sought to reduce a perfervid attachment to a calmer good will. On the former occasion, Emily wrote painfully to her brother: "how to grow up I dont know" (L115). It would appear that certain needs and desires became excusable, became tolerable to the poet, if they were given a childish context. In short, she could think of herself quite comfortably as a boy, freed not only of the onerous restrictions laid upon little girls, but relieved also of the deadly necessity of growing into a woman. On the other hand, she dared not wish to be a man and indeed repudiated the idea with a curious ferocity in the opening stanza of a poem somewhat neglected by the explicators:

> Rearrange a "Wife's" affection!
> When they dislocate my Brain!
> Amputate my freckled Bosom!
> Make me bearded like a man!   (1737)

To become a man involves, first, a destructive alteration of the brain, followed by a gruesome major surgery which evokes parallels with the castration fears common to men, completed by the humiliation of suffering a disfiguring growth upon one's cherished smooth skin. A male reader must need be remarkably naive to suppose these lines express a simple admiration. Indeed, they are so hysterical, so much in excess, as to suggest a particular occasion, a monition to a friend who might be showing an interest in the bearded sex. The manuscript has been destroyed, presumably by Mrs. Bianchi, the poet's niece, but not before it was copied by Mabel Loomis Todd and listed among the contents of Packet 8.[14] Most of the poems in this packet appear to have been written in the fall of 1861, when the now estranged Kate Turner was once more visiting Sue Dickinson next door, and one reproachful poem of this group (221) was sent across the lawn to her. If only (the poems imply) they could have been boys together forever! In default of such happiness on earth, Emily was driven to fix her eyes upon that life beyond death when, as Elizabeth Browning suggested in one of her scolding sonnets to George Sand, earthly sexual distinctions would be ended and they could be boys together for all eternity.[15]

Notes

1. Theodora Ward: *The Capsule of the Mind* (Cambridge, Mass., 1961), pp. 70, 73. In *The Long Shadow* (Princeton, N.J., 1964), pp. 286–292, Clark Griffith has given an incomplete and not wholly satisfactory psychoanalytic examination with a verdict of penis-envy. John Cody's *After Great Pain: The Inner Life of Emily Dickinson* (Cambridge, Mass., 1971), published after this article was completed, makes several disconnected references to a masculine identification, but pursues a different thesis. In general, the book offers occasional brilliant insights but in a context of confusion and contradiction.

2. Parenthetical numbers without prefix and numbers preceded by a capital L refer, respectively, to the numbers in the 1955 three-volume *Poems of Emily Dickinson* and to the numbers in the 1958 three-volume *Letters*, both edited by Thomas H. Johnson, with the assistance of Theodora Ward, for the Harvard University Press.

3. Ward, p. 14.

4. Ward, p. 8.

5. Hebrews 13:2.

6. Ward, pp. 12–14.

7. See George S. Merriam: *The Life and Times of Samuel Bowles* (New York 1885), I, 168.

8. It is a curious fact that the poet clipped the name "Timothy" from the title page of 1 Timothy, in her personal copy of the Bible (preserved in the Houghton Library, Harvard), and may have used it as signature in a letter to some friend familiar with her "Tim" identity—possibly Kate Turner, who had made a deep impression on her. In her first letter to this important new friend, the poet asks: "Dare you dwell in the *East* where we dwell?," meaning the east of the poetic imagination and not simply the hundred miles or so between Amherst, Massachusetts, and Cooperstown, New York. She adds: "All *we* are *strangers*—dear . . . We are hungry, and thirsty, sometimes—We are barefoot—and cold—" Her words are a paraphrase of Matthew 25: 35–36: "For I was an hungered, and ye gave me meat: I was thirsty, and ye gave me drink: I was a stranger, and ye took me in: Naked, and ye clothed me . . ." This highly charged letter concludes by describing Kate as the gorgeous rose worn on the poet's breast (L203).

9. Martha Dickinson Bianchi: *Emily Dickinson Face to Face* (Boston, 1932), p. 27. The poem that Emily Dickinson wrote and Bowles published in the Springfield *Republican* contains the phrase, "when a boy," but Mrs. Bianchi quoted the carefully neutralized version of first editor Mabel Loomis Todd, "when a child." In a curious way this would seem to guarantee the authenticity of an anecdote which exists quite independently of the Todd version chosen to illustrate it.

10. Charles Dickens: *The Old Curiosity Shop*, Chaps. 33, 36, 63. See also Jay Leyda: *The Years and Hours of Emily Dickinson* (New Haven, 1960), II, 277.

11. Merriam, I, 317.

12. That she liked to represent herself as a boy in her relations with Samuel Bowles throws a curious light on the currently fashionable thesis that Bowles was the object of her erotic poems. She loved him, no doubt, as faithfully as a "little boy" could love a wiser, older friend (he was only four years her senior, but she persistently edged him into her father's generation). As for the earlier and now fading myth of an erotic attachment to the middle-aged clergyman, the evidence shows that she depended on Charles Wadsworth, and somewhat desperately, to get her a ticket of admission to Heaven, and this dependence is largely confined to the years after her father's death. Far from wishing to be Wadworth's spirit bride, she aspired respectfully to be his little boy Willie, as a careful reading of her letters to his friends the Clarks will show.

13. In an interesting analysis of this poem, John Cody has pointed out that the "Eider-

Duck's Deep Pillow" "connotes the idea of a nest with its cosy security and maternal nurturing" ("Emily Dickinson's Vesuvian Face," *American Imago*, Fall 1967, 24: 175). More exactly, it connotes the female breast itself, an association she found in "The Custom-House" section of Hawthorne's *Scarlet Letter:* "her bosom has all the softness and snugness of an eider-down pillow." The "Doe" which this gun-woman hunts is equally feminine. Since she was acquainted with Tennyson's *The Princess*, she may well have remembered the description of the somewhat mannish Princess Ida as a "lovely, lordly creature" and "leader" of "a hundred airy does" (VI, 69–72). Prince Cyril's uncouth old father clarifies the metaphor:

> Man is the hunter; woman is his game.
> The sleek and shining creatures of the chase,
> We hunt them for the beauty of their skins.; . . . (V, 147–149)

In becoming a hunter of the doe, Emily Dickinson clearly usurped a male prerogative.

14. See R. W. Franklin: *The Editing of Emily Dickinson* (The University of Wisconsin Press, 1967), pp. 46–47.

15. Elizabeth Browning: *The Complete Poetical Works* (Boston, 1900), p. 103.

Vesuvius at Home:
The Power of Emily Dickinson   Adrienne Rich*

I am travelling at the speed of time, along the Massachusetts Turnpike. For months, for years, for most of my life, I have been hovering like an insect against the screens of an existence which inhabited Amherst, Massachusetts, between 1831 and 1884. The methods, the exclusions, of Emily Dickinson's existence could not have been my own; yet more and more, as a woman poet finding my own methods, I have come to understand her necessities, could have been witness in her defense.

"Home is not where the heart is," she wrote in a letter, "but the house and the adjacent buildings." A statement of New England realism, a directive to be followed. Probably no poet ever lived so much and so purposefully in one house; even, in one room. Her niece Martha told of visiting her in her corner bedroom on the second floor at 280 Main Street, Amherst, and of how Emily Dickinson made as if to lock the door with an imaginary key, turned and said: "Matty: here's freedom."

I am travelling at the speed of time, in the direction of the house and buildings.

Western Massachusetts: the Connecticut Valley: a countryside still full of reverberations: scene of Indian uprisings, religious revivals, spiritual confrontations, the blazing-up of the lunatic fringe of the Puritan coal. How peaceful and how threatened it looks from Route 91, hills gently curled above the plain, the tobacco-barns standing in fields sheltered with white gauze from the sun, and the sudden urban sprawl: ARCO, MacDonald's, shopping plazas. The country that broke the heart

*From *Parnassus: Poetry in Review*, 5 (Fall / Winter 1976), 49–74. Reprinted by permission of the author.

of Jonathan Edwards, that enclosed the genius of Emily Dickinson. It lies calmly in the light of May, cloudy skies breaking into warm sunshine, light-green spring softening the hills, dogwood and wild fruit-trees blossoming in the hollows.

From Northhampton bypass there's a 4-mile stretch of road to Amherst—Route 9—between fruit farms, steakhouses, supermarkets. The new University of Massachusetts rears its skyscrapers up from the plain against the Pelham Hills. There is new money here, real estate, motels. Amherst succeeds on Hadley almost without notice. Amherst is green, rich-looking, secure; we're suddenly in the center of town, the crossroads of the campus, old New England college buildings spread around two village greens, a scene I remember as almost exactly the same in the dim past of my undergraduate years when I used to come there for college weekends.

Left on Seelye Street, right on Main; driveway at the end of a yellow picket fence. I recognize the high hedge of cedars screening the house, because twenty-five years ago I walked there, even then drawn toward the spot, trying to peer over. I pull into the driveway behind a generous 19th-century brick mansion with wings and porches, old trees and green lawns. I ring at the back door—the door through which Dickinson's coffin was carried to the cemetery a block away.

For years I have been not so much envisioning Emily Dickinson as trying to visit, to enter her mind, through her poems and letters, and through my own intimations of what it could have meant to be one of the two mid-19th-century American geniuses, and a woman, living in Amherst, Massachusetts. Of the other genius, Walt Whitman, Dickinson wrote that she had heard his poems were "disgraceful." She knew her own were unacceptable by her world's standards of poetic convention, and of what was appropriate, in particular, for a woman poet. Seven were published in her lifetime, all edited by other hands; more than a thousand were laid away in her bedroom chest, to be discovered after her death. When her sister discovered them, there were decades of struggle over the manuscripts, the manner of their presentation to the world, their suitability for publication, the poet's own final intentions. Narrowed-down by her early editors and anthologists, reduced to quaintness or spinsterish oddity by many of her commentators, sentimentalized, fallen-in-love with like some gnomic Garbo, still unread in the breadth and depth of her full range of work, she was, and is, a wonder to me when I try to imagine myself into that mind.

I have a notion that genius knows itself; that Dickinson chose her seclusion, knowing she was exceptional and knowing what she needed. It was, moreover, no hermetic retreat, but a seclusion which included a wide range of people, of reading and correspondence. Her sister Vinnie said, "Emily is always looking for the rewarding person." And she found, at various periods, both women and men: her sister-in-law Susan Gilbert,

Amherst visitors and family friends such as Benjamin Newton, Charles Wadsworth, Samuel Bowles, editor of the Springfield *Republican* and his wife; her friends Kate Anthon and Helen Hunt Jackson, the distant but significant figures of Elizabeth Barrett, the Brontës, George Eliot. But she carefully selected her society and controlled the disposal of her time. Not only the "gentlewoman in plush" of Amherst were excluded; Emerson visited next door but she did not go to meet him; she did not travel or receive routine visits; she avoided strangers. Given her vocation, she was neither eccentric nor quaint; she was determined to survive, to use her powers, to practice necessary economies.

Suppose Jonathan Edwards had been born a woman; suppose William James, for that matter, had been born a woman? (The invalid seclusion of his sister Alice is suggestive.) Even from men, New England took its psychic toll; many of its geniuses seemed peculiar in one way or another, particularly along the lines of social intercourse. Hawthorne, until he married, took his meals in his bedroom, apart from the family. Thoreau insisted on the values both of solitude and of geographical restriction, boasting that "I have travelled much in Concord." Emily Dickinson—viewed by her bemused contemporary Thomas Higginson as "partially cracked," by the 20th century as fey or pathological—has increasingly struck me as a practical woman, exercising her gift as she had to, making choices. I have come to imagine her as somehow too strong for her environment, a figure of powerful will, not at all frail or breathless, someone whose personal dimensions would be felt in a household. She was her father's favorite daughter though she professed being afraid of him. Her sister dedicated herself to the everyday domestic labors which would free Dickinson to write. (Dickinson herself baked the bread, made jellies and gingerbread, nursed her mother through a long illness, was a skilled horticulturist who grew pomegranates, calla-lillies, and other exotica in her New England greenhouse.)

Upstairs at last: I stand in the room which for Emily Dickinson was "freedom." The best bedroom in the house, a corner room, sunny, overlooking the main street of Amherst in front, the way to her brother Austin's house on the side. Here, at a small table with one drawer, she wrote most of her poems. Here she read Elizabeth Barrett's "Aurora Leigh," a woman poet's narrative poem of a woman poet's life; also George Eliot; Emerson; Carlyle; Shakespeare; Charlotte and Emily Brontë. Here I become, again, an insect, vibrating at the frames of windows, clinging to panes of glass, trying to connect. The scent here is very powerful. Here in this white-curtained, high-ceilinged room, a redhaired woman with hazel eyes and a contralto voice wrote poems about volcanoes, deserts, eternity, suicide, physical passion, wild beasts, rape, power, madness, separation, the daemon, the grave. Here, with a darning-needle, she bound these poems—heavily emended and often in variant versions—into booklets, secured with darning-thread, to be found and read after her death. Here she knew "freedom," listening from above-stairs to a visitor's piano-playing, escaping from the pantry where she was mistress of the household bread and puddings, watching, you feel, watching ceaselessly, the life of sober Main Street below. From this room she glided downstairs, her hand on the polished bannister, to meet the complacent magazine editor, Thomas Higginson, unnerve him while claiming she herself was unnerved. "Your scholar," she signed herself in letters to him. But she was an independent scholar, used his criticism selectively, saw him rarely and always on *her* premises. It was a life deliberately organized on her terms. The terms she had been handed by society—Calvinist Protestantism, Romanticism, the 19th-century corseting of women's bodies, choices, and sexuality—could spell insanity to a woman genius. What this one had to do was retranslate into a dialect called metaphor: her native language. "Tell all the Truth—but tell it Slant—." It is always what is under pressure in us, especially under pressure of concealment—that explodes in poetry.

The women and men in her life she equally converted into metaphor. The masculine pronoun in her poems can refer simultaneously to many aspects of the "masculine" in the patriarchal world—the god she engages in dialogue, again on *her* terms; her own creative powers, unsexing for a woman, the male power-figures in her immediate environment—the lawyer Edward Dickinson, her brother Austin, the preacher Wadsworth, the editor Bowles—it is far too limiting to trace that "He" to some specific lover, although that was the chief obsession of the legend-mongers for more than half a century. Obviously, Dickinson was attracted by and interested in men whose minds had something to offer her; she was, it is by now clear, equally attracted by and interested in women whose minds had something to offer her. There are many poems to and about women, and some which exist in two versions with alternate sets of pronouns. Her latest biographer, Richard Sewall, while rejecting an earlier Freudian biographer's theory that Dickinson was essentially a psycho-pathological case, the by-product of which happened to be poetry, does create a context in which the importance, and validity, of Dickinson's attachments to women may now, at last, be seen in full. She was always stirred by the existences of women like George Eliot or Elizabeth Barrett, who possessed strength of mind, articulateness, and energy. (She once characterized Elizabeth Fry and Florence Nightingale as "holy"—one suspects she merely meant, "great.")

But of course Dickinson's relationships with women were more than intellectual. They were deeply charged, and the sources both of passionate joy and pain. We are only beginning to be able to consider them in a social and historical context. The historian Carroll Smith-Rosenberg has shown that there was far less taboo on intense, even passionate and sensual, relationships between women in the American 19th-century "female world of love and ritual," as she terms it, than there was later in the 20th century. Women expressed their attachments to other women both physically and verbally; a marriage did not dilute the strength of a female friendship, in which two women often shared the same bed during long visits, and wrote letters articulate with both physical and emotional longing. The 19th-century close woman friend, according to the many diaries and letters Smith-Rosenberg has studied, might be a far more important figure in a woman's life than the 19th-century husband. None of this was condemned as "lesbianism." We will understand Emily Dickinson better, read her poetry more perceptively, when the Freudian imputation of scandal and aberrance in women's love for women has been supplanted by a more informed, less misogynistic attitude toward women's experiences with each other.

But who, if you read through the seventeen hundred and seventy-five poems—who—woman or man—could have passed through that imagination and not come out transmuted? Given the space created by her in that corner room, with its window-light, its potted plants and work-table, given that personality, capable of imposing its terms on a household, on a whole community, what single theory could hope to contain her, when she'd put it all together in that space?

"Matty: here's freedom," I hear her saying as I speed back to Boston along Route 91, as I slip the turnpike ticket into the toll-collector's hand. I am thinking of a confined space in which the genius of the 19th-century female mind in America moved, inventing a language more varied, more compressed, more dense with implications, more complex of syntax, than any American poetic language to date; in the trail of that genius my mind has been moving, and with its language and images my mind still has to reckon, as the mind of a woman poet in America today.

In 1971, a postage stamp was issued in honor of Dickinson; the portrait derives from the one existing daguerrotype of her, with straight, center-parted hair, eyes staring somewhere beyond the camera, hands poised around a nosegay of flowers, in correct 19th-century style. On the first-day-of-issue envelope sent me by a friend there is, besides the postage stamp, an engraving of the poet as popular fancy has preferred her, in a white lace ruff and with hair as bouffant as if she had just stepped from a Boston beauty-parlor. The poem chosen to represent her work to the American public is engraved, alongside a dew-gemmed rose, below the portrait.

> If I can stop one heart from breaking
> I shall not live in vain
> If I can ease one life the aching
> Or cool one pain
> Or help one fainting robin
> Unto his nest again
> I shall not live in vain.

Now, this is extremely strange. It is a fact, that in 1864, Emily Dickinson wrote this verse; and it is a verse which a hundred or more 19th-century versifiers could have written. It is undistinguished language, as in its conventional sentiment, it is remarkably untypical of the poet. Had she chosen to write many poems like this one we would have no "problem" of non-publication, of editing, of estimating the poet at her true worth. Certainly the sentiment—a contented and unambiguous altruism—is one which even today might in some quarters be accepted as fitting from a female versifier—a kind of Girl Scout prayer. But we are talking about the woman who wrote:

> He fumbles at your Soul
> As Players at the Keys
> Before they drop full Music on—
> He stuns you by degrees—
> Prepares your brittle Nature
> For the Ethereal Blow
> By fainter Hammers—further heard—
> Then nearer—Then so slow
> Your breath has time to straighten—
> Your brain—to bubble Cool—
> Deals—One—Imperial—Thunderbolt—
> Then scalps your naked Soul—
>
> When winds take Forests in their Paws—
> The Universe—is still—

(#315)

Much energy has been invested in trying to identify a concrete, flesh-and-blood male lover whom Dickinson is supposed to have renounced, and to the loss of whom can be traced the secret of her seclusion and the vein of much of her poetry. But the real question, given that the art of poetry is an art of transformation, is how this woman's mind and imagination may have used the masculine element in the world at large, or those elements personified as masculine—including the men she knew; how her relationship to this reveals itself in her images and language. In a patriarchal culture, specifically the Judeo-Christian, quasi-Puritan culture of 19th-century New England in which Dickinson grew up, still inflamed with religious revivals, and where the sermon was still an active, if perishing, literary form, the equation of divinity with maleness was so fundamental that it is hardly surprising to find Dickinson, like many an early mystic, blurring erotic with religious experience and imagery. The poem I just read has intimations both of seduction and rape merged with the intense force of a religious experience. But are these metaphors for each other, or for something more intrinsic to Dickinson? Here is another:

> He put the Belt around my life—
> I heard the buckle snap—

And turned away, imperial,
My Lifetime folding up—
Deliberate, as a Duke would do
A Kingdom's Title Deed
Henceforth, a Dedicated sort—
Member of the Cloud.

Yet not too far to come at call—
And do the little Toils
That make the Circuit of the Rest—
And deal occasional smiles
To lives that stoop to notice mine—
And kindly ask it in—
Whose invitation, know you not
For Whom I must decline?

(#273)

These two poems are about possession, and they seem to me a poet's poems—that is, they are about the poet's relationship to her own power, which is exteriorized in masculine form, much as masculine poets have invoked the female Muse. In writing at all—particularly an unorthodox and original poetry like Dickinson's—women have often felt in danger of losing their status as women. And this status has always been defined in terms of relationships to men—as daughter, sister, bride, wife, mother, mistress, Muse. Since the most powerful figures in patriarchal culture have been men, it seems natural that Dickinson would assign a masculine gender to that in herself which did not fit in with the conventional ideology of womanliness. To recognize and acknowledge our own interior power has always been a path mined with risks for women; to acknowledge that power and commit oneself to it as Emily Dickinson did was an immense decision.

Most of us, unfortunately, have been exposed in the schoolroom to Dickinson's "little-girl" poems, her kittenish tones, as in "I'm Nobody! Who Are You?" (a poem whose underlying anger translates itself into archness) or

I hope the Father in the skies
Will lift his little girl—
Old fashioned—naughty—everything—
Over the stile of "Pearl."

(#70)

or the poems about bees and robins. One critic—Richard Chase—has noted that in the 19th century "one of the careers open to women was perpetual childhood." A strain in Dickinson's letters and some—though by far a minority—of her poems was a self-diminutization, almost as if to offset and deny—or even disguise—her actual dimensions as she must have experienced them. And this emphasis on her own "littleness," along with the deliberate strangeness of her tactics of seclusion, have been, until recently, accepted as the prevailing character of the poet: the fragile poetess in white, sending flowers and poems by messenger to unseen friends, letting down baskets of gingerbread to the neighborhood children from her bedroom window; writing, but somehow naively. John Crowe Ransom, arguing for the editing and standardization of Dickinson's punctuation and typography, calls her "a little home-keeping person" who, "while she had a proper notion of the final destiny of her poems . . . was not one of those poets who had advanced to that later stage of operations where manuscripts are prepared for the printer, and the poet's diction has to make concessions to the publisher's stylebook." (In short, Emily Dickinson did not wholly know her trade, and Ransom believes a "publisher's style-book" to have the last word on poetic diction.) He goes on to print several of her poems, altered by him "with all possible forbearance." What might, in a male writer—a Thoreau, let us say, or a Christopher Smart or William Blake—seem a legitimate strangeness, a unique intention, has been in one of our two major poets devalued into a kind of naïveté, girlish ignorance, feminine lack of professionalism, just as the poet herself has been made into a sentimental object ("Most of us are half in love with this dead girl," confesses Archibald MacLeish. Dickinson was fifty-five when she died.)

It is true that more recent critics, including her most recent biographer, have gradually begun to approach the poet in terms of her greatness rather than her littleness, the decisiveness of her choices instead of the surface oddities of her life or the romantic crises of her legend. But unfortunately anthologists continue to plagiarize other anthologies, to reprint her in edited, even bowdlerized versions; the popular image of her and of her work lags behind the changing consciousness of scholars and specialists. There still does not exist a selection from her poems which depicts her in her fullest range. Dickinson's greatness cannot be measured in terms of twenty-five or fifty or even 500 "perfect" lyrics, it has to be seen as the accumulation it is. Poets, even, are not always acquainted with the full dimensions of her work, or the sense one gets, reading in the one-volume complete edition (let alone the three-volume variorum edition) of a mind engaged in a lifetime's musing on essential problems of language, identity, separation, relationship, the integrity of the self; a mind capable of describing psychological states more accurately than any poet except Shakespeare. I have been surprised at how narrowly her work, still, is known by women who are writing poetry, how much her legend has gotten in the way of her being re-possessed, as a source and a foremother.

I know that for me, reading her poems as a child and then as a young girl already seriously writing poetry, she was a problematic figure. I first read her in the selection heavily edited by her niece which appeared in 1937; a later and fuller edition appeared in 1945 when I was sixteen, and

the complete, unbowdlerized edition by Johnson did not appear until fifteen years later. The publication of each of these editions was crucial to
me in successive decades of my life. More than any other poet, Emily
Dickinson seemed to tell me that the intense inner event, the personal and
psychological, was inseparable from the universal; that there was a range
for psychological poetry beyond mere self-expression. Yet the legend of
the life was troubling, because it seemed to whisper that a woman who
undertook such explorations must pay with renunciation, isolation, and
incorporeality. With the publication of the *Complete Poems*, the legend
seemed to recede into unimportance beside the unquestionable power and
importance of the mind revealed there. But taking possession of Emily
Dickinson is still no simple matter.

The 1945 edition, entitled *Bolts of Melody*, took its title from a poem
which struck me at the age of sixteen and which still, thirty years later, ar-
rests my imagination:

> I would not paint—a picture—
> I'd rather be the One
> Its bright impossibility
> To dwell—delicious—on—
> And wonder how the fingers feel
> Whose rare—celestial—stir
> Evokes so sweet a Torment—
> Such sumptuous—Despair—
>
> I would not talk, like Cornets—
> I'd rather be the One
> Raised softly to the Ceilings—
> And out, and easy on—
> Through Villages of Ether
> Myself endured Balloon
> By but a lip of Metal
> The pier to my Pontoon—
>
> Nor would I be a Poet—
> It's finer—own the Ear—
> Enamored—impotent—content—
> The License to revere,
> A privilege so awful
> What would the Dower be,
> Had I the Art to stun myself
> With Bolts of Melody!
>
> (#505)

This poem is about choosing an orthodox "feminine" role: the receptive
rather than the creative; viewer rather than painter, listener rather than
musician; acted-upon rather than active. Yet even while ostensibly choosing this role she wonders "how the fingers feel / whose rare-celes-

tial—stir— / Evokes so sweet a Torment—" and the "feminine" role is praised in a curious sequence of adjectives: "Enamored—*impotent*—content—*.*" The strange paradox of this poem—its exquisite irony—is that it is about choosing not to be a poet, a poem which is gainsaid by no fewer than one thousand seven hundred and seventy-five poems made during the writer's life, including itself. Moreover, the images of the poem rise to a climax (like the Balloon she evokes) but the climax happens as she describes, not what it is to be the receiver, but the maker and receiver at once: "A Privilege so awful / What would the Dower be / Had I the Art to stun myself / With Bolts of Melody!"—a climax which recalls the poem: "He fumbles at your soul / As Players at the Keys / Before they drop full Music on—" And of course, in writing those lines she possess herself of that privilege and that "dower." I have said that this is a poem of exquisite ironies. It is, indeed, though in a very different mode, related to Dickinson's "little-girl" strategy. The woman who feels herself to be Vesuvius at home has need of a mask, at least, of innocuousness and of containment.

> On my volcano grows the Grass
> A meditative spot—
> An acre for a Bird to choose
> Would be the General thought—
>
> How red the Fire rocks below—
> How insecure the sod
> Did I disclose
> Would populate with awe my solitude.
>   (#1677)

Power, even masked, can still be perceived as destructive.

> A still—Volcano—Life—
> That flickered in the night—
> When it was dark enough to do
> Without erasing sight—
>
> A quiet—Earthquake style—
> Too subtle to suspect
> By natures this side Naples—
> The North cannot detect
>
> The Solemn—Torrid—Symbol—
> The lips that never lie—
> Whose hissing Corals part—and shut—
> And Cities—ooze away—
>   (#601)

Dickinson's biographer and editor Thomas Johnson has said that she often felt herself possessed by a demonic force, particularly in the years

1861 and 1862 when she was writing at the height of her drive. There are many poems besides "He put the Belt around my Life" which could be read as poems of possession by the daemon—poems which can also be, and have been, read, as poems of possession by the deity, or by a human lover. I suggest that a woman's poetry about her relationship to her daemon—her own active, creative power—has in patriarchal culture used the language of heterosexual love or patriarchal theology. Ted Hughes tells us that

> the eruption of (Dickinson's) imagination and poetry followed when she shifted her passion, with the energy of desperation, from (the) lost man onto his only possible substitute,—the Universe in its Divine aspect . . . Thereafter, the marriage that had been denied in the real world, went forward in the spiritual . . . just as the Universe in its Divine aspect became the mirror-image of her "husband," so the whole religious dilemma of New England, at that most critical moment in its history, became the mirror-image of her relationship to him, of her "marriage" in fact.[1]

This seems to me to miss the point on a grand scale. There are facts we need to look at. First, Emily Dickinson did not marry. And her non-marrying was neither a pathological retreat as John Cody sees it, nor probably even a conscious decision; it was a fact in her life as in her contemporary Christina Rossetti's; both women had more primary needs. Second: unlike Rossetti, Dickinson did not become a religiously dedicated woman; she was heretical, heterodox, in her religious opinions, and stayed away from church and dogma. What, in fact, *did* she allow to "put the Belt around her Life"—what *did* wholly occupy her mature years and possess her? For "Whom" did she decline the invitations of other lives? The writing of poetry. Nearly two thousand poems. Three hundred and sixty-six poems in the year of her fullest power. What was it like to be writing poetry you knew (and I am sure she did know) was of a class by itself—to be fuelled by the energy it took first to confront, then to condense that range of psychic experience into that language; then to copy out the poems and lay them in a trunk, or send a few here and there to friends or relatives as occasional verse or as gestures of confidence? I am sure she knew who she was, as she indicates in this poem:

> Myself was formed—a carpenter—
> An unpretending time
> My Plane—and I, together wrought
> Before a Builder came—
>
> To measure our attainments
> Had we the Art of Boards
> Sufficiently developed—He'd hire us
> At Halves—

> My Tools took Human—Faces—
> The Bench, where we had toiled—
> Against the Man—persuaded—
> We—Temples Build—I said—
>
> (#488)

This is a poem of the great year 1862, the year in which she first sent a few poems to Thomas Higginson for criticism. Whether it antedates or postdates that occasion is unimportant; it is a poem of knowing one's measure, regardless of the judgments of others.

There are many poems which carry the weight of this knowledge. Here is another one:

> I'm ceded—I've stopped being Theirs—
> The name They dropped upon my face
> With water, in the country church
> Is finished using, now,
> And They can put it with my dolls,
> My childhood, and the string of spools,
> I've finished threading too—
>
> Baptized before, without the choice,
> But this time, consciously, of Grace—
> Unto supremest name—
> Called to my Fill—the Crescent dropped—
> Existence's whole Arc, filled up
> With one small Diadem.
>
> My second Rank—too small the first—
> Crowned—Crowing—on my Father's breast—
> A half unconscious Queen—
> But this time—Adequate—Erect—
> With Will to choose—or to reject—
> And I choose—just a Crown—
>
> (#508)

Now, this poem partakes of the imagery of being "twice-born" or, in Christian liturgy, "confirmed"—and if this poem had been written by Christina Rossetti I would be inclined to give more weight to a theological reading. But it was written by Emily Dickinson, who used the Christian metaphor far more than she let it use her. This is a poem of great pride—not prideful, but *self*-confirmation—and it is curious how little Dickinson's critics, perhaps misled by her diminutives, have recognized the will and pride in her poetry. It is a poem of movement from childhood to womanhood, of transcending the patriarchal condition of bearing her father's name and "crowing—on my Father's breast—." She is now a conscious Queen, "Adequate—Erect / With Will to choose, or to reject—."

There is one poem which is the real "onlie begetter" of my thoughts here about Dickinson; a poem I have mused over, repeated to myself, taken into myself over many years. I think it a poem about possession by the daemon, about the dangers and risks of such possession if you are a woman, about the knowledge that power in a woman can seem destructive, and that you cannot live without the daemon once it has possessed you. The archetype of the daemon as masculine is beginning to change, but it has been real for women up until now. But this woman poet also perceives herself as a lethal weapon:

> My life had stood—a Loaded Gun—
> In Corners—till a Day
> The Owner passed—identified—
> And carried me away—
>
> And now We roam in Sovereign Woods—
> And now we hunt the Doe—
> And every time I speak for Him—
> The Mountains straight reply—
>
> And I do smile, such cordial light
> Upon the Valley glow—
> It is as a Vesuvian face
> Had let its pleasure through—
>
> And when at Night—our good Day done—
> I guard My Master's Head—
> 'Tis better than the Eider-Duck's
> Deep Pillow—to have shared—
>
> To foe of His—I'm deadly foe—
> None stir the second time—
> On whom I lay a Yellow Eye—
> Or an emphatic Thumb—
>
> Though I than he—may longer live
> He longer must—than I—
> For I have but the power to kill,
> Without—the power to die—

(#754)

Here the poet sees herself as split, not between anything so simple as "masculine" and "feminine" identity but between the hunter, admittedly masculine, but also a human person, an active, willing being, and the gun—an object, condemned to remain inactive until the hunter—the *owner*—takes possession of it. The gun contains an energy capable of rousing echoes in the mountains and lighting up the valleys; it is also deadly, "Vesuvian;" it is also its owner's defender against the "foe." It is the gun, furthermore, who *speaks for him*. If there is a female consciousness in this poem it is buried deeper than the images: it exists in the ambivalence toward power, which is extreme. Active willing and creation in women are forms of aggression, and aggression is both "the power to kill" and punishable by death. The union of gun with hunter embodies the danger of identifying and taking hold of her forces, not least that in so doing she risks defining herself—and being defined—as aggressive, as un-womanly, ("and now we hunt the Doe") and as potentially lethal. That which she experiences in herself as energy and potency can also be experienced as pure destruction. The final stanza, with its precarious balance of phrasing, seems a desperate attempt to resolve the ambivalence; but, I think, it is no resolution, only a further extension of ambivalence.

> Though I than he—may longer live
> He longer must—than I—
> For I have but the power to kill,
> Without—the power to die—

The poet experiences herself as loaded gun, imperious energy; yet without the Owner, the possessor, she is merely lethal. Should that possession abandon her—but the thought is unthinkable: "He longer *must* than I." The pronoun is masculine; the antecedent is what Keats called "The Genius of Poetry."

I do not pretend to have—I don't even wish to have—explained this poem, accounted for its every image; it will reverberate with new tones long after my words about it have ceased to matter. But I think that for us, at this time, it is a central poem in understanding Emily Dickinson, and ourselves, and the condition of the woman artist, particularly in the 19th century. It seems likely that the 19th-century woman poet, especially, felt the medium of poetry as dangerous, in ways that the woman novelist did not feel the medium of fiction to be. In writing even such a novel of elemental sexuality and anger as *Wuthering Heights*, Emily Bronte could at least theoretically separate herself from her characters; they were, after all, fictitious beings. Moreover, the novel is or can be a construct, planned and organized to deal with human experiences on one level at a time. Poetry is too much rooted in the unconscious; it presses too close against the barriers of repression; and the 19th-century woman had much to repress. It is interesting that Elizabeth Barrett tried to fuse poetry and fiction in writing "Aurora Leigh"—perhaps apprehending the need for fictional characters to carry the charge of her experience as a woman artist. But with the exception of "Aurora Leigh" and Christina Rossetti's "Goblin Market"—that extraordinary and little-known poem drenched in oral eroticism—Emily Dickinson's is the only poetry in English by a woman of that century which pierces so far beyond the ideology of the "feminine" and the conventions of womanly feeling. To write it at all, she had to be willing to enter chambers of self in which

> Ourself behind ourself, concealed—
> Should startle most—

and to relinquish control there, to take those risks, she had to create a relationship to the outer world where she could feel in control.

It is an extremely painful and dangerous way to live—split between a publicly acceptable persona, and a part of yourself that you perceive as the essential, the creative and powerful self, yet also as possibly unacceptable, perhaps even monstrous.

> Much Madness is divinist sense—
> To a discerning Eye—
> Much sense—the starkest Madness.
> 'Tis the Majority
> In this, as All, prevail—
> Assent—and you are sane—
> Demur—you're straightway dangerous—
> And handled with a chain—
>
> (#435)

For many women the stresses of this splitting have led, in a world so ready to assert our innate passivity and to deny our independence and creativity, to extreme consequences: the mental asylum, self-imposed silence, recurrent depression, suicide, and often severe loneliness.

Dickinson is *the* American poet whose work consisted in exploring states of psychic extremity. For a long time, as we have seen, this fact was obscured by the kinds of selections made from her work by timid if well-meaning editors. In fact, Dickinson was a great psychologist; and like every great psychologist, she began with the material she had at hand: herself. She had to possess the courage to enter, through language, states which most people deny or veil with silence.

> The first Day's Night had come—
> And grateful that a thing
> So terrible—had been endured—
> I told my soul to sing—
>
> She said her Strings were snapt—
> Her Bow—to Atoms blown—
> And so to mend her—gave me work
> Until another Morn—
>
> And then—a Day as huge
> As Yesterdays in pairs,
> Unrolled its horror in my face—
> Until it blocked my eyes—
>
> My Brain—begun to laugh—
> I mumbled—like a fool—

And tho' 'tis years ago—that Day—
My brain keeps giggling—still.

And Something's odd—within—
That person that I was—
And this One—do not feel the same—
Could it be Madness—this?

(#410)

Dickinson's letters acknowledge a period of peculiarly intense personal crisis; her biographers have variously ascribed it to the pangs of renunciation of an impossible love, or to psychic damage deriving from her mother's presumed depression and withdrawal after her birth. What concerns us here is the fact that she chose to probe the nature of this experience in language:

The Soul has Bandaged moments—
When too appalled to stir—
She feels some ghastly Fright come up
And stop to look at her—

Salute her—with long fingers—
Caress her freezing hair—
Sip, Goblin, from the very lips
The Lover—hovered—o'er—
Unworthy, that a thought so mean
Accost a Theme—so—fair—

The soul has moments of Escape—
When bursting all the doors—
She dances like a Bomb, abroad,
And swings upon the hours . . .

The Soul's retaken moments—
When, Felon led along,
With shackles on the plumed feet,
And staples, in the Song,

The Horror welcomes her, again,
These, are not brayed of Tongue—

(#512)

In this poem, the word "Bomb" is dropped, almost carelessly, as a correlative for the soul's active, liberated states—it occurs in a context of apparent euphoria, but its implications are more than euphoric—they are explosive, destructive. The Horror from which in such moments the soul escapes has a masculine, "goblin" form, and suggests the perverse and terrifying rape of a "bandaged" and powerless self. In at least one poem, Dickinson depicts the actual process of suicide:

He scanned it—staggered—
Dropped the Loop
To Past or Period—
Caught helpless at a sense as if
His mind were going blind—
Groped up—to see if God was there—
Groped backward at Himself—
Caressed a Trigger absently
And wandered out of Life.

                    (#1062)

The precision of knowledge in this brief poem is such that we must assume that Dickinson had, at least in fantasy, drifted close to that state in which the "Loop" that binds us to "Past or Period" is "dropped" and we grope randomly at what remains of abstract notions of sense, God, or self, before—almost absent-mindedly—reaching for a solution. But it's worth noting that this is a poem in which the suicidal experience has been distanced, refined, transformed through a devastating accuracy of language. It is not suicide that is studied here, but the dissociation of self and mind and world which precedes.

Dickinson was convinced that a life worth living could be found within the mind and against the grain of external circumstance: "Reverse cannot befall / That fine prosperity / Whose Sources are interior—." (#305) The horror, for her, was that which set "Staples in the Song"—the numbing and freezing of the interior, a state she describes over and over:

There is a Languor of the Life
More imminent than Pain—
'Tis Pain's Successor—When the Soul
Has suffered all it can—

A Drowsiness—diffuses—
A Dimness like a Fog
Envelopes Consciousness—
As Mists—obliterate a Crag.

The Surgeon—does not blanch—at pain
His Habit—is severe—
But tell him that it ceased to feel—
That creature lying there—

And he will tell you—skill is late—
A Mightier than He—
Has ministered before Him—
There's no Vitality.

                    (#396)

I think the equation surgeon-artist is a fair one here; the artist can work with the materials of pain; she cuts to probe and heal; but she is powerless at the point where

> After great pain, a formal feeling comes—
> The nerves sit ceremonious, like Tombs—
> The stiff Heart questions was it He, that bore,
> And Yesterday, or Centuries before?
>
> The Feet, mechanical, go round—
> Of Ground, or Air, or Ought—
> A Wooden way
> Regardless grown,
> A Quartz contentment, like a stone—
>
> This is the Hour of Lead
> Remembered, if outlived
> As Freezing persons, recollect the Snow—
> First—Chill—then Stupor—then the letting go—
>
> (#341)

For the poet, the terror is precisely in those periods of psychic death, when even the possibility of work is negated; her "occupation's gone." Yet she also describes the unavailing effort to numb emotion:

> Me from Myself—to banish—
> Had I Art—
> Impregnable my Fortress
> Unto All Heart—
>
> But since Myself—assault Me—
> How have I peace
> Except by subjugating
> Consciousness?
>
> And since We're mutual Monarch
> How this be
> Except by Abdication—
> Me—of Me?
>
> (#642)

The possibility of abdicating oneself—of ceasing to be—remains.

> Severe Service of myself
> I—hastened to demand
> To fill the awful longitude
> Your life had left behind—
>
> I worried Nature with my Wheels
> When Hers had ceased to run—

When she had put away her Work
My own had just begun.

I strove to weary Brain and Bone—
To harass to fatigue
The glittering Retinue of nerves—
Vitality to clog

To some dull comfort Those obtain
Who put a Head away
They knew the Hair to—
And forget the color of the Day—

Affliction would not be appeased—
The Darkness braced as firm
As all my strategem had been
The Midnight to confirm

No drug for Consciousness—can be—
Alternative to die
Is Nature's only Pharmacy
For Being's Malady—

(#786)

Yet consciousness—not simply the capacity to suffer, but the capacity to experience intensely at every instant—creates of death not a blotting-out but a final illumination:

This Consciousness that is aware
Of Neighbors and the Sun
Will be the one aware of Death
And that itself alone

Is traversing the interval
Experience between
And most profound experiment
Appointed unto Men—

How adequate unto itself
Its properties shall be
Itself unto itself and none
Shall make discovery.

Adventure most unto itself
The Soul condemned to be—
Attended by a single Hound
Its own identity.

(#822)

The poet's relationship to her poetry has, it seems to me—and I am not speaking only of Emily Dickinson—a twofold nature. Poetic language—the poem on paper—is a concretization of the poetry of the world at large, the self, and the forces within the self; and those forces are rescued from formlessness, lucidified, and integrated in the act of writing poems. But there is a more ancient concept of the poet, which is that she is endowed to speak for those who do not have the gift of language, or to see for those who—for whatever reasons—are less conscious of what they are living through. It is as though the risks of the poet's existence can be put to some use beyond her own survival.

> The Province of the Saved
> Should be the Art—To save—
> Through Skill obtained in themselves—
> The Science of the Grave
>
> No Man can understand
> But He that hath endured
> The Dissolution—in Himself—
> That man—be qualified
>
> To qualify Despair
> To Those who failing new—
> Mistake Defeat for Death—Each time—
> Till acclimated—to—
>
> (#539)

The poetry of extreme states, the poetry of danger, can allow its readers to go further in our awareness, take risks we might not have dared; it says, at least: "Someone has been here before."

> The Soul's distinct Connection
> With immortality
> Is best disclosed by Danger
> Or quick Calamity—
>
> As Lightning on a Landscape
> Exhibits Sheets of Place—
> Not yet suspected—but for Flash—
> And Click—and Suddenness.
>
> (#974)

> Crumbling is not an instant's Act
> A fundamental pause
> Dilapidation's processes
> Are organized Decays.

'Tis first a cobweb on the Soul
A Cuticle of Dust
A Borer in the Axis
An Elemental Rust—

Ruin is formal—Devil's work
Consecutive and slow—
Fail in an instant—no man did
Slipping—is Crash's law.
                    (#997)

I felt a Cleaving in my Mind
As if my Brain had split—
I tried to match it—Seam by Seam—
But could not make them fit.

The thought behind, I strove to join
Unto the thought before—
But Sequence ravelled out of Sound
Like Balls—upon a Floor
                    (#937)

There are many more Emily Dickinsons than I have tried to call up here. Wherever you take hold of her, she proliferates. I wish I had time here to explore her complex sense of Truth; to follow the thread we unravel when we look at the numerous and passionate poems she wrote to or about women; to probe her ambivalent feelings about fame, a subject pursued by many male poets before her; simply to examine the poems in which she is directly apprehending the natural world. No one since the 17th century had reflected more variously or more probingly upon death and dying. What I have tried to do here is follow through some of the origins and consequences of her choice to be, not only a poet but a woman who explored her own mind, without any of the guidelines of orthodoxy. To say "yes" to her powers was not simply a major act of nonconformity in the 19th century; even in our time it has been assumed that Emily Dickinson, not patriarchal society, was "the problem." The more we come to recognize the unwritten and written laws and taboos underpinning patriarchy, the less problematical, surely, will seem the methods she chose.

Note

1. Ted Hughes, *A Choice of Emily Dickinson's Verse* (London, 1968), p. 11.

Naming As History:
Dickinson's Poems of Definition   Sharon Cameron*

In the following pages I shall consider the problems that arise when a poem's beginning is more forceful than its conclusion; when the name or definition it contains bears no relation or a problematic relation to its context; when a word in such a poem lacks adequate contextual specification. I shall then examine a group of poems in which definitions successfully require their contexts, temporal or otherwise; which exist in an effort to clarify an internal state or to clear up an external confusion; which open rather than close the issues they consider; and in which the complexity of definition is revelatory of the complexity of the speaker's situation and the need for its exegesis.

There are frequent instances in Dickinson's definitional poems where the poem's conclusion follows poorly from its beginning. Sometimes, as in the following poem, it is redundant and hence gratuitous:

> Hope is a subtle Glutton—
> He feeds upon the Fair—
> And yet—inspected closely
> What Abstinence is there—
>
> His is the Halcyon Table—
> That never seats but One—
> And whatsoever is consumed
> The same amount remain—[1]

The second stanza glosses the first. It explains the fact that Hope's table is prosperous (a restatement of line 2), and that Hope's consumption in no way depletes the fare of reality, since Hope feasts only in supposition (an idea contained in the last two lines of the first stanza). The problem with the restatement is that it is not particularly interesting. Similarly, the opening of the following poem has an exactitude that its conclusion lacks:

> Longing is like the Seed
> That wrestles in the Ground,
> Believing if it intercede
> It shall at length be found.
>
> The Hour, and the Clime—
> Each Circumstance unknown,
> What Constancy must be achieved
> Before it see the Sun!
>
> (P1255)

*From Sharon Cameron, *Lyric Time: Dickinson and the Limits of Genre* (Baltimore and London: Johns Hopkins Univ. Press, 1979) pp. 34–44. Reprinted by permission of the Johns Hopkins University Press, © 1979.

Similes recognize that we fail at direct names because we fail at perfect comprehension, and that certain experiences evade mastery and hence definition—the best we can do is approximate or approach them; a simile is an acknowledgment of that failure and contains within it the pain of imperfect rendering. What is evocative about the simile in P 1255 is the way in which it gets the verb to enact the tension between being, which is manifest, and presence, which is hidden. This tension is precisely the essence of longing, and externalizing it reveals the conflict: it can never be perfectly rendered because, half-hidden with its object, it can never be perfectly apprehended. Dickinson is using the word "intercede" to suggest that surfacing of longing which would be tantamount to its acknowledgment, its open coming between the speaker and an instigating source. What might be "found" at such a moment is not simply the shape of the buried feeling, but also its object, which, one presumes, is similarly absent or unavailable. In the poem's following lines, however, both the representation of tension between presence and being and the recognition that it is this tension that makes longing so difficult to represent are abandoned, and the simile is "extended" with little regard for the significance of its original distinction. Here, then, as in the previous poem, the most complex part of the assertion is the name itself. In such an instance, an explanation of, or rationale for, the genesis of the name after the fact of it cannot help but affect the reader as gratuitous.

As in the following poem, the definition exists for the purpose of dismissing the situation with which it purports to deal:

> Remorse—is Memory—awake
> Her Parties all astir—
> A Presence of Departed Acts—
> At window—and at Door—
>
> Its Past—set down before the Soul
> And lighted with a Match—
> Perusal—to facilitate
> Of its Condensed Despatch
>
> Remorse is cureless—the Disease
> Not even God—can heal—
> For 'tis His institution—and
> The Complement of Hell—
>   (P 744)

The emphasis in the first two stanzas is on the excruciating sense in which we can be inhabited by a past that will not stay still. Remorse awakens memory and memory prevents calmness (perhaps literally prevents sleep, as the metaphor in the first line suggests) by lighting our minds with unwanted thoughts. Remorse (for that is the match) illuminates the past so that the flash revealed to us is simply accusatory. If we did not distort the past by condensing it, if we knew not to simplify, the accusation would be less clear. The speaker is defining a situation in which our experiences play upon our minds in such a way that we cannot doubt them to be ours, yet robbed of their specificity, we cannot see them as they in fact happened to us. The hell of remorse is that it blinds us to the real meanings of our experiences and simultaneously convinces us that the distortion we are seeing in place of that meaning is reality.

Our sense of the speaker in the first two stanzas is that of someone who is naming or defining an experience in order to achieve mastery over it. But in the third stanza, control is secured as a consequence of ascribing blame, so the focus of the poem narrows to exclude experience. The definitions in the first two stanzas are concerned with the quality of remorse. In them the speaker makes clear the way in which remorse is experiential hell. The definition in the third stanza is concerned with its cause. There we are told about the way in which it is a complement of theological Hell. That remorse is God's institution may be a matter of fact or, more important, a matter of belief, but it shifts the speaker's role in the experience by predicating an agent for the affliction. A relationship exists between these two factors but the poem is not positioned with respect to that relationship.

In the following poem, a disjunction between the initial naming in line one and the lines that follow it leads the reader to interpretive despair, for there is no way to figure the confusion that ensues:

> Doom is the House without the Door—
> 'Tis entered from the Sun—
> And then the Ladder's thrown away,
> Because Escape—is done—
>
> 'Tis varied by the Dream
> Of what they do outside—
> Where Squirrels play—and Berries die—
> And Hemlocks—bow—to God—
>
> (P 475)

If the statement in line one is literal, it perhaps refers to the grave. But it need not be literal, perhaps cannot be literal, as line two suggests. Maybe then the speaker is using "Doom" as a metaphor for an inevitability one may come to dwell in (like a house) but be unaware of (and therefore enter like a doorless house). The second stanza, far from clarifying these concerns, only confuses them, for the shape of the two realities implicitly being compared remains too ambiguously sketched for the reader to see a coherent picture.

The lack of explicit connection between the statements in a definitional poem sometimes results in speech that is almost unintelligible:

> Experience is the Angled Road
> Preferred against the Mind

By—Paradox—the Mind itself—
Presuming it to lead

Quite Opposite—How Complicate
The Discipline of Man—
Compelling Him to Choose Himself
His Preappointed Pain—

(P 910)

The distinctions are so coiled here that it is difficult to understand them. One way of interpreting the first stanza is to assume that experience is chosen above the mind (preferred against it) even though (and this is the paradox) the mind itself states its preference for experience. But it is not clear what the mind presumes experiences will "lead / Quite Opposite [to]," since the line breaks in the middle of the thought. If we infer that the object of the implicit preposition is "pain," this is still awkward sense, and it is certainly awkward syntax. The real problem, however, is that the focus of the poem shifts in stanza two. There "The Discipline of Man," an idiosyncratic but in no way interesting (because not made relevant) periphrasis for the mind, is called "Complicate," and this is then stated as the reason man chooses his "Preappointed Pain," itself an unexplained paradox. "Preappointed," moreover, has resonances of a final judgment, though whether of salvation or damnation is not clear. These resonances come from the word itself and our inferences about how Dickinson might be likely to use it rather than from the poem's context. While there is too little linguistic specificity to substantiate inference, one wonders if the speaker is choosing between the immediacy of this world and the promise of the next only to discover that any choice must confront the inevitability of pain. The problem with my reading is that while the mind has been rendered as complex, it has not been so rendered in terms of these specific issues. The problem with the poem and particularly with that suggestive last phrase is that it insinuates my reading without confirming it.

The poems about which I have been speaking have become progressively more difficult to understand, and the efforts at understanding them progressively less rewarding. In "Hope is a subtle Glutton" we found that the poem repeated without elaborating upon its initial name; in "Longing is like the Seed" and "Remorse is Memory awake" that complex situations were stated only to be dismissed by the poems' conclusions; in "Doom is the House without the Door" and "Experience is the Angled Road" that context and conclusion bore such an ambiguous relation to the initial names that we literally could make no sense even of the names themselves. The problem with these poems and with the many like them is twofold. First, they raise the question of the point in an experience at which one's awareness of it yields a name. For whether a name seems gratuitous or appropriate is contingent upon its relationship to the rest of the experience being narrated. Second, there is the problem of how a given speaker manifests the need of, or reason for, the name at which she arrives. It is not here my intention to theorize on criteria for fictional coherence, but it ought to be obvious that one credits speech in direct presence, and no less in poems, that issues out of a discernible and describable situation and that is functional in nature. In a discussion of the following poems, I will examine the quite specific and complex tasks that naming and definition-making can perform.

Sometimes the point of a definition can be to reveal the speaker's knowledge of its inadequacy, as, for example, in the following:

> A Coffin—is a small Domain,
> Yet able to contain
> A Citizen of Paradise
> In it's diminished Plane.
>
> A Grave—is a restricted Breadth—
> Yet ampler than the Sun—
> And all the Seas He populates
> And Lands He looks upon
>
> To Him who on it's small Repose—
> Bestows a single Friend—
> Circumference without Relief—
> Or Estimate—or End—
>
> (P 943)

The first stanza, at least nominally, answers the question of what space a person inhabits after death. It is notable, therefore, that the second stanza should return to that question. Maybe the speaker returns to the literal facts of death in order to anchor herself in a reality that is not speculative, as if the positive assertiveness of the first stanza were more bravado than belief. We know further that the reason she is not free of her initial question is that her manner of dealing with it has not spoken to the anxiety implicit in its insistence.

So the definitional voice comes back like the voice of reality: "A Grave—is a restricted Breadth—." Because in stanza one the limited space of the coffin has been juxtaposed to the infinity of the dead person's new dwelling place, we might suppose the speaker is again minimizing the grave's size in order to point to the spaciousness of an afterlife. But the infinity to which she now refers is inside of her and is of the everlastingness of loss. Similarly overwhelmed, another of Dickinson's speakers has spoken of "a Wilderness of Size" (P 856). The shift in definition has been occasioned by the shift in the speaker's perspective, for this is a poem in which awe discovers its origin and its proper object. It discovers that its object is not elsewhere at the supposition of another life, but rather here at the fact that this one is mortal.

Definition, then, can be a way of coming to terms with a discrepancy between what one believes and what one feels, of growing knowledgeable about one's feeling.[2] For the first definition is insufficient not because it is untrue, but rather because it is irrelevant. In the following definitional poem, renunciation is the strategy for coming to terms with loss:

> Renunciation—is a piercing Virtue—
> The letting go
> A Presence—for an Expectation—
> Not now—
> The putting out of Eyes—
> Just Sunrise—
> Lest Day—
> Day's Great Progenitor—
> Outvie
> Renunciation—is the Choosing
> Against itself—
> Itself to justify
> Unto itself—
> When larger function—
> Make that appear—
> Smaller—that Covered Vision—Here—
>
> (P 745)

This poem, unlike "A Coffin is a small Domain," begins with the tone of a voice aware of the situation's complexity. It is the tone of someone trying to convince herself of something she finds both difficult and imperative to believe—that renunciation is a virtue; that it is piercing she knows. The pain of the conflict is woven into the first three lines and enacted in the direct discourse of "Not now—." The force of the imperative moves the speaker back to a more bounded place where she can more safely (because the danger of capitulation is less real) define renunciation with specificity: "The putting out of eyes— / Just Sunrise—." Sight must be avoided at all costs because it will inform her that day surpasses "Day's great Progenitor—." Of course the very presumption that if she could see God's light it would be judged dim compared to the light of day is itself a judgment. In 1885 Dickinson had written to Maria Whitney: "I fear we shall care very little for the technical resurrection, when to behold the one face that to us comprised it is too much for us, and I dare not think of the voraciousness of that only gaze and its only return" (L 969). And almost twenty years earlier, to the Hollands: "If God had been here this summer, and seen the things that I have seen—I guess that He would think His Paradise superfluous" (L 185). More soberly, she had expressed the belief that the reason earthly bliss does not last is that, if it did, " 'Twould supersede the Heaven—" (P 393). "I have never believed [Paradise] to be a superhuman site," she had insisted (L 391).

At the point in the poem at which the speaker exhibits a clear preference for this world, a second definition is formulated, perhaps as an explanation for why she is opting for what she does not want. The syntax of lines ten to thirteen is convoluted because the idea that renunciation is a matter of one's best interest is a convoluted idea involving, as the lines literally do, several iterations of the concept of self: the sense in which renunciation is an act that violates the self; the sense in which it is an act that legitimates the self; and the sense in which the self stands as ambivalent arbiter between the two. The diction of the last three lines lacks the precision of the rest of the poem, but, to paraphrase what I believe to be the speaker's conclusion, she is saying: "My act of renunciation will be justified when the vision of God makes this world appear insignificant." Though she concedes that God's revelation will dwarf that of this world, she clearly indicates that with the eyes she now has, a presence looks better than an expectation. The speaker's last word is "Here," for the most significant fact about this world is its presence.

The relationship between renunciation and loss remains tentative throughout the poem, as I suspect it remained tentative throughout Dickinson's life. In 1882, she had written to James D. Clark, "No Verse in the Bible has frightened me so much from a Child as 'from him that hath not, shall be taken even that he hath' " (L 788), and we can speculate that the speaker's willingness to give up this world is contingent upon her recognition of the requirement of doing so. Definition here, then, is a way of teaching the will to desire what a force external to it has deemed necessary.

The following definitional poem establishes familiarity with a subject about which we ordinarily feel profound and disquieting ignorance:

> Death is the supple Suitor
> That wins at last—
> It is a stealthy Wooing
> Conducted first
> By pallid innuendoes
> And dim approach
> But brave at last with Bugles
> And a bisected Coach
> It bears away in triumph
> To Troth unknown
> And Kindred as responsive
> As Porcelain
>
> (P 1445)

One of the most striking characteristics of this utterance is the speaker's awareness that while death is always with her, his relationship to her is always changing. Therefore the definition takes the form of a progression. Isolating the steps in the process is a strategy for asserting knowledge over something, half of whose threat lies in its insistence that we cannot know it. Though we are told about death's activities, and not about the speaker's, the poem is itself a telling insofar as it is clear by the second line that the speaker is repelled by the suit. If death is company of which the speaker cannot be rid, then the speech is uttered in his presence the way an insult would be.

Once in an effort to define the "Porcelain" quality of death to which she here refers, Dickinson found words for the terrible transformation she witnessed:

> 'Twas warm—at first—like Us—
> Until there crept upon
> A Chill—like frost upon a Glass—
> 'Till all the scene—be gone.
>
> The Forehead copied Stone—
> The Fingers grew too cold
> To ache—and like a Skater's Brook—
> The busy eyes—congealed—
>
> It straightened—that was all—
> It crowded Cold to Cold—
> It multiplied indifference—
> As Pride were all it could—
>
> And even when with Cords—
> 'Twas lowered, like a Weight—
> It made no Signal, nor demurred,
> But dropped like Adamant.
>
> (P 519)

In the space created by the words, at the center of which lies recognition (as in the space created by the lowering of the corpse, at the center of which lies grief), definition is by default.

The effort to understand the incomprehensible frequently depended upon definitions that took scrupulous note of the progressions of experience whose totality evaded the grasp. If one could at least chart the stages whereby a thing passed into incomprehensibility, one might come to terms with the fact that process itself and the loss with which it concludes is not sudden, as it appears, but has stages. Here the person neutered by death becomes unrecognizable in direct proportion to the speaker's perception of his / her loss of feeling. " 'Twas warm— / at first—like Us," but the ultimate abdication of human life is the numbing and final absence of sensation, interpreted from a mortal perspective as "Pride": the power to remain unmoved. Dickinson had observed a related progression when she noted: "The Living—tell— / The Dying—but a Syllable— / The Coy Dead—None—" (P 408).

Definitions that had their genesis in the stages of a situation were useful precisely because, through their recapitulation, a speaker might perceive a relationship between the first and final steps of a phenomenon that seemed otherwise of inexplicable origin. The definition of such a phenomenon was thus a reconstruction of its history:

> Crumbling is not an instant's Act
> A fundamental pause
> Dilapidation's processes
> Are organized Decays.
>
> 'Tis first a Cobweb on the Soul
> A Cuticle of Dust
> A Borer in the Axis
> An Elemental Rust—
>
> Ruin is formal—Devil's work
> Consecutive and slow—
> Fail in an instant, no man did
> Slipping—is Crash's law.
>   (P 997)

Here we are told that the beginning of a process contains and predicts its conclusion. Though in retrospect we are capable of understanding the relationship between one part of an experience and another, at the time they may seem radically disconnected. Effecting a connection often comes, as in the following poem about disillusionment, only after it is too late:

> Finding is the first Act
> The second, loss,
> Third, Expedition for
> The "Golden Fleece"
>
> Fourth, no Discovery—
> Fifth, no Crew—
> Finally, no Golden Fleece—
> Jason—sham—too.
>   (P 870)

In this case the step past the final one is really the step upon which all other deceptions are predicated. Jason is mentioned last as something absolutely unforgettable would be. We note, too, that his deception cannot be formulated serially; it is too large. It is because Medea made this discovery last that she was not saved from making the other, earlier discoveries.

Notes

1. All selections of Dickinson's poems are from *The Poems of Emily Dickinson*, ed. Thomas H. Johnson (Cambridge, Mass., 1955) and will be indicated in the text by the capital letter P followed by the poem number and enclosed in parentheses as (P 1547).

2. In *Emily Dickinson's Poetry* (Chicago, 1975), Robert Weisbuch discusses a similar phenomenon in Dickinson's definitional poems when he observes that they sometimes propose analogues that the rest of the poem revises or even overthrows (see pp. 63–71).

Doing Without: Dickinson as Yankee Woman Poet

Jane Donahue Eberwein*

"Sisters are brittle things," Emily Dickinson wrote to the Hollands in 1859, reporting on Lavinia's sickness. Instead of resolving to extend her circle of kindred spirits, however, she went on characteristically to celebrate the value of uniqueness: "*One* is a dainty sum! One bird, one cage, one flight; one song in those far woods, as yet suspected by faith only!" One sister, then, must suffice, although Dickinson occasionally welcomed "Sister Sue" Dickinson and eventually "Little Sister" Mrs. Holland within the family circle. For the admiring readers, however, who have wanted to claim sisterhood with Emily Dickinson on the basis of shared concerns and constraints, the Amherst poet has herself proven a brittle friend. Where other women might reach out socially to protect themselves from isolation, Dickinson drew in upon her own household and evaluated the problem of isolation as one to be solved in her dealings with God rather than in relationships with other people: "God was penurious with me, which makes me shrewd with Him." The vocabulary here is commercial, and the economic system is one of scarcity. Like any Yankee girl trained from childhood in habits of thrift, Dickinson instinctively conserved her resources rather than trying to extend them, and she applied to sisterhood the same practical prudence with which she learned to "Use it up, wear it out, / Make it do, or do without." In a family whose prosperous and socially prominent mother devoted herself to mending her student son's shirts, Emily Dickinson cultivated a pride in thrift which would have extraordinary influence on the poetry she wrote and the attitude she took toward herself as a writer. She would be resourceful, careful, shrewd. She would make do with what she had or do without whatever she lacked.

This Yankee parsimony distances Dickinson from many modern admirers who wish she had been a more assertive woman and a more conscious representative of her sex. We who live in a twentieth-century middle-class economy of abundance unconsciously apply our own fiscal metaphors to social and artistic issues, and we raise questions about Dickinson's strategies in accordance with cultural assumptions which she never shared. For us, who imagined until recently that the world's

*This essay was written specifically for this volume and appears here for the first time by permission of the author.

resources might be infinite, it makes no sense to make do with little or do without; those who find themselves deprived should demand more. Improvement, for us, tends to be associated with expansion. Success is measured in terms of profit and celebrity. Responsibility involves identification with other people, especially those who share similar deprivations, and it requires social solidarity for the common good. Given such assumptions it is no wonder that we find Emily Dickinson so mysterious, even at times so alienating. That she, the greatest woman poet in nineteenth-century America and quite possibly the most brilliant female artist this country has yet produced, should never have earned money for her poems, never have seen her name in print except for winning a baking prize, never exerted her influence to assist her artistically deprived sisters seems to us a waste of ability. Assuming that she wanted the opportunities modern women have learned to demand, we tend to think of Emily Dickinson as a victim of cultural limitations, especially of those restrictions her society placed on gently-bred young women. We regard her as a silent and generally ineffective rebel against social conventions, writing secretly like some Soviet dissident with no assurance of ever reaching an audience. We take it for granted that she needed to break out of the limitations her culture placed around her and that she, and we, would have benefited from greater freedom.[2]

Yet Dickinson herself remained silent on the issue of cultural restraints against women. While other women in nineteenth-century America demanded opportunities or simply settled down to doing tasks normally regarded as male preserves, Dickinson withdrew into austerely private domesticity and made no complaints—except protests against the few efforts other people made to draw her out. Anne Bradstreet, fully two centuries earlier, had shown more spunk in asserting her woman's right to expression; and the lady editors of even the most genteel Victorian womens' magazines self-consciously defended their role in a literary world still considered masculine. Dickinson, however, made no such claims and seemed unaware of a problem. No poem asserts female artistic abilities like Bradstreet's "Prologue;" no surviving letter even mutely echoes Margaret Fuller's feminist demands or Sara Josepha Hale's protestations. Why not?

Dickinson appreciated the literature written by other women, of course, and seemed to take their stature for granted. She admired Elizabeth Barrett Browning, George Eliot, and the Bronte sisters; and Emily Stipes Watts makes a good case for the theory that she profited as well from the tradition of women's writing in the United States, including the work of such sentimental poetesses as the Sweet Singer of Hartford.[3] Many of her favorite books were written by members of her own sex or by men who, like Ik Marvell, calculatedly directed their work to an audience of genteel ladies. The sentimental and gothic conventions of such popular literature permeate her poems and letters to an extent we cannot afford to ignore. Perhaps because of this tradition, in the best of which she took justifiable pride, Dickinson felt no need to defend her aspirations as a woman poet if, indeed, she thought of herself in such terms.

From the evidence of her poems it would seem that Dickinson applied a human but surprisingly impersonal vocabulary to poetry and thought of "The Poet" in asexual terms. Rather than redefine poet to admit women within its range of denotation or add the word poetess to her vocabulary, she made do with what she had. To avoid sexual pronouns which might limit the range of poet, she adopted resourceful expedients. Often she chose the plural form to suggest inclusiveness: "The Martyr Poets—did not tell—," "The Poets light but Lamps," "I reckon—when I count at all— / First—Poets—Then the Sun—." Even her elegy for Mrs. Browning used the plural form in its celebration of the Anglo-Florentine. Sometimes she chose an abstract singular form, without any accompanying personal pronoun, as in "Shall I take thee, the Poet said." It is revealing that, for a writer so devoted to first-person statements, she never spoke of the poet in terms of I except in the final stanza of "I would not paint—a picture—," where her denial of poetic ambition served only to illustrate the romantic preference for aesthetic responsiveness over craftsmanship.

In the one poem which directly defines poet, Dickinson avoided personal and relative pronouns as long as possible, substituting two grammatically startling demonstrative pronouns to frame a strikingly impersonal definition:

> This was a Poet—It is That
> Distills amazing sense
> From ordinary Meanings—
> And Attar so immense
>
> From the familiar species
> That perished by the Door—
> We wonder it was not Ourselves
> Arrested it—before—
>
> Of Pictures, the Discloser—
> The Poet—it is He—
> Entitles Us—by Contrast—
> To ceaseless Poverty—
>
> Of Portion—so unconscious—
> The Robbing—could not harm—
> Himself—to Him—a Fortune—
> Exterior—to Time—
>
> (P, 448)

By spotlighting the central word of the opening line in this way, she called attention to the term Poet itself. Without tracing its etymological roots, a convention of lexicography denied to the poet, she suggested them. Dickinson, who had studied Latin, presumably knew that the word *poeta*, like *agricola*, occupies an odd linguistic station in that both use a feminine declension to express a supposedly masculine idea. But the concepts of expression and cultivation are surely so basic to human nature as to defy sexual classification. So too with distilling and disclosing, the kinds of work by which Dickinson defines her poet's functions. It is only when she ventures into the language of property in the two closing stanzas that she resorts to the masculine pronoun and represents herself as part of the general "we" who feel the impoverishment of creative failure. The language of possession and power resonates with reflexive masculine pronouns, "Himself—to Him—a Fortune," which separate the writer of these lines from the term she is defining. Yet the functions she designates for the poet here describe her own writing more than anyone else's.

Note that Dickinson's poet reveals himself as a Fortune rather than acquiring one and does so by shrewd use of universally available resources. Rather than painting pictures, the poet discloses them— presumably by eliminating overlays of grime and erasing surface distractions. Rather than producing a new substance, the poet distills the essence from ordinary reality, squeezing eternity out of the temporal. Rather than asserting new truths, the poet releases "amazing sense," an emotional and physical complex, from "ordinary Meanings." Like Emerson's poet, Dickinson's apprises us not of his own wealth but of the common wealth. Her key word in the poem is "Distills," the first transitive verb and one that applies equally to the masculine work of distilling liquor from grain and the feminine activity of distilling perfume from flowers. The lasting essence of organic matter must be forced into usefulness by pressure at once destructive and liberating.

"Essential oils are wrung," Dickinson wrote elsewhere, in her most remarkable testament to the vitality of art:

> Essential Oils—are wrung—
> The Attar from the Rose
> Be not expressed by Suns—alone—
> It is the gift of Screws—
>
> The General Rose—decay—
> But this—in Lady's Drawer
> Make Summer—When the Lady lie
> In Ceaseless Rosemary—
>   (P, 675)

Art, being "Exterior—to Time," could achieve immortal remembrance even for a lady who hid it like a sachet in a drawer to continue its influence when the artist herself lay in the "Spiceless Sepulchre" or "Ceaseless Rosemary" she considered in two versions of the poem.

Given this emphasis on wringing, distilling, and disclosing as keys to expression, it may be enlightening to examine the socio-cultural limitations of Dickinson's life to identify the pressures she spoke of as both pains and values. She led a restricted existence, even more so than the conventions of Victorian America seemed to demand of ladies, and it is hard for her readers not to feel that she missed out on experiences she would have found fulfilling. Whether pitying "Poor Emily" for her spinsterish seclusion and enshrining her as a sentimental victim of blighted love or assailing her unpublished condition as evidence of the political, social, and economic discrimination which stultifies female artistic growth, her modern admirers share T.W. Higginson's puzzlement at her ability to make do with so little stimulus or reward—to do without the conditions by which we normally define happiness.

Recent studies in nineteenth-century American women's history and in the development of feminine literary traditions provide ample evidence of the limiting cultural factors which bounded Emily Dickinson's life. Barbara Welter borrows a satiric Dickinson phrase to title her social and literary analysis, *Dimity Convictions: The American Woman in the Nineteenth Century*, which investigates the assumptions about female intellectual and physical incapacity in Victorian America and the expedients women adopted to escape their conventional restrictions to pious, self-effacing, innocent behavior. In *The Feminization of American Culture*, Ann Douglas explores the curious parallels between middle-class American women from 1830 to 1860, especially those with literary ambitions, and the liberal clergy: both groups victims of an economic and political disestablishment which forced them to seek moral influence through manipulation of feelings. Restricting her studies to literature, Emily Stipes Watts details, in *The Poetry of American Women from 1632 to 1945*, the emergence of a distinctively feminine literary tradition which culminated in Dickinson's own poetry. From such books, from Sewall's Dickinson biography with its overwhelming emphasis on the poet's local milieu, and from a wealth of more narrowly focused studies of Dickinson's habitual theme of deprivation, it is possible to identify a number of crucially important limiting factors in her life—limitations which she shared with untold numbers of her female contemporaries.[4] It is worthwhile to review some of those cultural restrictions here in an attempt to comprehend their influence on her art and in an effort to determine whether her literary distinction resulted from rebellion against restrictive cultural norms for women or from conformity to them. The consistent pattern that emerges from comparing Dickinson's personal experience with those cultural limitations is that her background almost never exemplified these limiting factors to an extreme degree, although sexual and social constraints were always present. What happened, however, is that Dickinson herself tightened the screws on each restriction. By her own choices, she immured herself within the magic prison which paradoxically liberated her art.

The first limitation was one which Dickinson shared with most American contemporaries: that of small-town provincialism. Amherst's population was small and, except for a few Irish servants, heterogeneously Yankee; its citizens all knew each other. People there had little opportunity to appreciate most kinds of artistic excellence. Aside from one concert by Jenny Lind, whom she pitied as an exile more than she enjoyed as a singer, Emily Dickinson never heard an internationally acclaimed musical performance. She could not have seen great paintings or sculpture except in reproductions. Theater, dance, and opera entered her life only by hearsay. Amherst, however, had its college and whatever cultural stimulation it could offer the community either directly by sponsoring events or indirectly by assembling a group of highly literate people, some of whom became the poet's friends. The combination of cultural appetite with artistic deprivation forced this community toward language for expression and enjoyment. Lecturers could be hired even in a small town, and books could be sent for. For Dickinson, as for Hawthorne in Salem and Thoreau in Concord, literature was the only art form familiar enough to be understood, imitated, and eventually created. That Dickinson turned inward toward books and eventually substituted written correspondence for almost every other kind of communication was, then, only an intensification of a general cultural pattern. If books opened to her a world beyond Amherst and more interesting, she was prepared to renounce the town. Luckily, when she withdrew from the town's lectures, concerts, and tableaus, she had adequate literary resources to make up the loss: a steady supply of books, including popular novels and magazines; correspondents like Sue Dickinson, the Norcross cousins, and Higginson who appreciated her allusive habits; and the good taste to appreciate literary greatness. (She told Higginson that, "after long disuse of her eyes she read Shakespeare & thought why is any other book needed."[5]) When her preceptor invited her to join his Boston salon of artistic ladies, she stayed home.

Home, of course, was another constraining factor in her life. The conventional family pattern to which the Dickinsons adhered was patriarchal and role-restrictive. As the children of Edward Dickinson, Amherst's leading citizen and self-conscious representative of its values, Emily, Lavinia, and Austin grew up deeply aware of the responsibilities which accompanied their status. The expectations of success and the public obligations bore most heavily upon Austin, but the girls felt social pressures and the burdens of maintaining domestic order. Even the close ties which bound the family together in mutual support could prove restrictive, as the parents held tightly to their children and the siblings to each other. With such comforts at home and so much sense of being needed, none could ever justify leaving—not even Austin, who gave up his hopes of a law practice in Chicago to move into the house Edward Dickinson built next door to the Homestead. Yet Emily Dickinson's eventual resolve that "I do not cross my Father's ground to any House or town" surely carried the familial closeness to an extreme.[6] Obeying her parents on points of domestic duty, she increasingly resisted their efforts to have her represent the family outside. She exploited the protection her family offered her and the willingness of her brother, sister, and friends to do her errands as a means of avoiding all but the most basic responsibilities, thereby simplifying her life to the point where she could almost control it. "Truth," she once wrote, "like Ancestor's Brocades can stand alone," and it was the armament of family pride which secured Dickinson's independence.[7]

Within her father's house and everywhere she went beyond it, she experienced the spiritual domination of Calvinist religion, another crucial limiting factor in her environment. Even in religion, however, she was spared the extremes of evangelical fire-and-brimstone terror, on the one hand, and broad-minded intellectual vapidity on the other.[8] At home, in church, and in school, Dickinson confronted the awesome contrast between human weakness and divine omnipotence; she knew her radical insufficiency—her depraved natural condition. She felt great pressure from the people who loved her to accept Jesus as her savior, although she knew that she must wait for conversion and cipher at its signs. There was particular pressure on girls to be religious. They were thought to be more vulnerable to early death than boys, more naturally pious, more in need of spiritual protection. Dickinson's friends Abiah Root and Abby Wood found themselves converted in adolescence, as did Lavinia; and Dickinson's letters at the time show her somewhat envious awareness of the peace Christian girls enjoyed. Although she never recognized herself as converted and never joined a church, she continued to value the idea of election and hoped God would choose her. Although Edward Dickinson's minister found Miss Dickinson theologically sound, however, she paid little attention to doctrine and none to piety or communal worship: the visible signs of religion in her community. Dickinson's intense religious passion focused, instead, on the intimate encounter between herself and God—an interchange in which she hoped, by shrewdness since not by power, to snatch the prize of immortality.[9]

She had ample chance to hope for immortality and to exercise her imagination in attempting to comprehend her "Flood subject" because experience confronted her steadily with the ultimate human limitation of death. She and almost everyone else she knew suffered from chronic poor health. Emily Dickinson's letters to friends, especially in adolescence and young womanhood, depended for substance on inquiries about her correspondents' health, reports on her own indispositions, and news of all the sickness that came to her attention. A typical comment reads, "Mother has been an invalid since we came *home*. . . . I don't know what her sickness is, for I am but a simple child, and frightened at myself."[10] She worried that Austin got sick every time he left Amherst, yet she kept narrating medical problems at home. Physical and emotional weakness often interfered with planned activities and hoped-for achievements. This obsession with bodily infirmity probably derived from her own lifelong pattern of sickness which has yet to be diagnosed. Richard B. Sewall and Martin Wand attribute her headaches, intolerance of light, and cyclic medical crises to a congenital eye disorder that she shared with her mother and sister and for which she sought medical help in Cambridge.[11] Jerry Ferris Reynolds thinks Dickinson a victim of lupus.[12] Other analysts, notably John Cody, attribute her problems to a psychological disturbance culminating in a major breakdown just before her most productive poetic years. All these theories attempt to define her physical limitations though none, of course, explains the uses she made of her illness.

Recent attention to Dickinson's background, especially Barbara Welter's chapter on "Female Complaints" in *Dimity Convictions*, focus attention on cultural expectations in middle-class Victorian America.[13] Gently bred Americans of the time, whether male or female, worried more about health and expressed their concerns more articulately than any previous generation. And the cultural fascination with sickness emphasized female disabilities. Women were considered physiologically weaker than men, though spiritually stronger, and they were expected to suffer from potentially fatal though unspecified ailments throughout their lives, with the period from first menstruation to first confinement being especially critical. No wonder so many ladies of that physically and emotionally vulnerable age turned to religion for security or to sentimental literature for the consolation of glamor. Poe, after all, could think of no more melancholy subject than the death of a beautiful woman, and James Gates Percival opened his poem "Consumption" with the assertion that "There is sweetness in a woman's decay." Decay could be useful as well as sweet, if the privileges of invalidism were shrewdly used, and Emily Dickinson, whose health seems not to have been markedly worse than that of her female relatives, exploited physical limitations—like social ones—for artistic ends. Illness, expected within her culture, encouraged both her social withdrawal and her literary emergence. Many letters began with such confessions as "I am sick today, dear Susie, and have not been to church. There has been a pleasant quiet, in which to think of you, and I have not been sick eno' that I cannot write to you."[14] Invalidism could provide a woman with time for art even as it provided a man with topics.

Partly as a consequence of adolescent illness and even more because of restrictive notions about feminine needs, most girls of Dickinson's generation were educated less rigorously than their brothers. Intellectual limitations followed upon social and physical limitations. Even people who thought girls might have adequate intelligence for formal education worried about the physical strain of schooling and questioned the usefulness of a masculine curriculum for young ladies. Few girls attended school regularly beyond the primary grades, undertook higher education, or studied the classical languages and mathematics that would equip them for the learned professions. Domestic skills, the social graces, religious principles, and superficial artistic and intellectual attainments prepared a lady sufficiently to ornament her husband's genteel household. Margaret Fuller, given a classical education by her father, complained that girls studied more subjects than boys but were never expected to use their knowledge independently. Emily Dickinson's education, however, improved in most respects upon the feminine norm. She studied philosophy, Euclid, and Latin—much the same curriculum Austin faced, and she endured the alarms of public examinations only slightly less rigorous than those which challenged boys. She fortified herself for these ordeals, as her brother probably did, by remembering her father's confidence "that I shall not disgrace myself."[15] Under the governance of Mary Lyons, the female seminary at Mount Holyoke set high academic standards. There were entrance examinations, which many girls failed, and a demanding curriculum which educated students for competence and service rather than for display. Miss Lyons took special pride in the alumnae who undertook mission assignments. But Dickinson spent only a year at South Hadley, and even that period—like her previous academy experiences—was interrupted by parentally mandated intervals at home for rest and domestic activity. Too much intellectual pressure might threaten health. Dickinson returned with relief from the seminary to her home, but she continued her education independently. With Benjamin Newton as a tutor and Higginson as a preceptor, she concentrated her extraordinary intellectual and imaginative force on her poetic growth.

Both at school and at home, a young woman could exercise her mind in comparative safety by reading imaginative literature, and Dickinson's letters reveal the enthusiasm with which she used fiction and poetry to counteract educational deprivation. She seems to have read almost anything recommended to her by her like-minded friends: Shakespeare, of course, and Emerson, Thoreau, Hawthorne, and the Brownings—but also Longfellow, Marvell, and a host of popular writers. It was the current sentimentalism which dominated her early letters, probably because society approved such reading for young ladies—if indulged in moderately so as not to round the shoulders or erode common sense. The popular fiction reinforced the values to which the society conditioned its girls. It accorded kind attention to women, both as characters and authors, even as it narrowed their aspirations.

By fixing attention on domestic life and locating heroism in meek acceptance of suffering, sentimental literature exalted women in their capacities as dutiful daughters, sacrificing mothers, and model Christians. It presented life as sad but beautiful without examining the economic or political bases for the sadness—preferring to justify all crises as moral tests. Such writing, which implicitly honored the limitations of genteel Christian womanhood, promoted the reputations of writers as diverse as Harriet Beecher Stowe, Lydia Sigourney, Lucy Larcom, and Frances Osgood. Women demonstrated that they could turn a profit out of their ostensibly timid calls upon public attention, and they established magazines to publish the edifying fiction for which the public appetite appeared insatiable. But Dickinson—always an elitist—refused to superimpose ordinary, culturally acceptable meanings on the amazing sense of her poetry, and she never availed herself of the feminine literary marketplace to which both male and female literati willingly consigned all imaginative ladies—even Emily Dickinson.

Her community, through all its familial, religious, educational, and social institutions, assumed for women of Dickinson's class a culturally predetermined life-pattern which was presumably ordained by God. Woman was made for marriage and maternity. Only a home of her own could shield her against the economic, physical, and spiritual threats to which she was exposed. Most women would marry men from backgrounds like their own, would live near their home communities in close touch with their mothers, and would find pleasure in maintaining their homes and fulfillment in obeying their husbands and nurturing their children. Only a small percentage of young ladies would earn their own livings, even for as much as a year; and Dickinson's friends illustrated the limited options available to Amherst women whom financial necessity forced into employment. Factory jobs were below them, of course, as were shop positions and hiring out as domestics. (Moving in with distant family members to help out on an unpaid basis was, of course, meritorious.) Susan Gilbert went to Baltimore to teach at a private girls' school before becoming engaged to Austin, and other young ladies taught briefly in similarly protective institutions. The most glamorous vocation in Amherst eyes was the missionary work that attracted Abby Wood, but female missionaries needed husbands to guard them. Women could be professional writers, of course, but they were expected to plead financial pressures to justify such temerity—the claims of aged parents, invalid husbands, and starving children. For someone of Dickinson's class, there was no non-financial justification for employment, and her father gave her no reason for considering it. Her letters treat working friends—even men—with compassion, never envy.

The other alternative was spinsterhood, which her society regarded as a slightly unnatural condition unless the unclaimed jewel attracted sympathy with a sad history of unrequited love (such as the Wadsworth story Dickinson's family may have fabricated on her behalf) or earned respect by charitable service. This option, too, irritated Dickinson, whose notion of charitable duty to anyone but close friends prompted this explosion to Jane Humphrey: ". . . work makes one strong, and cheerful—and as for society what neighborhood so full as my own? The halt—the lame—and the blind—the old—the infirm—the bed-ridden—and superannuated—the ugly, and disagreeable—the perfectly hateful to me—all *these* to see—and be seen by—an opportunity rare for cultivating meekness—and patience—and submission—and for turning my back to this very sinful, and wicked world. Somehow or other I incline to other things—and Satan covers them up with flowers, and I reach out to pick them."[16] Her solution, characteristically, was to choose the most constricted option of all—turning her back more fully to the sinful and wicked world than the teachers she mimicked in this letter ever imagined and settling for the inviolate privacy of an aristocratic New England recluse—responsible only to herself and God.

The women who felt themselves exceptional in Dickinson's society had few alternatives to the conventionally supportive domestic role. Essentially they had to create new patterns for their lives. Modern feminists admire Margaret Fuller for her anticipation of a pattern now considered liberating: refusal to make choices between sexuality and intellect, security and independence, marriage and career. She broke out of the circle of limitations in which her sisters were entrapped, and Fuller's life—despite its frustrations and its tragic but easily sentimentalized end—demonstrated that an aggressive, self-confident woman could do everything. Dickinson, however, did just the opposite. Instead of smashing through limitations, she drew them in upon herself—deliberately narrowing her life beyond the cultural norms she assimilated.

Dickinson demonstrated her independence of society by making negative choices which carried her culture's values for women to an extreme of self-assertion masked as self-effacement. In doing so, she followed a cultural pattern which allowed men to think in terms of active choices and women of passive ones. A woman should wait for a man to choose her in marriage. She should conform her will to parental choices and those her husband would make for her. She should, of course, obey God's laws and hope for signs of divine approval. Her will should manifest itself in obedience to choices made by others. To emphasize such constraints on female choices, however, is to exaggerate a problem. Women did have important areas of freedom. Religious salvation loomed so large as a goal in Calvinist communities that women were given considerable freedom in seeking it. As Ann Douglas has shown, women often chose their own churches and were more likely than men to change from one sect to another. A woman's soul was as valuable as a man's, and she was independently responsible for saving it. Within the home, also, a woman could exercise a great many choices about furniture, clothing, and medical treatment. Although some women used their privileges to acquire fashionable property, defining themselves by their possessions, the

Yankee women of Dickinson's community were more likely to use freedom in making negative choices. They demonstrated thrift and prudence by showing what they could do without; the best taste reflected itself in discriminations. Mocking this tendency, Emily Dickinson amused herself in several letters with references to a neighbor's potentially fatal fastidiousness: " 'Mrs. Skeeter' is very feeble, 'cant bear Allopathic treatment, cant have Homeopathic'—dont want Hydropathic—Oh what a pickle she is in—should'nt think she would deign to *live*—it is so decidedly vulgar!"[17] Yet her life and poems carry to an extreme the habits of selecting, discriminating, excluding.

In subject matter, Dickinson's poems stress both sides of a woman's situation. She could express delight at being chosen—the passive beneficiary of a more powerful being's option, as in "He touched me, so I live to know" (P, 506). But she also communicated the painful power of making exclusions: "Of all the Souls that stand create—" (P, 664); "The Soul selects her own Society—" (P, 303); and "Renunciation—is a piercing Virtue—" (P, 745). At her most ebullient, describing herself as self-sufficient and self-defined, she claimed the right to positive choice: characteristically, a grand one. "With Will to choose, or to reject," she chose "just a Crown—" (P, 508). Even this coronation, however, came by a process of negative choices, rejection of the names and roles her family and friends chose for her:

> I'm ceded—I've stopped being Theirs—
> The name They dropped upon my face
> With water, in the country church
> Is finished using, now,
> And They can put it with my Dolls,
> My childhood, and the string of spools,
> I've finished threading—too—

She asserted her right to do without many of the satisfactions she had been taught she needed.

In her life, Dickinson exploited the opportunity to make negative choices, recognizing that her tendency to deny opportunities marked her off as eccentric. "Odd, that I, who say 'no' so much, cannot bear it from others," she wrote to Louise Norcross, "Odd, that I, who run from so many, cannot brook that one turn from me."[18] Wanting to be chosen by important others, she habitually abstained from positive choices herself. Exclusions, especially in emotionally vulnerable relationships, offered her protection. Whether she ever actually rejected a marriage proposal, as she is said to have denied Judge Lord, we shall probably never know, but it seems unlikely that she ever truly wished marriage, as distinct from love. Despite the powerful evidence in the poems and letters (especially the Master letters) that Dickinson craved the sense of being chosen, accepted, and loved by a man as well as by God, there is little textual evidence for interest in matrimony. Marriage, as the lawyer's daughter probably knew, meant loss of identity. As the reader of sentimental fiction understood, it meant submission to a man who might prove unworthy. Young Emily's letter to Sue Gilbert expressing adolescent attraction to sexual experience and fear of it can be used as evidence of her divided feelings, but it also stands as an uncannily prescient anticipation of Sue's own history with Austin: "How dull our lives must seem to the bride, and the plighted maiden, whose days are fed with gold, and who gathers pearls every evening; but to the *wife*, Susie, sometimes the *wife forgotten*, our lives perhaps seem dearer than all others in the world; you have seen flowers at morning, *satisfied* with the dew, and those same sweet flowers at noon with their heads bowed in anguish before the mighty sun; think you these thirsty blossoms will *now* need naught but—*dew*? No, they will cry for sunlight, and pine for the burning noon, tho' it scorches them, scathes them; they have got through with peace—they know that the man of noon, is *mightier* than the morning and their life is henceforth to him. Oh, Susie, it is dangerous . . ."[19] Sentimental fiction played itself out right next door, and Dickinson felt the pain that others found in marriage. Why would she choose it? For loving companionship, such as she already found at home and knew she could depend upon? For economic support that her father provided, even posthumously? For motherhood: one of the few female roles she never played in her poetic fantasies? For romantic love, which seems never to have been offered her—her standards being high and Robert Browning unique? For social connections, when she increasingly craved solitude? To imagine that Emily Dickinson would ever have enjoyed the public responsibilities and private obligations of a minister's or lawyer's wife in small-town New England is to capitulate totally to the conventions of sentimental domestic fiction.

From a purely artistic point of view, Dickinson enjoyed the most privileged literary life in nineteenth-century America. While Emerson was delivering lectures on the frontier, Lowell grumbling about the stolid despair of the author turned editor, Hawthorne picking up government jobs in an effort to finance periods of retirement for writing, and Melville writing that dollars damned him, Dickinson was simply writing. She never haggled for a publisher's advance, stopped work on a project because it might not sell, or worried about financial obligations. In a sense, Edward Dickinson presented her with a lifelong creative writing fellowship as her birthright. While other women authors scribbled with children tugging at their skirts and husbands awaiting dinner, Dickinson took for granted what Virginia Woolf would later say every woman artist craves: a room of her own.

But what about publication? Writing is a form of communication; and Dickinson, who described her verse as "my letter to the World" (P, 441), must have needed an audience. The few poems which reached print anonymously and in corrupted texts reveal an initial willingness to share her work even as they partially justify her eventual protectiveness of it. Clearly she hoped that Bowles and Higginson would help her to publish in well-read, respectable journals.[20] When they failed her, however, she apparently made another major negative choice: to refrain from offering her poetry to the plethora of literary magazines which might have printed some. It was hardly impossible for women poets to publish in nineteenth-century America, but those who succeeded often did so by pandering to conventional tastes and commercial pressures. Too proud to join Hawthorne's infamous "d——d mob of scribbling women," Dickinson tucked her booklets away in drawers.

In "Publication—is the Auction / Of the Mind of Man—" (P, 709), she expressed her contempt for commercial composition. To read this poem only as an ironic attempt at disguising her authorial pain is to miss the genteel Yankee pride that spits out the key word "Auction." Recall Thoreau's sneers at auctions in *Walden*, the association he draws between bodily death and material accumulation; and remember Frost's New England reversal of consumerist values: "The having anything to sell is what / Is the disgrace in man or state or nation."[21] Dickinson, a lady comfortably provided, had nothing to sell in the grand garage sale of the mind. She substituted the concept of stewardship for that of possession in the statement "Thought belong to Him who gave it— / Then-to Him Who bear / It's Corporeal illustration—" and refused to reduce her proud spirit "To Disgrace of Price—." If her talent belonged to God, he would somehow get the value of it. Her work was to wait—live in hope and die a poet.

She made no money from her writing and probably never wanted to. She never saw her name in print and most likely gave thanks for the privacy. She did, however, find a few appreciative readers. Her correspondence with Susan Gilbert Dickinson on "Safe in their Alabaster Chambers—" reveals a better editor next door than in the offices of the *Springfield Republican* or *Atlantic Monthly*.[22] The eventual editing history of Dickinson's poetry, especially the contributions of Mabel Loomis Todd, demonstrates that the poet had access to responsive, critical readers—most of them women. The enthusiasm for literature of all sorts among middle-class American ladies and their habit of writing long, literate, tonally-varied letters resulted in the development of a reading audience capable of artistic discrimination beyond the level the commercial marketplace assumed—capable of welcoming Dickinson's poems when they appeared in 1890.

Dickinson's habit of pulling in upon the limitations she encountered influenced her poetry in powerful ways: the artistic equivalent, at best, of crushing the atom. Not only are many of her poems about negative decisions, but they are generally also examples of such. To a great extent her poetry may be understood as a stylization of conventional genteel feminine fiction by eliminating narrative and moral elements. The result, of course, was to distill amazing sense from ordinary meanings and fragrant attar from rotten literary materials.

Although Dickinson read sketches, tales, and novels and enjoyed such long narrative poems as Longfellow's "Kavanagh" and Mrs. Browning's "Aurora Leigh," she wrote very few narrative poems, most of which—like "A little East of Jordan" (P, 59)—adopted familiar stories to protect her from having to develop character and plot. A good case can be made for the theory that more poems build on suppressed narrative situations she borrowed from conventional fiction.[23] In this sense her cautionary note to Higginson declaring the I of her poems an imaginary person is revealing. The situations in which the speaker finds herself may well be derivative. A poet who played the roles of boys, empresses, and ballerinas could also enact such stock roles of sentimental fiction as the betrayed lover or languishing maiden or the equally familiar role of hypersensitive gothic victim. A narrative background is suggested in many poems but never developed. Readers, naturally wanting to know how the speaker reached her condition of emotional crisis, speculate about preceding events and possible conclusions. It may be an indication of how close our popular culture comes to nineteenth-century storytelling conventions that the underlying narratives most readers find embedded in this literature (generally assuming it to be autobiographical rather than fictive) are overwhelmingly sentimental.

Dickinson's exclusion of narrative meaning from poetry extended also to that other staple of nineteenth-century female writers: moral message. Long anticipating MacLeish's dictum in "Ars Poetica" that "A poem should be equal to: Not true," Dickinson rejected the assumption that literature ought to be didactic and that it should reinforce the pious conventions of middle-class Protestant culture. Sometimes she sported with such expectations by proclaiming as moral aphorisms such startling notions as "A Bomb upon the Ceiling / Is an improving thing—" (P, 1128), such discomfiting announcements as "An actual suffering strengthens / As Sinews do, with age—" (P, 686), or such near-sinful advice as "Tell all the Truth but tell it slant—" (P, 1129). Almost inevitably, given Dickinson's fascination with choices, her poems suggest moral crises and hint at moral issues, but one could hardly send a reader to her collected poems for advice on how to live. The emotional ordeal of moral crisis lives in the poems, but the conclusions—if any—have been excluded. One need only consider those of her poems which didactic twentieth-century editors have selected for school anthologies to notice how atypical such moralizing was in her work and how great a disservice is done to her art by the assumption that poems should be useful to the general reader. "Success is counted sweetest," "I never saw a Moor—," and "There is no Frigate like a Book" should teach us gratitude that Emily Dickinson was never forced by circumstances to churn out the platitudinous verses her culture expected from ladies.

Dickinson's greatest poems strip away all narrative and moral context from emotion—even all paraphraseable ideas—to give us powerfully distilled images. The character of the speaker means nothing to us, nor the specific situation, the preceding or successive episodes, or the setting. If they were in the back of her mind sometime in the process of composition, they have been ruthlessly expunged from the actual poem. "After great pain, a formal feeling comes—" (P, 341) encapsulates the physiological numbness resulting from any tragedy which drives body and mind beyond the limits of anguish to numb calm. Who knows the circumstances attending "Mine—by the Right of the White Election!" (P, 528), but questions about its spiritual, romantic, or artistic context do nothing to dull the sense of triumphant entitlement ringing throughout the poem. Such poetry, cutting away even the conventional elements of meaning allowed within the cultural tradition in which Dickinson was educated, attain a universality denied to the literature which, like *Uncle Tom's Cabin*, made emphatic use of sentimental literary conventions or, like *Woman in the Nineteenth Century*, assailed their limitations. Dickinson's poetry pressed down upon the conventional elements of ladylike literature and distilled away the meanings generally noticed in her time and place to arrest the universally surprising sense experience discoverable although usually lost in familiar literary materials.

Emily Dickinson's poems are recognizable products of mid-nineteenth-century genteel New England feminine culture. Had she written out the stories suggested by her verses, she might have produced Amherst local-color sketches in a sentimental mode. These are not the poems of a rebel against her culture nor models for the twentieth-century authors who call themselves her sisters. Paradoxically, however, the poems eliminate so much of the local and ephemeral from consideration that they become—by a process of exclusion—extraordinarily inclusive. Rather than pushing against the cultural limitations she encountered, Dickinson pressed in upon them and exploited them for artistic purposes in her effort to explore the general limitations at the margin of all human life. Her most fruitful themes, after all, had little to do with romantic disappointment or any other sentimental material. She was at her best and most honest when pressing at the limits of sanity, consciousness, and mortality. The poems continually explore extreme sensations and anticipate the feelings of death. She insisted in such poems as "I heard a Fly buzz—when I died—" (P, 465), on detailing fragments of an untellable but compelling story, with no discernible moral. Existence, after all, has limits for everyone—even men and modern careerwomen, and Dickinson made Circumference her business.

Even her poetic style assumed and exploited limitations. She chose an habitual verse form too slight for her ambitious themes and then refined it by a process of excision. Unparaphraseable, her lines call for expansion by readers intent on restoring meanings to the distilled sense. But the flowers of rhetoric have been crushed to render essence, and any filling in of syntax or situation proves puzzling. Often Dickinson's cryptic style seems purely idiosyncratic, and at times it leaves nothing but fragments. By the end of her most productive decade, she was focusing attention on the inadequacy even of the word as "portion of the Vision" (P, 1126); later she would present "This loved Philology" in sacramental terms (P, 1651). Given her penchant for her lexicon and her delight in bursting the limits of the most reductive literary forms, it seems natural that many of her most memorable poems began as definitions of terms as diverse as renunciation, remorse, presentiment, and publication. No wonder she wrote a definition of poetry that—without one feminine pronoun—described her alone among contemporary writers.

But the definition is hardly the most reductive literary form, nor was it culturally resticted to women. Dr. Johnson himself had demonstrated the combination of logic, imagination, and language which could exploit the potential of individual words. Perhaps Dickinson's most delightful experiment in turning cultural conventions in upon themselves to release imagination came in the following familiar verse:

> To make a prairie it takes a clover and one bee,
> One clover, and a bee,
> And revery.
> The revery alone will do,
> If bees are few.
>
> (P, 1755)

This, of course, is cookbook language: a recipe for the American sublime. Take a little of this and enough of that. Mix them together until they feel right. Only one ingredient is really essential. Leave out the others, if unavailable. Note, typically, how she suggests no desirable additions; even her recipe varies only by deletion.[24] The result, of course, will be the landscape Bryant took 124 lines of blank verse to describe and Cooper massive novels.

Whereas Whitman, speaking for the newer national culture of aggrandizement, proclaimed himself the representative American poet by agglomerating everything into himself, the Yankee Emerson stressed in "The Poet" that artistic triumph must come through a series of willingly accepted renunciations: "Thou shalt leave the world, and know the muse only. Thou shalt not know any longer the times, customs, graces, politics, or opinions of men, but shall take all from the muse." Dickinson, in many ways the typical Yankee woman of her time, left the world in a more than Emersonian sense and proceeded to demonstrate that she could "Make it do, or do without" to draw poetry out of privation. If distillation of meaning into sense defines the essence of her poetry, we should stop pitying "Poor Emily" her negative choices and instead count it providential that she had a room of her own, some recycled paper, the social exemptions allowed a Yankee spinster, and revery in a New England town that expected no genius in its daughters but nevertheless provided the conditions in which one of them could both choose and create.

Notes

1. In preparing this essay, I have consulted Thomas H. Johnson's editions of *The Letters of Emily Dickinson*, Volumes I–III, and *The Poems of Emily Dickinson*, Volumes I–III (Cambridge, Mass.: Harvard University Press, 1958). Citations from the letters will be identified in the notes by *Letters* and Johnson's identifying number (*Letters*, 207), and quotations from the poems in the text by P and his number (P, 448).

2. These assumptions underlie Elsa Greene's argument in: "Emily Dickinson Was a Poetess," *College English*, 34 (1972), 63–70, that Dickinson's New England background differed from that of her male literary contemporaries and that her growth as a poetess required her to overcome cultural conditioning in self-denial. To be a poet at all, therefore, a woman of Dickinson's time must have been a social rebel.

3. Chapters 3 through 5 of *The Poetry of American Women from 1632 to 1945* (Austin: University of Texas Press, 1977) place Dickinson in a feminine literary tradition of which she became the most distinguished representative. Watts finds that E.D.'s themes, forms, and voice show the influence of other women poets, especially sentimentalists. Similar linkages between Dickinson and her female contemporaries, using a cross-cultural British and American frame of reference, may be found in Sandra M. Gilbert's and Susan Gubar's study, *The Madwoman in the Attic: The Woman Writer and the Nineteenth-Century Literary Imagination* (New Haven: Yale University Press, 1979).

4. A number of articles and dissertations probe Dickinson's theme of scarcity in various manifestations, generally building on John Cody's *After Great Pain: The Inner Life of Emily Dickinson* (Cambridge, Mass.: Harvard University Press, 1971), which traces the poet's psychological difficulties and artistic achievements to early deprivation of maternal love. In "Thirst and Starvation in Emily Dickinson's Poetry," *American Literature*, 51 (1979), 33–49, Vivian R. Pollak studies Dickinson's "ethic of abstention" in terms of the cultural tensions she shared with other women of her generation. In her 1978 Indiana University dissertation, "When a Writer is a Daughter," Barbara Ann Clarke Mossberg argues that Dickinson exaggerated her lack of nurture in order to reject her mother's domestic role and replace it with an artistic self-image: *DAI* 38: 6729A.

5. *Letters*, 342 b.

6. *Letters*, 330.

7. *Letters*, 368.

8. Ann Douglas surveys the theological decline into sentimentalism among the liberal nineteenth-century northeastern clergy in *The Feminization of American Culture* (New York: Alfred A. Knopf, 1977), but the Amherst congregation of Dickinson's time seems to have remained more orthodox in its Calvinism. The poet's contempt for liberalizing religious trends may be gathered from her satire in "He preached upon 'Breadth' till it argued him narrow—" (P, 1207). Her letters and poems reveal a sentimentalized image of heaven, however, which Barton Levi St. Armand links with Elizabeth Stuart Phelps's popular novel, *The Gates Ajar*, in "Paradise Deferred: The Image of Heaven in the Work of Emily Dickinson and Elizabeth Stuart Phelps," *American Quarterly*, 29 (1977), 55–78.

9. Karl Keller explores the poet's relationship to her Calvinist heritage in *The Only Kangaroo among the Beauty: Emily Dickinson and America* (Baltimore: Johns Hopkins University Press, 1979), pointing out in his comparison of Bradstreet and Dickinson that "One of early Puritanism's best legacies to the modern world is the promise of the elevation of women," p. 9.

10. *Letters*, 182.

11. " 'Eyes Be Blind, Heart Be Still': A New Perspective on Emily Dickinson's Eye Problem," *New England Quarterly*, 52 (1979), 400–6.

12. A summary of Reynolds's thesis, published in the 1979 *Markham Review*, appeared in an article by Herbert Black for the *Boston Globe*, February 19, 1980, p. 28: "Theory on Beethoven and Dickinson: they both suffered from lupus disease."

13. *Dimity Convictions: The American Woman in the Nineteenth Century* (Athens: Ohio University Press, 1976). This chapter previously appeared in the 1970 *Journal of the History of Medicine*.

14. *Letters*, 177.

15. *Letters*, 20.

16. *Letters*, 30.

17. *Letters*, 82.

18. *Letters*, 245.

19. *Letters*, 93.

20. Ruth Miller makes a particularly strong case for Dickinson's early hope of publication in *The Poetry of Emily Dickinson* (Middletown, Conn.: Wesleyan University Press, 1968). By 1876, however, Dickinson was turning to Higginson for protection against Helen Hunt Jackson's insistence on printing some of the poems: "She was so sweetly noble, I would regret to estrange her, and if you would be willing to give me a note saying you disapproved it, and thought me unfit, she would believe you—I am sorry to flee so often to my safest friend, but hope he permits me—"(*Letters*, 476).

21. *Walden* may well be the closest parallel in American literature to Dickinson's assessment of values, and it resembles her work in its paradoxical application of Yankee economics to spiritual growth. "When a man dies he kicks the dust," Thoreau wrote in his chapter on "Economy" and his neighbors buy the dust (even a dried tapeworm) at auctions. The Frost excerpt comes from "New Hampshire," which contrasts New England pride in scarcity with a national zeal for surplus. Edward Taylor had speculated in "Gods Selecting Love in the Decree" that his neighbors would reject salvation itself, if allowed to haggle over it.

22. *Letters*, 238.

23. John Evangelist Walsh makes suggestions about possible fictive borrowings as narrative backgrounds for Dickinson poems in *The Hidden Life of Emily Dickinson* (New York: Simon and Schuster, 1971).

24. She offered a typically cryptic prose recipe in this letter: "Will Mrs Hills please break an Ounce Isinglass in a Quart of fresh Milk, placing in boiling Water till quite dissolved, adding afterward four table spoons Chocolate shavings and two of Sugar, boiling together fifteen minutes and straining before turning into molds" (*Letters*, 376).

"Everyone Else is Prose": Emily Dickinson's Lack of Community Spirit

Barbara Antonina Clarke Mossberg*

Our sense that Emily Dickinson's achievement as a writer is a phenomenon—and she the Dark Horse of American literature—is par-

*This essay was written specifically for this volume and appears here for the first time by permission of the author.

tially a function of her image, accurate or not, as a literary isolato—in her words, a "Nobody" (P. 288) or a "Kangaroo among the Beauty."[1] In fact, she does not just see herself standing out as an exotic if ungainly creature who belongs in another country's habitat, she sees herself as the "only" one. To Thomas Wentworth Higginson, editor of *The Atlantic Monthly* and Dickinson's chosen literary confidante and "Preceptor," she writes,

> Will you tell me my fault, frankly as to yourself, for I had rather wince, than die. Men do not call the surgeon, to commend—the Bone, but to set it, Sir, and fracture within, is more critical. And for this, Preceptor, I shall bring you—Obedience—the Blossom from my Garden, and every gratitude I know. Perhaps, you smile at me. I could not stop for that—My Business is Circumference—An Ignorance, not of Customs, but if caught with the Dawn—or the Sunset see me—Myself the only Kangaroo among the Beauty, Sir, if you please, it afflicts me, and I thought that instruction would take it away.

Whether or not Dickinson really thought she needed it, Higginson criticized among other things her "lack of control,"[2] and later would call her "wayward" and accuse her of admitting the "little" mistake but not the "large."[3] Dickinson's response is to present herself as a lone, singular transgressor, at odds with tradition and culture. As a "Kangaroo" she does not belong with figures of the literary establishment (the "Beauty" according to Dickinson) who share their culture's implicit sanction and even expectation of literary activity. She knows the "customs" for women and for poetry as well, and pretends to fear any reprisals for her usurpation in her writing or for her trespass in literary terrain. Higginson's "instruction" could "save" her and at least would provide a form of sanction for her poetic efforts—and successes.

It certainly could appear from reading American literary criticism, at least that written before the mid-nineteen sixties, that Dickinson formulates a rather troublesome bulge in theories of the "Beauty," based on trends, movements, and philosophies of what is a masculine community, the existence of female "scribblers" notwithstanding. She is left out of such major studies of nineteenth-century American literature as F. O. Mathiessen's *American Renaissance*, R. W. B. Lewis's *The American Adam*, Leo Marx's *The Machine in the Garden*, Quentin Anderson's *The Imperial Self*; studies which span her genre or period such as *The Language of Canaan*, *Classic Americans*, *The Golden Age of American Literature*; and other studies of American realism, transcendentalism, renaissance, social criticism, European influence, regionalism, romanticism, humor, gothic, the influence of the West, religion, democratic humanism, and so on—all the traditional categories and methods of approach.[4] Either they do not seem applicable to her work, or for one reason or another, it is simply more convenient from a scholarly point of view to leave her out. The significance of Dickinson's absence in these studies is a

book-length topic in itself. Her omission can reflect her relatively late entrance into American literary history with the posthumous publication of
her poems culminating in 1955,[5] but it also parallels the poet's own sense
of estrangement from the writing community in her own life, for which
she is both helpless and responsible.

No one was more aware than she that she was a "Kangaroo," and in
fact she cultivated a stance of ironic distance towards literary tradition
and her milieu. In her letters and poetry, she stresses and develops her
uniqueness as a writer to such an extreme that Higginson could hardly
believe, given the "quality" of her thought, that she lived, as she told him,
"so very alone."[6] Later critics would find her uninfluenced in any particular way by literary sources.[7] She seemed to have come out of nowhere.
Even though Jack Capps was able to document and to provide compelling
evidence for Dickinson's use of other writers' materials in her own work,
these influences are obscured because of her idiosyncratic style and her
corresponding self-image as a literary oddball.[8] Henry Wells suggests that
she belongs in a literary tradition, not of her own century or region, but
with great poets in general, while Capps, along with Jay Leyda, argues
that Dickinson does belong in the context of her age.[9] Karl Keller—fit-
tingly under the title *The Only Kangaroo Among the Beauty*—does illuminate Dickinson's affinities with other major American authors.[10] But
others, like Yvor Winters, find her different from every other major New
England writer of the nineteenth century, and Conrad Aiken finds the
"meagreness of literary allusions" in her letters to be "astounding." "She
appears to have existed in a vacuum." She "hardly mentions" the literary
events breaking all around her, considering that "she came to full consciousness at the very moment when American Literature came to flower.
That she knew this, there cannot be any question; nor that she was
stimulated and influenced by it."[11]

But the point is that Dickinson did not always act very "stimulated"
by these literary events and figures in her letters. Towards major male
writers she could be critical, offhand, irreverent, and ironic. Towards a
relative outsider in the literary community like Walt Whitman, she
wrote, "I was told he was disgraceful."[12] Of Poe she admitted, "I know
too little to think."[13] Toward William Dean Howells and Henry James she
felt, "one hesitates."[14] Of the Brahmin Longfellow she wrote,
"Longfellow's 'golden legend' has come to town I hear—and may be seen
in state on Mr. Adams' bookshelves."[15] As for the other authors in the store
of 'language texts' she half expects to hear that they have "flown some
morning and in their native ether revel all the day."[16] The reasons for her
detachment may seem more clear perhaps if we recognize the degree of
wistfulness with which Dickinson *hears about* the literary personalities
and events of her day, and the envy in her sarcasm. From an early age,
Dickinson yearned to be "somebody" herself. "For our sakes," she continues in her letter about Longfellow's latest work, "who please ourselves

with the fancy that we are the only poets, and everyone else is *prose*, let us hope that they will yet be willing to share our humble world and feed upon such ailment as *we* consent to do!" While she does not share their privileges, then, she feels considerably above them: "prose" is her term for the conventionally expressed, for conventional thinking itself, and for the patriarchal enforcement of "prose" orthodoxy,[17] and "real life."[18] "Prose" is antithetical to poetry, by which Dickinson means the kind of poetry she writes, which embodies freedom of expression and spirit, a certain rebelliousness against customs and tradition, and, of course, genius. "Poetry" is so unique that only she and Susan Gilbert are poets—and later she sees herself as the only one.

Even though Dickinson styles herself after Emerson's prescriptive vision of "The Poet"[19] and incurs her father's displeasure by identifying herself with "modern Literati" (such as when she reads Melville),[20] she feels cut off from the possibility of ever being part of the literary establishment, or the "Beauty." As she implies in her letter to Higginson ("Will you tell me my fault, . . ." quoted above) she lacks the necessary privileges of education and the cultural and familial support that such an education embodies. She is wanted at home to bake her father's daily bread, and is shuttled back and forth during her short time at Mt. Holyoke at her father's whim, with no serious regard for her education or vocation. She thus is spared the fate of Prose, but still, when her education ends, she is frustrated, if resigned to her father's will. She sighs to a girlfriend, "We'll finish an education sometime, won't we?"[21] But it will be an education of her own making, and hence an illicit education of which her father—she can count on it—will disapprove.

Thus towards the literary community which was constantly being paraded before her eyes in books and periodicals and newspapers (and even in the visitors to her brother's house next door), Dickinson felt an ambivalence rooted in the idea that she could only "look on," and never hope nor wish to be a participant. While acknowledging the odds against her achieving greatness in her culture, she still decides to be distinguished. "It's a great thing to be great," she tells her cousin Louisa with some authority, "and you and I might tug for a lire, and never accomplish it, but no one can stop our looking on . . . You know some cannot sing . . . what if we learn, ourselves, someday! Who indeed knows?"[22] Dickinson intends to do more than "look on," then, like a wallflower at the dance of literary immortality. If she is not asked to dance, she will not attend the ball. But she still may dance outside, by herself, to use her own metaphor for her poetry:

> I cannot dance upon my Toes—
> No Man instructed me—
> But oftentimes, among my mind,
> A Glee possesseth me,

That I had Ballet knowledge—
Would put itself abroad
In Pirouette to blanch a Troupe—
Or lay a Prima, mad,

And though I had no Gown of Gauze—
Nor Ringlet to my Hair,
Nor hopped to Audiences—like birds,
One Claw upon the Air,

Nor tossed my shape in Eider Balls
Nor rolled on wheels of snow
Till I was out of sight, in sound,
The House encore me so—
Nor any know I know the Art
I mention—easy—Here—
Nor any placard boast me—
It's full as Opera—

(P.326)

She may lack "instruction" in how to dance (male instruction), and she
may not stoop to gratify the popular taste in poetic fashions, especially for
female authors, but her art is grand nevertheless—not despite the fact
that she is self-taught, but because of it. Although Dickinson approached
Higginson as a person desperately in need of an instructor or Preceptor,
she asked if perhaps "melody" could not, like witchcraft, be taught, at
least by a man;[23] and she confessed to a girlfriend that in her literary pursuit of immortality she was heeding the advice of no one, a fact which
Higginson knew very well.[24]

Dickinson confesses that she wants a destiny that is quite out of keeping with traditional women's aspirations. To Susan Gilbert she writes,
when she is twenty, "You and I would *try* to make a little destiny to have
for our own."[25] We note that while Dickinson keeps her plans for a
distinguished career secret from her family (she writes at night), she does
initially try to share her ambitions with her group of female friends,
whom she addresses as a literary support group. She consistently tries to
rally her friends to outwit society by avoiding the traps set to keep women
from being "great." She describes herself dreading the fate of the "wife
forgotten" who longs for a girl's independence, freedom, and possibility.[26]
When Susan Gilbert arrives home without the male escort who has been
sent for her, Dickinson writes, "Three cheers for American Independence!"[27]

In view of her estrangement from a social world in which she defines
herself as the one at a party who neither is "enamored" with a boy nor
cares to stand around and eat while the lovers "sigh," it is significant that
she casts her alienation in terms of her feelings about the male literary

community. She urges her friends not to get married and fears for the ones that do, determined herself not to "yield" because the "big *future*" awaiting her pivots on espousing traditional female fulfillment in marriage:

> I do think it's wonderful, Susie, that our hearts don't break, *every day*, when I think of all the whiskers, and all the gallant men, but I guess I'm made with nothing but a hard heart of stone, for it dont break any, and dear Susie if mine is strong your's is stone, upon stone, for you never yield *any* . . . Are we going to *ossify* always, say, Susie—how will it be? When I see the Popes and the Pollacks, and the John-Milton Browns, I think we are *liable*. But I dont know! I am glad there's a big *future* waiting for me and you. You would love to know what I read—I hardly know what to tell you, my catalogue is so small.
>
> I have just read three little books not great, not thrilling—but sweet and true. "The Light in the Valley," "Only," and "A House upon a Rock"—I know you would love them all—yet they dont *bewitch* me any. There are no walks in the wood—nor low and earnest voices, no moonlight, nor stolen love, but pure little lives, loving God, and their parents, and obeying the laws of the land; yet read, if you meet them, Susie, for they will do one good.[28]

She affirms her desire to remain single and singular, and encourages Susan Gilbert, to whom the above letter was written, to use the pen herself to attain the "big" destiny: "Write! Comrad, write!"[29] She then follows this exhortation with a poem of her own (P. 4) as evidence of her own resolution. It is one of the first poems she saved as part of her decision to seriously write poetry.

But as her friends begin to occupy their lives with marriage and children and sewing and musical societies, and become religious, even "born again," and her own sister is apparently content to dust the stairs and perform other domestic chores, Dickinson feels gradually isolated even within her female community. She describes herself as lonely, yet she is convinced that her gamble for literary greatness, while wicked, is not "wrong." She has "dared to do strange—bold things," and has asked no advice from any—"I have heeded beautiful tempters, yet do not think I am wrong." She is in fact extremely self-reliant and unrepentant, even in her isolation: "Nobody *thinks* of the joy, nobody *guesses* it."[30] She can still discuss her aspirations and poetry with her sister-in-law, Susan Gilbert, and can hint of her future fame. After they had discussed "Safe in their Alabaster Chambers," Dickinson wrote that she would "gain taller feet" if she could make her brother and Susan "proud—sometime—a great way off."[31] But Susan's response is often ambivalent, and the relationship is strained because of family politics.[32] Susan Gilbert was an immediate audience (Dickinson wrote her over 200 letters, most of them containing poems), but she could not be committed wholeheartedly to Dickinson's career. By the time Dickinson takes herself seriously as a poet when she is in her early thirties, she is still defining herself as a kind of brave, defiant moral outlaw, from both the female as well as the male worlds. She estranges herself from the female world by her refusal or inability to marry or to accept Christ or to be conventionally "sociable," and the male world will not take her work seriously—that is, it will not publish her.

It is a myth that Dickinson did not want to publish. She not only was sending her poetry regularly to Higginson, who was in a position to publish her, but also to Samuel Bowles, editor of *The Springfield Republican*, Dr. Holland, editor of *Scribner's*, and finally to Thomas Niles, head of Roberts Brothers Publishing house. But for whatever reason, they did not take her up, and she then pretended that publishing was never her intent: "I smile when you suggest that I delay 'to publish'—that being foreign to my thought, as Firmament to Fin—."[33] Besides, her poetry was unique in theme and style; it not only did not resemble the other poetry that was being written by females or males, but did not, some claimed, resemble "poetry" at all.[34] When it was finally published after her death, it was "regularized," made to conform to conventional poetry, and even after this doctoring, it was still new and bold.

Emily Dickinson's dwelling upon a self-image as strange and estranged, a poet of isolation and betrayal, makes sense given her assessment of her age's literary values and her own experience. But, although the image might make sense, it does not mean that she actually did not have support, *if she had wanted it.* Recent scholarship has focused attention on the affinities among nineteenth century women writers in such studies as Gilbert and Gubar's *The Madwoman in the Attic*, Suzanne Juhasz's *Naked and Fiery Forms*, and Ellen Moers's *Literary Women*, which show Dickinson operating within a female literary tradition and milieu. What we must remember is that there were actually *two* literary communities for Dickinson. One, the male literary establishment from which she felt hopelessly estranged. But the other, the largely British community of women writers, could provide role models and a distinct feminine literary tradition in which to work. Dickinson obviously had little rapport with the American women writers of her day, "Fannie Fern," "Minnie Myrtle," or even the women who wrote of "pretty little lives" loving God and their country.[35] But Dickinson read and idolized George Eliot, George Sand, the Brontes, Christina Rossetti and Elizabeth Barrett Browning, and made it a point to know about their lives. The publication of George Eliot's biography for example was a momentous event to her.[36] In her own country, Dickinson could identify with the success of writers like Helen Hunt Jackson, also from Amherst, who was championed by Higginson, Bowles, and even Emerson—Dickinson's own coterie of potential mentors.[37] Helen Hunt Jackson offered to do what Dickinson's male editors did not—she would put forth Emily Dickinson to the American literary community.[38] She tried, again and again, to get Dickinson to publish—even offered to be her literary executor—and finally succeeded only in submitting a poem of Dickinson's into a "No Name" series, where it was published anonymously, and with Dickinson's permission.

Therefore it is all the more remarkable that Dickinson should insist upon a self-image of isolation and betrayal, and in her letters should even project her sense of estrangement and repression upon these other women writers. For example, she purported to empathize with George Sand, George Eliot, and Barrett Browning in terms of the significance of a repressed childhood for a female writer:

> "Now, *my* George Eliot. The gift of belief which her greatness denied her, I trust she receives in the childhood of the kingdom of heaven. As childhood is earth's confiding time, perhaps having no childhood, she lost her way to the early trust, and no later came.[39]

> "That Mrs. Browning fainted we need read *Aurora Leigh* to know, when she lived with her English aunt; and George Sand 'must make no noise in her grandmother's bedroom.' Poor children! Women, now, queens, now! And one in the Eden of God. I guess they both forget that now, so who knows but we, little stars from the same night, stop twinkling at last?[40]

Dickinson often embraces these women writers in her letters, and assumes an intimacy, even possessiveness about them ("*my* George Eliot") especially when she writes to other women. She is admiring and rapt: "What do I think of *Middlemarch*?' What do I think of glory—"[41] But she can be sarcastic about women in general to her male correspondents and friends. To Higginson she said, "Women talk: men are silent. That is why I dread women."[42] Rebuked once by Bowles for her chauvinistic attitudes towards her own sex, she replied, "I am sorry I smiled at women. Indeed, I revere holy ones, like Mrs. Fry and Miss Nightengale. I will never be giddy again."[43] Perhaps Dickinson felt that she had to dissociate herself from women if she was to be taken seriously by men. Perhaps her sense that "woman poet" was a contradiction in terms led to her own ambivalence about her sex.

Certainly in her poetry Dickinson presents a female identity as a liability to be overcome if she were to be a great writer. Dickinson presents herself as a woman who has desexed herself by her choice of writing over marrying, an either / or decision to her. Assuming people's shock when her poems are discovered after her death, and she is exposed as a poet, she imagines her corpse and her psychology as being "rearranged" to conform to our image of "the poet:"

> Rearrange a "Wife's" Affection!
> When they dislocate my Brain!
> Amputate my freckled Bosom!
> Make me bearded like a Man!
> (from P. 1737)

In retrospect we will change her gender. Scores of poems record such identity conflict, which is based on her conviction that she is supposedly inappropriately sexed to be a poet—or at least a *published*, recognized poet. In many cases she taunts her reader with society's foolishness and flaunts her feminine poetic abilities with defiance and glee.

But there are also many poems of anguish, and these poems, which describe her identity being annihilated, fragmented by civil war into various states of animation and gender, possessed, mutilated, and hounded, are the more remarkable when we see that they are not really necessary, or even fair. Dickinson had evidence that a woman could be a successful poet, even married. Why, then, did she insist on seeing and presenting herself as isolated and estranged? Thomas Higginson repeatedly invited her to Boston to introduce her to the leading literary figures of the day, and she refused. That is understandable, considering her ambivalence about social encounters and travel and her own physical and emotional problems.[44] But her refusal to be nurtured by her sister writers, at least in terms of her own identity, does not make sense. That is, it does not make sense unless one considers Emily Dickinson's rejection of *both* the female and male literary communities in the light of her cultivation of the role of the rebellious daughter to her mother and the patriarchy in which she existed.

Emily Dickinson's mother played a major role in her daughter's development, not because she was a powerful personality but because she was, simply, Dickinson's mother. There is a paradox in what she represents, namely, an innocent force. She was the type of wife and mother her culture (and in particular, her husband) called for and theoretically esteemed: dutiful, obedient, passive, meek, submissive, modest, unassuming, timid, religious, self-sacrificing, and eager-to-please. But then her adherence to this feminine ideal was held against her. Her husband, frequently away on business, did not trust her management of the household and children, and treated her patronizingly. Her efforts to be independent were treated derisively. He once joked about a time in which she had displayed "decision of character," and assumed the "air of *authority* and independence."[45] She must not have manifested these traits often or effectively. In fact she was an invalid, emotionally and physically dependent, weak, fluttering, and plaintive. Knowing that a growing daughter cannot help but identify with her mother, we can imagine the conflict it caused a fiercely proud Emily Dickinson to see her mother viewed as so powerless and insignificant that her death does not even cause a "ripple," according to what Austin Dickinson, Emily's brother, told Mabel Loomis Todd.[46] Dickinson herself seems to have dealt with her conflict by contributing to the derogatory remarks, as if to dissociate herself from her mother, and hence her mother's fate. She is patronizing about her mother's inability to take care of herself. Dickinson tended to her invalid mother's "dear little wants," low intellectual faculties, her narrow piety, and her use of cliches.[47] Thus in her letters Dickinson wittily points out her mother's ordinary mind and moral conventionality in order to show how she herself is different—intellectually progressive, sophisticated, *smart*.[48] She is not her mother's daughter, she seems to say, and her mother means little to her, so little, in fact, that Dickinson actually denies her existence. She maintains to an editor that "I never had a mother."[49] She notes, "I always ran Home to Awe when a Child, if anything befell me. He was an awful mother, but I liked him better than none."[50] She purports to have no one but her sister to dress her, to tell her right from wrong, and complains, "How to grow up I don't know."[51] In other words, she mourns the lack of a mother at the same time as she complains about the one she has.

But Emily Dickinson's rebellion from what her mother stands for takes the form of more than recriminations. She refuses to become "born again," in spite of her mother's fervent urgings, and in fact, practices a kind of skepticism as regards institutionalized Christianity. She makes irreverent jabs at God, the church, the deacons, the sermons, and the Bible, and refuses to go to Church. Despite the pressure to conform, and her acknowledged need of spiritual solace, she refuses to be nurtured by religion when she sees that obedience to the Father and Son team is the identical obedience that has eclipsed and diminished her mother.[52] Similarly, she feels awkward about her own sexuality, and, as I have mentioned, vows not to marry, convinced that marriage and family will reduce her to her mother's fate. In refusing to attend sewing and musical groups, and finally, even to entertain visitors, she rebels not only from formal religious structures but also from her social world, even at the price of unhappiness and feelings of loneliness and isolation. As for the domestic life within the house, she tries to escape it, mentally and physically: "How I love to run fast and hide away from them all."[53] Only when her mother is sick does Dickinson enter the kitchen, and at that with trepidation. She writes that she wants to make the food which is immortal (words), not the food that perishes. She is miserable, and feels put upon, the "Queen of Calvary." Catching herself saying "my kitchen", she exclaims, "*My* kitchen I think I called it, God forbid that it was or shall be my own—God keep me from what they call households."[54] Dickinson extends her rejection of her mother and her mother's world, then, to any convention to which she, as a woman, is expected to submit: courtship, marriage, church, family, housework, sewing society. She cultivates a self-image that is alienated from any form of the feminine ideal. She is defiant, sassy, crabby, stubborn, wicked.

Dickinson's rebellion from the maternal matrix has as much to do with the situation of women in her culture as with her mother, an unquestioning product of this culture. It has to do with women's status. Dickinson wants to be "great, Someday" and her rejection of her mother is a way to circumvent her mother's destiny. Dickinson feels that writing poetry is her only way to procure immortality and fame. She also knows that women get jobs teaching; she knows that women travel; she knows women who lead their own lives. Yet she never leaves home to establish a career and independent identity, and in fact, never gives up her primary identity as a daughter. She continues to define and present herself in her letters and in her poetry as a daughter—albeit rebellious—functioning in reference to her mother and her father. This means that even as she proclaims her independence from society, she responds to the world as a child does, in terms of protesting her dependence, powerlessness, insignificance, lack of autonomy, and "small size." Even in her fifties Dickinson complains about her household tasks, such as her "gymnastic destiny" in caring for her mother.[55] At a time when her contemporaries are grandmothers—even great-grandmothers—she sulks about repression, persecution, abandonment, lack of nurture. She imagines herself pouting in heaven "where it's Sunday all the time," "recess never comes," and God "never takes a nap" to give her some reprieve from an eternity of good behavior (P. 413).

Similarly, Dickinson approaches the men in her life as father figures, whether suitors, editors, tutors or God. Even in her late forties, with Judge Otis Lord, her father's contemporary, she presents herself as a wicked little girl who will *try* not to misbehave, who promises her obedience, who vows to be "quiet." She also tries to elicit notice and esteem of her intellectual and poetic talent, trying to get powerful men to nurture her potential as a poet. Her own father was reportedly too busy to notice her and was critical of and probably even bewildered by Dickinson's precocity. He was stern, authoritarian, and dominating. Dickinson turned to other men for father-substitutes, trying to evoke and then maintain their interest by a combination of lip-service to the requisite humility and docility (designed to flatter) and transparent intellect and wit (designed to intrigue). But if Dickinson submerged her resentment at being dependent upon male power in her relationships with men, she used her writing to take irreverent pot-shots at patriarchal authority. Her father is thus reduced in her letters about him to a tyrant buffoon at cross-purposes with himself, "*mad*, and silly" and "amused."[56] God is a jealous bully who flexes his spiritual bicep to keep people in line (P. 597). He is a negligent parent, setting the table "too high for us" (P. 640). The Bible is written by "faded old men" (P. 1545). She takes jabs at the dignified and the sacred. Yet Dickinson also purports to scorn daughters, so that when a friend has another "little *daughter*" Dickinson is snide: "Very promising Children I understand. I dont doubt if they live they will be ornaments to society." Being an ornament to society, a dispensable trimming, is not Dickinson's idea of a "promising" destiny.[57] Another time she speaks of "pretty girls, very simple hearted and happy—and would be very interesting if they had anybody to teach them."[58] Dickinson's ire is not against daughters *per se*, but with a daughter's possibilities, so limited that she once exclaimed, "Why can't *I* be a delegate to the great Whig convention—dont I know all about Daniel Webster, and the Tariff, and the Law?"[59] Admitting the futility of such an ambition, given her culture, Dickinson rejects the political system itself: "George Washington was the Father of his Country—'George Who?' That sums all Politics to me—" Feeling outside of the political system, Dickinson doesn't "like this country at all, and I shant stay here any longer!" *Her* country is "Truth," and her native land is her mind.[60] And, in fact, in her own poetry Dickinson shows us rather sensational accounts of the life of a singular daughter engaged in breaking laws, confessing ambivalence to God, and parents, and living a life which is only superficially "little," and is not "pretty."

Dickinson remains a daughter in her attitude, dress, manner, themes, and style: although she rebels, she never leaves what she always terms her "father's House," because the daughter who chafes at restrictions placed upon her sex is motivated to write poetry. In her poems about art and hunger, Dickinson is explicit about her conviction that her poems, and the identity and self-esteem they confer, come only from her sense of deprivation and the accompanying need to reject any form of society's nurture. "It was given to me by the Gods" (P. 454) makes her deprivation a "gift" which she retains only by not eating or drinking or sleeping. The result is that she "wins" the gold. In another, she describes writing in order to appease her "Clamoring for gold" (P. 810), a hunger so intense it can hardly "be borne;" but her hands are "fitter" for her "Want." Saying "no" gives her power; being deprived is actually a sign of the unique destiny in store for her. Thus we see that apparent self-pity in poems such as "God gave a Loaf to every Bird— / But just a Crumb to me— / I dare not eat it who I starve— / My poignant Luxury" (P. 579), "I want—it pleaded all its Life" (P. 731), "Deprived of other Banquet" (P. 773), and "It would have starved a Gnat" (P. 612) are evidence that her deprivation either makes her superior or manifests her uniqueness. In P. 579 especially, she is the Princess whose squeamishness and intestinal fragility are royal. Common food makes her sick.

Dickinson may feel herself deprived of metaphoric food as a poet—the nurture of encouragement, praise, and sanction—but Dickinson converts her "kangaroo" status among the literary establishment from a liability into a strength. She is superior because she says no: "To earn it by disdaining it / Is Fame's consummate Fee—" (P. 1427). Therefore she disdains any nurture.

We may say that Dickinson's spurning of what the world could offer her if it chose to do so is a defensive tactic, designed to ease her pain at being denied her place among the American literati. But it is significant that Dickinson puts fame, recognition, acceptance, identity, wealth, and independence in the language of food—the language, that is, of mother-daughter interaction at the earliest and most profound stage of the relationship. To profess to refuse nurture when it is offered (as in P. 579, or

"Fame is a fickle food," P. 1659) is a metaphoric way of rebelling against the mother or what she stands for. Not to eat, as studies of anorexia in young girls have shown, is a way to avoid becoming *like* one's mother. Physiologically, we know, it also postpones a woman's sexual development.

Thus we can understand Dickinson's seemingly unwarranted portrait of herself as an isolato. Perhaps her refusal to let herself find support in the existence of a female literary community is a function of her need to say "no" to her mother and the feminine world which she sees threatening her ambition to be "great, Someday." She may have retained her self-image as an isolated "Kangaroo" as an aesthetic strategy, to keep herself hungry and alienated enough to write poetry. For words come out of her need to belong, to commune, to reconcile and to alleviate her sense of separation. Dickinson needs a mother, but as a poet that is a luxury she cannot afford; she needs a community, but she cannot let herself have one; she must be mother and community to herself, feeding herself the words (in her terms, the "precious food," P. 1587) which make poems—and immortality—come into being. To be her own community is Dickinson's way to transcend a traditional female destiny—but even more importantly, to sustain the *need* to communicate and break the barrier of her self-imposed isolation.

This may be why Emily Dickinson continues to present herself in her poetry as alienated—her reading of other nineteenth-century women authors notwithstanding—and in her own life keeps herself physically removed from any supportive community outside of the upstairs realm in her own home. Her mother and sister, the only people she really sees and interacts with, are not even aware that she writes poetry. She needs a self-maintained distance from both male and female literary communities, in order to maintain her necessary rebellion from what she feels the world expects of dutiful daughters. Thus she suffers the identity conflict arising from being in her own eyes a neuter freak, with beard and without breasts. And thus, when she writes her elegy to Elizabeth Barrett Browning, she writes, "This was a poet . . . It is he. . . ." (P. 448). And from this identity conflict which she imposes upon the female literary community, which could have given her a healing sense of normality about herself and her ambitions, she forges a community of one at odds with self and society. Ironically, her lonely yet snobbish celebration of being alienated from society places her in the American literary tradition of Thoreau, Melville, Cooper, Hawthorne, *et al.* And her portrayal of being at odds with her *self* places her in the very bosom of the nineteenth-century women writers. Dickinson would seem to deny both communities, but she freely used them in her work, and she existed within them, immersing and even baptising herself as a poet, as Joseph Conrad's character Stein advised in *Lord Jim*, in the "destructive element."

Notes

1. *The Letters of Emily Dickinson*, 3 vols., ed. Thomas H. Johnson and Theodora Ward (Cambridge, Mass.: Belknap Press of Harvard University Press, 1958), p. 412. Subsequent references will be in the Notes as *Letters* followed by volumes and page number.

2. *Letters*, II, p. 409.

3. *Letters*, II, p. 415.

4. Examples of kinds of studies which omit Dickinson include Mason Lowance, Jr., *The Man of Letters in New England and the South: Essays on the History of the Literary Vocation in America* (1973); Austin Warren's *The New England Conscience* (1966); Lawrence Buell, *Literary Transcendentalism* (1973); *Four Makers of the American Mind: Emerson, Thoreau, Whitman, and Melville*, ed. Thomas E. Crawley, (1976); Harold Kaplan, *Democratic Humanism and American Literature* (1972). It is not that Dickinson necessarily should be included in these or scores of other recent studies which apply to aspects of her art, literary terrain, region, and so on; it is that the cumulative effect of her omission from so many scholarly approaches does make her appear to be the "kangaroo" she considered herself to be.

5. *The Poems of Emily Dickinson*, 3 vols. ed. Thomas H. Johnson (Cambridge, Mass.: Belknap Press of Harvard University Press, 1955). See Ralph Franklin, *The Editing of Emily Dickinson* (Madison, Milwaukee, and London: University of Wisconsin Press, 1967).

6. *Letters*, II, p. 461.

7. For example, George Whicher, *This Was a Poet* (New York: Charles Scribner's Sons, 1938), p. 224; Richard Chase, *Emily Dickinson* (New York: William Sloane, 1951), p. 206.

8. Jack L. Capps, *Emily Dickinson's Reading* (Cambridge, Mass.: Harvard University Press, 1966). See also John E. Walsh, *The Hidden Life of Emily Dickinson* (New York: Simon and Schuster, 1971); Richard B. Sewall, *The Life of Emily Dickinson* (New York: Farrar, Straus, and Giroux, 1974), pp. 668–705; Ellen Moers, *Literary Women* (New York: Doubleday, 1977).

9. Henry Wells, "Romantic Sensibility," in *Emily Dickinson: A Collection of Critical Essays*, ed. Richard B. Sewall (Englewood Cliffs, N.J.: Prentice-Hall, 1963); *Introduction to Emily Dickinson* (Chicago: Packard and Company, 1947); pp. xvi–xvii. Jay Leyda, *The Years and Hours of Emily Dickinson* (New Haven: Yale University Press, 1960), pp. xx, ff.

10. Karl Keller, *The Only Kangaroo Among the Beauty: Emily Dickinson and America* (Baltimore and London: Johns Hopkins University Press, 1979). Keller's thesis of affinities is overdue and compellingly drawn: "My intent is to set her squarely in the center of American literary history," p. 4.

11. Yvor Winters, "Emily Dickinson and the Limits of Judgement," *Collected Essays on Emily Dickinson*, ed. Sewall, op. cit., p. 39. Conrad Aiken, "Emily Dickinson" Ibid., p. 11.

12. *Letters*, II, p. 404.

13. *Letters*, II, p. 649.

14. *Letters*, II, p. 649.

15. *Letters*, I, p. 144.

16. *Letters*, I, p. 144.

17. See *Letters*, II, pp. 373, 475; I, p. 144.

18. *Letters*, I, p. 161.

19. Dickinson's reading of Emerson has been amply documented, especially by Sewall and Capps. I am thinking particularly of his advice to "The Poet" in his essay of that name, a page of which Dickinson (we believe) not only marked but actually folded over. She appears to have taken to heart his advice:

Doubt not, O poet, but persist. Say "It is in me, and shall out." Stand there, balked and dumb, stuttering and stammering, hissed and hooted, stand and strive, until at last rage draw out of thee that *dream*-power which every night shows thee is thine own; a power transcending all limit and privacy, and by virtue of which a man is the conductor of the whole river of electricity. Nothing walks, or creeps, or grows, or exists, which must not in turn arise and walk before him as exponent of his meaning. . . .

. . . The conditions are hard, but equal. Thou shalt leave the world, and know the muse only. Thou shalt not know any longer the times, customs, graces, politics, or opinions of men, but shalt take all from the muse. For the time of towns is tolled from the world by funereal chimes, but in nature the universal hours are counted by succeeding tribes of animals and plants, and by growth of joy on joy. God wills also that thou abdicate a manifold and duplex life, and thou be content that others speak for thee. Others shall be thy gentlemen and shall represent all courtesy and worldly life for thee; others shall do the great and resounding actions also. Thou shalt lie close hid with nature, and canst not be afforded to the Capitol or the Exchange. The world is full of renunciations and apprenticeships, and this is thine; thou must pass for a fool and a churl for a long season. This is the screen and sheath in which Pan has protected his well-beloved flower, and thou shalt be known only to thine own, and they shall console thee with tenderest love. And thou shalt not be able to rehearse the names of thy friends in thy verse, for an old shame before the holy ideal. *Essays, Second Series*, 1844.

20. *Letters*, II, p. 427.

21. *Letters*, I, p. 10.

22. *Letters*, II, p. 346.

23. *Letters*, II, p. 404.

24. *Letters*, I, p. 95.

25. *Letters*, I, p. 144.

26. *Letters*, I, pp. 209–10.

27. *Letters*, I, p. 202.

28. *Letters*, I, pp. 144–45.

29. *Letters*, I, p. 226.

30. *Letters*, I, p. 95.

31. *Letters*, II, p. 380.

32. For an impartial account of this conflict, see Sewall, *The Life of Emily Dickinson*, Vol. I, pp. 161–234.

33. *Letters*, II, p. 408.

34. The reception of Dickinson's poetry in the 1890's is documented and discussed in works such as Caesar R. Blake and Carlton F. Wells, *The Recognition of Emily Dickinson* (Ann Arbor: University of Michigan Press, 1964); Millicent Todd Bingham, *Ancestor's Brocades* (New York and London: Harper Bros., 1945), which used the scrapbooks of Mabel Loomis Todd; Franklin's *The Editing of Emily Dickinson*, op. cit.; Klaus Lubbers, *Emily Dickinson, The Critical Revolution* (Ann Arbor: University of Michigan Press, 1960).

35. *Letters*, I, p. 95.

36. See *Letters*, III, pp. 725–26, 768–69, 864–65.

37. See Sewall, and John Cody, *After Great Pain: The Inner Life of Emily Dickinson* (Cambridge, Mass.: Belknap Press of Harvard University Press, 1971).

38. See *Letters*, II, pp. 563–67, p. 639; III, pp. 841–42.

39. *Letters*, III, p. 700.

40. *Letters*, II, p. 376.

41. *Letters*, II, p. 506.

42. *Letters*, II, p. 573.

43. *Letters*, p. 366; see also III, p. 929.

44. See Sewall, *The Life*, pp. 577–592.

45. *Letters*, I, p. 77.

46. Bingham, *Ancestor's Brocades*, p. 8 (quoting Mabel Loomis Todd).

47. See *Letters*, I, pp. 111, 116, 137–38; II, pp. 454, 667; III, p. 675.

48. For example, see *Letters*, II, p. 622.

49. *Letters*, II, p. 475.

50. *Letters*, II, pp. 517–18.

51. *Letters*, II, p. 508 and I, p. 241.

52. *Letters*, I, pp. 26–27, 30–31, 67–68.

53. *Letters*, I, p. 193.

54. *Letters*, I, pp. 97–100.

55. *Letters*, III, p. 687.

56. *Letters*, I, p, 121.

57. *Letters*, I, p. 17.

58. *Letters*, I, p. 200.

59. *Letters*, I, p. 212; see also II, p. 368.

60. *Letters*, III, p. 849.

INDEX